PLACE OF HEALING

When talented cook Jess is betrayed by her boyfriend and best friend, she has to get away, so she books a holiday cottage in a remote corner of Somerset. And Higher Neston immediately feels like home, her landlady Elsie like family. Jess lacks confidence in her own instincts, yet finding herself caught in the middle of family quarrels and old rivalries, she must learn to listen to her heart and decide who is trustworthy . . .

PAULA WILLIAMS

◆

PLACE
OF HEALING

Complete and Unabridged

LINFORD
Leicester

First published in Great Britain in 2010

First Linford Edition
published 2011

British Library CIP Data

Williams, Paula.
  Place of healing. - -
  (Linford romance library)
  1. Women cooks- -Fiction. 2. Families- -
England- -Somerset- -Fiction. 3. Love stories.
4. Large type books.
  I. Title II. Series
  823.9′2–dc22

  ISBN 978–1–4448–0635–9

Published by
F. A. Thorpe (Publishing)
Anstey, Leicestershire

Set by Words & Graphics Ltd.
Anstey, Leicestershire
Printed and bound in Great Britain by
T. J. International Ltd., Padstow, Cornwall

This book is printed on acid-free paper

1

Jess stood in the doorway of Matt's kitchen, her brain refusing to accept what her eyes were telling her. Sophie — her best friend, colleague and flatmate — was wrapped around Jess's boyfriend, Matt, like a vine leaf around a dolmade and getting creative with Jess's beautifully made chocolate mousse in a way that definitely wasn't on the menu.

Jess stared at the small butterfly tattoo on Sophie's left shoulder blade and had the most bizarre flashback, to her schooldays, of all things. To her physics teacher droning on about the Butterfly Effect. The theory that tiny differences in input can result in overwhelming differences in output. Like, for example, he explained, how a butterfly flapping its wings in Brazil could cause a tornado in Texas.

Now, for the first time, Jess knew

exactly what he meant. Only in her case, it wasn't a butterfly causing the tornado, but a slice of cheesecake.

If she hadn't eaten that last slice of lemon cheesecake, she wouldn't have gained an extra pound last week. And if she hadn't forgotten to sew on the button on her grey woollen trousers when the strain of the extra slice of cheesecake proved too much for her overstrained waistband, then she wouldn't have had to waste precious time this morning hunting for a pair of trousers with its full complement of buttons.

In which case, she'd have been around to stop Sophie going off without the whipped cream. If she'd done that, she'd have been spared the shock of standing in the doorway, unable to move, speak or think of anything other than butterflies and cheesecake. Unable to say or do anything to alert them to her presence. They were so absorbed in each other and the chocolate mousse, they wouldn't have noticed an entire

SAS regiment yomping through the room, least of all one small, slightly overweight woman, wild-eyed with disbelief, clutching a bowl of whipped cream to her chest as if it was the Crown Jewels.

In one of those weird hiccups of time that can happen to people in shock, Jess felt as if she was seeing the entire scene through the wrong end of a very long telescope.

She considered hurling the whipped cream, one heaped spoonful at a time, over the pair of them. She imagined watching it slither down their faces, cling to their hair and trickle down their necks, the shock and guilt in their eyes blanked out by huge white dollops of cream that stuck to their eyes and swirled in the smear of chocolate on Matt's nose that Sophie's catlike tongue had missed.

But the cream remained safely in the bowl as Jess placed it on the kitchen table, mumbled something like 'I should have knocked', then turned and fled back to her car.

It wasn't until she got back to the flat that the shock began to wear off and the first stirrings of anger, along with a deep sense of betrayal, began to wash over her in waves.

How could they? Matt was not only Jess's boyfriend but one of their clients. He was entertaining a group of Japanese businessmen and wanted to impress them with lunch in his loft style apartment. This is where Simply The Best, Sophie's company, came in, providing smart, elegant food for the clients to claim as their own if they wished. Sophie dealt with the customers, while Jess did the cooking. It was an arrangement that had suited them both perfectly. Until now.

Now Jess didn't know what to believe. She'd only taken the cream to Matt's as a favour to Sophie, who, according to the story she'd told Jess last night, was to be meeting her mother for lunch today so would be pushed for time. Obviously a lie.

And Matt's meeting with the Japanese businessmen? Was that a lie too? Had she spent all yesterday afternoon, creating such a beautiful lunch, thinking she was doing something to help Matt further his career, when all the time, it was for Matt and Sophie, to . . . ? She broke off as images of asparagus dripping in butter swam into her tortured mind.

★ ★ ★

Jess went to the kitchen cupboards and took out her emergency supply of Chocolate Hobnobs then took them in to her bedroom with her and started packing. She was on her second suitcase — and fourth Hobnob — when she heard the door of the flat open.

'Jess?' It was Sophie. 'Oh, my God, I'm so, so sorry. Look, we've got to talk about this. Can I come in?'

'It's your flat,' Jess muttered as she yanked a drawer out of the chest and tipped the entire contents into her suitcase. Sophie had a rich father who bought his precious daughter whatever she asked for, including the flat they shared and the premises and equipment needed to set up their business. Correction: Sophie's business. Whatever Sophie wanted, Daddy would get it for her.

And now, it appeared, she wanted Matt. Only this time Sophie didn't need Daddy. She'd been well capable of getting him herself.

Sophie stood in the doorway, her eyes downcast, her long elegant fingers twirling a strand of hair round and round. 'We didn't mean it to happen, Jess,' she said in a subdued voice.

'Oh, really?' Jess slammed the lid of her second suitcase shut and stuffed the remainder of the packet of biscuits in her shoulder bag. 'You mean, the chocolate mousse jumped out of the bowl, knocked Matt out and you were giving him mouth to mouth resuscitation. Was that it?'

'I meant we didn't mean to fall in

love. I'm sorry — we tried not to and neither of us wanted you to find out like that.'

'Oh? And how did you mean me to find out? By email? Twitter? Or a full page advert in the Times?'

Jess's uncharacteristically harsh tone made Sophie look up. She shrugged, defensively. 'But it's not as if you were so very keen on him, were you? You were mad as hell with him when you found he asked you out because your mother had asked him to, remember? So in a way . . . '

'Look, Sophie. Do me a favour.' Fear of losing control and either bursting into tears or strangling Sophie with her own irritatingly beautiful long blonde hair gave Jess the necessary amount of self control to keep her voice level. 'Just . . . stay away for an hour or so, while I pack, will you?'

'But you're not walking out on me, are you? What about the business? How am I going to manage? Jess, surely we can talk about this, can't we?'

Jess shook her head. 'You'll manage fine,' she said. 'You always do. All you need is someone else to do the cooking for you. There are plenty of agencies in the phone book. Please, Sophie. All I ask is half an hour to finish my packing. I promise you I won't make off with the TV or anything that doesn't belong to me.'

'Take it. Take whatever you need,' Sophie said. 'You can have the DVD player if you — '

'What I need — ' Jess stopped. She'd been about to say that what she needed was her boyfriend back. But that sounded pathetic. So she walked to the door, held it open and looked her ex-friend firmly in the eye. 'What I need is half an hour to finish my packing and get out of your life,' she said with quiet and, to her mind, astonishing dignity.

Sophie opened her mouth to protest, then shrugged and walked out, leaving Jess biting back tears as the front door closed behind her.

Jess let herself into Simply The Best's small kitchen and looked around it for the last time. She'd come here with such hopes and excitement, thrilled at the thought of being in at the beginning of a business that she and Sophie had talked about since they'd first become friends at college.

She collected the few items she had brought with her — an old food mixer that she'd known and loved all her life, her grandmother's ancient frying pan and a set of chef's knives that cost more than everything else she owned put together. As she was fitting them into a box, her phone rang.

'Jessica?' It was her mother, the only person apart from a stiff-backed music teacher at school who called her Jessica. 'Are you all right? Is something wrong?'

How did she do that? Jess wondered, guiltily wiping biscuit crumbs from her mouth, even though the rational part of her brain knew her mother couldn't see her. Her mother had an uncanny way of knowing when Jess was at her lowest.

9

When she was at school, it always seemed as if her mother knew when she'd messed up an exam or failed to get a part in the play before Jess did herself.

'How do you mean?' Jess asked.

'Come on, darling. I can tell just by the sound of your voice something's wrong. Unless, of course, you're starting a cold?'

Jess sighed. Might as well get it over with, even though she'd have liked a little more time to work out how she was going to tell people that she and Matt had broken up. She took a deep breath and began to tell her mother how it was all over between her and Matt. Because? Because Matt was all over Sophie — and all over chocolate mousse. She shook her head. Would she ever get that image out of her head? With an effort, she forced herself to focus on what her mother was saying.

' . . . and so at the end of the day, darling, it sounds as if you're rather making a fuss over nothing.'

'Nothing?' For the second time that day, Jess was shocked into speaking more sharply than was normal for her. 'My best friend's having an affair with my boyfriend and you say that's nothing?'

Her mother tutted. 'I always said you read too many romantic novels, didn't I? Those books do huge amounts of harm, giving foolish young girls like yourself the idea that everything's happy ever after. So Matt's got a wandering eye? He's a good looking chap. Hardly surprising.'

'But he — '

'For heaven's sake, don't be such a wet,' her mother snapped. 'Your father's had countless affairs, all our married life, and we're still together. It doesn't mean a thing. Just get over it.'

'Dad's had affairs?' Jess was deeply shocked. She'd often noticed tension between her parents but had never thought it was anything significant. Instead, she'd always assumed they were, on the whole, happily married, despite the fact that a man would need the patience of an entire cathedral full of saints to put up with her mother.

'Still has them as far as I know,' her mother said, 'Although personally I think he's getting a bit long in the tooth for that sort of thing now. But there you go — welcome to the real world.'

Well, if that's your real world, you can keep it, Jess thought and, as she did so, realised that there was no way she could go back to her parents' home, not even in the short term while she sorted herself out. She was still trying to come to terms with splitting up from Matt without trying to make sense of her mother's casual reference to the fact that her father was a . . . Jess floundered for a suitable world before settling for philanderer.

As if reading her thoughts, which she seemed to do so often, her mother went on, 'Still, if you really have left Sophie's, then you're going to have to come home for a while, aren't you? Your old room is always ready for you, you know that.'

Did she? Jess wondered if now was the time to remind her mother that the last few times Jess had suggesting coming home for the weekend, she'd come up with various excuses for putting her off. The room was being decorated, they were away for the weekend, the cat had a tummy bug.

'Well, actually, I thought I might — '

'Nonsense. Of course you must come home. Where else would you go at such a time? And this whole thing couldn't have come at a better time, as far as I'm concerned. Because that's why I'm ringing you. Your father's wining and dining a party of Americans and, apparently, they're not in to what they call 'fancy restaurants'. All they want is a bit of good, old fashioned home cooking. Roast beef, apple pie and clotted cream. You know, all that ghastly, horrifically calorific stuff that you're so good at, darling. So, I thought you could — '

'No, Mother, I'm sorry. I can't — '

'For heaven's sake, why not?' Her

mother, not used to being said no to, asked crossly. 'Look, things are bad enough as it is. Heaven knows your father isn't going to be too pleased about you breaking up with Matt. It's going to make things very awkward for him at work, you do know that.'

Matt was one of the up and coming associates in her father's law firm and Jess hoped fervently that it was Matt who was going to find things awkward, not her father.

'Then perhaps you should have thought of that before you set me up with him,' Jess picked up a magazine she'd 'liberated' from her dentist's waiting room because it had a particularly good recipe for a salmon and asparagus quiche. Not much point now she supposed.

'Now come on darling. You're being hysterical. And I know you. You'll sit around all day, watching daytime TV and moping. Best thing is to keep busy. That's what I always do. Besides, if you don't come home, where else will you go?'

'As a matter of fact I've booked a holiday.' Jess said, as the magazine flipped open on the pages of small ads for holiday accommodation and settling for the first one her eye rested on, she added, 'In Somerset.'

'Somerset? In March? Now I know you've gone completely mad. You can't go to the countryside at this time of the year. You'll be up to your ankles in mud and goodness knows what else.'

At any other time, Jess would have laughed at the horror in her voice. Now, it just made her even more determined to do the exact opposite to what her mother wanted.

'I'll be in touch,' she said, rang off, then picked up the magazine and dialled the number in the advert.

★　★　★

The woman who answered the phone had a delightful soft West Country burr, which Jess simply loved.

'I'm ringing about your advert in The

15

Lady,' Jess said, 'For your holiday cottage, The Old Dairy. I wonder if it's available this week?'

'Are you sure you've got the right number? I haven't run an advert for some months.'

'It's quite an old magazine,' Jess admitted. 'And I know it's probably out of season, but I'm desperate.'

'I can certainly offer you Bed and Breakfast in the farmhouse. It's got en suite facilities, and the best cooked breakfast in the country. Guaranteed.'

Jess thought of the suitcases and boxes that were going to fill the back of her elderly hatchback. Bed and Breakfast was no good. She needed a cottage, preferably with a second bedroom.

'Look, I'm sorry,' she said, 'It sounds absolutely lovely but not quite what I'm looking for. I need — ' she swallowed hard, trying to keep from sounding too desperate. 'I need a bit of space, to sort myself out. The Old Dairy sounds ideal — and I'm quite willing to pay over the odds. I'll pay the peak season rate, seeing as it's such short notice. But it's got to be today.'

'Today? Oh, I don't think that's possible.'

'You mean it's let?'

'I mean I don't think I can get the place vacated by then. It's got to be cleaned through and aired and all — '

'I'll do it. I'll help you. Please don't worry about that. And I'm prepared to pay a whole month in advance. But it's got to be today.'

Jess could sense the woman's hesitation. 'Well, I suppose I could get it all ready for you by five o'clock.'

'Three would be better,' Jess said firmly, knowing full well she'd be fit for nothing by five o'clock.

Jess put the phone down with a sigh of satisfaction. It was not like her to be so forceful, but today was far from a normal day. When she got there, she'd apologise to — she glanced at the name she'd written down on the pad — Mrs Russell, but she knew that if she didn't find a place to stay tonight, she'd be back at her mother's and back, too, to the endless parade of 'suitable' young men.

Matt had been a one off, in that he was the only one of her mother's 'suitable' young men that she had liked — and look where that had got her.

She closed the door of Simply The Best, got in her car and began the long drive down to Somerset.

2

Jess wasn't a fast driver so she was astonished to find she'd made much better time on the drive down to Somerset than she'd expected until she realised the reason had nothing to do with any change in her driving, simply that she hadn't stopped for lunch. For the first time in her life, she'd forgotten to eat.

Had she discovered a new diet? She could call it the Heartbreak Diet and sell millions of books. Then Matt would be sorry for dumping her. The thought comforted her until she realised the biscuits she'd eaten while packing probably had more to do with her uncharacteristic loss of appetite, for Jess's normal healthy appetite (gargantuan was her mother's disparaging description) only increased when she was unhappy, as she turned to food for comfort.

She drove carefully along the narrow, high-banked lanes and, thanks to Mrs Russell's excellent directions, found the T-junction that was just half a mile away from the farmhouse without any problems.

She checked her watch. She was way too early. She'd already bullied the poor lady into letting her come at three. She could hardly turn up almost an hour early.

She pulled in to a nearby gateway and got out of the car, revelling in the chance to ease her stiff limbs and stretch her aching back. As she did so, she became aware of the deep silence around her. Except, as she listened she realised it wasn't silent at all. There was the drone of a tractor in the distance and, in a nearby field, a young lamb bleated for its mother. The air was alive with the sound of bird song, one bird in particular pouring out its pure notes, rich and silken as molten silver, into the still afternoon air.

'Will you listen to that old blackbird,

Jessie. He's singing his heart out.'

The voice was her grandmother's. For a second, she felt the pressure of her hand on her shoulder, smelt the scent of the Devon Violets perfume she always used to wear. She'd died when Jess was just eight years old. Jess had loved her very much and missed her dreadfully. If only she was still alive, Jess wouldn't have had a problem of where to go today.

Her grandmother had lived in a tiny village deep in rural Suffolk, a long way from Somerset and different landscape, but there was something about the quality of the air, the stillness that gave Jess a sense of homecoming.

Her mother had hated growing up in the country and had, according to her 'shaken the mud off her wellies the day she left for University'. She came back rarely and then under sufferance, but Jess had adored it and felt more at home with her grandmother than she ever did in her parents' smart London home.

As she listened to the blackbird's song and the ewes calling their lambs, she thought with a pang of homesickness, that she'd never felt for her parents' home, of her grandmother's kitchen, always full of warmth from the range, crowded with dogs and cats and rich with the smell of freshly baked scones or bread.

She smiled as a group of young cattle came towards her, necks outstretched, large amber eyes wide with curiosity. Their breath came in noisy gusts as they inched ever closer. She watched, fascinated, as one of them reached towards some long grass in the hedge, reaching under the barbed wire to get at them. When she was almost within reach, she put out her tongue, and with the very tip, wrapped it gently around the grass and pulled it towards her.

Jess watched for a second, fascinated, until another image of an outstretched tongue, this time reaching not for grass but for chocolate mousse landed in her brain with a thud. She blinked hard and focussed on the cattle. Would she ever get away from that image? Was it going to be forever running through her head like a bad tune?

But then, like slides at a presentation, the image slid away and was replaced by another, even more unexpected one. For as the young heifer moved away, the grass dangling like spaghetti verdi from her mouth, her bony hips reminded Jess of Sophie's coat-hanger shoulder blades and she began to laugh. The sudden sound caused the nervy young cattle to take a collective jump back.

'What the devil do you think you're doing?' A man's angry voice behind her made her jump as violently as the cattle. She whirled round, her heart thudding, to see a man coming towards her down the lane, a stick in his hand and a black and white dog at his heels like a shadow.

'I'm sorry?' Jess tried to sound unafraid.

'I asked what you were doing?'

Close to, he looked even angrier than he had at a distance — and his dog, the sort Jess preferred to see on a TV screen herding sheep into a pen, didn't look too friendly either. Jess, never at ease with dogs or angry men, come to that, took an instinctive step backwards, crunching her hip on the car's wing mirror as she did so.

'But I'm not doing any harm,' she protested, rubbing at what she was sure was going to be a huge bruise. 'I was just — '

'Blocking my gateway for one thing. Disturbing my livestock for another.'

'I'd just stopped to stretch my legs. Surely you can't object to that?'

She was relieved to see the anger fade from his deep brown eyes and his dark eyebrows, which had been drawn together in a straight heavy frown, started to relax.

'I've had a lot of trouble from sheep rustlers lately,' he said.

'And I look like your typical rustler, do I?' Jess snapped. All the turmoil of her rotten day erupted in one burst of sarcasm as she slapped her hip, not a wise move as it was still sore from its encounter with the wing mirror and said: 'Well, yee-haw!'

His facial expression was as cold as one of those killer winds you see in sci-fi films, that turns everything in its path to ice. 'Rustling may be a source of amusement where you come from,' he said, 'But around here it's no laughing matter. Not only does it affect my livelihood, but I happen to care about the welfare of my animals. Rustlers do not. And neither do the idiots who leave field gates open.'

She could tell he was dying to add, *Idiots like you*, and wished he had. At least then she could have denied the charge. She flushed, feeling bad about her flippant remark. She didn't usually go around being rude to strangers. After all, he'd every right to ask what she was doing on his land, although if he'd asked it in a less confrontational manner, she wouldn't have minded.

But she did mind, damn it. She was tired of people walking all over her, taking her for granted and thinking, *It's only old Jess, she won't mind*. Because she did. She minded very much that her boyfriend had gone off with her best friend, that her mother only wanted to know her when she needed something, that she had nowhere to live and that her hip was hurting now where she'd banged it. This rude farmer was the final straw.

The last straw? Oh, dear, how appropriately agricultural and how awful that, in the face of his anger she could feel her lips beginning to twitch and realised, to her dismay, that she was about to laugh. Matt was always telling her she had an 'inappropriate sense of humour'.

'I'm sorry.' She cleared her throat and inspected her fingernails so that he couldn't see her face. 'I didn't mean to offend you. And I promise I haven't done any damage. Now, if you'll excuse me, I'll be on my way.'

'Where are you going anyway?'

Jess was tempted to say it was none of his business, but decided against it. His dog was still giving her that, *Go ahead, punk, make my day* look, like he'd welcome the chance to take a bite out of her ankle at the slightest provocation on her part. 'I'm headed for a place called Higher Neston Farm. It's just down the lane, I believe?'

'About half a mile.' He glanced into her well-laden car and those dark, expressive brows drew together in yet another frown. 'You're staying with Elsie? I didn't know she was still doing B&B.'

'I'm not going B&B. I'm booked in at the Old Dairy for — ' She broke off, as she realised she had no idea how long she was going to stay. 'For a week or so,' she said vaguely.

'Really?' He looked surprised, then shrugged. 'Well, as long as you keep on this lane and don't take the right turn that's coming up, you'll be fine.'

'And if I do take the right turn?' Jess

couldn't resist asking, this time allowing her smile to break through.

'Then you could end up on the moor — where people have got themselves lost and it's taken them days to find their way back. Still,' he looked again at the back of her car, one eyebrow raised, an answering smile tugging at his mouth, 'You look as if you'll be okay. You don't exactly travel light, do you?'

Jess followed his gaze to the boxes on the back seat of her car, where her dear old food mixer and grandmother's ancient frying pan nestled.

'I couldn't fit the kitchen sink in, so I hope they have such modern luxuries this deep into rural Somerset,' she said as she got back into her car, wondering what he'd say if he'd seen the set of chef's knives that were buried somewhere between her nighties and a tangle that looked like a pair of mating octopuses but was in fact an unknown number of pairs of tights.

She was still smiling to herself as she came to the sign that said Higher

Neston Farm and pulled in to the yard with a sigh of pleasure.

The country air was doing her good already. On a day when she'd thought she'd never smile again she'd smiled twice, laughed out loud once and even managed a yee-haw!

She got out of the car and looked around. She was in the middle of what she supposed must once have been a farmyard, although from the clean condition of the concrete it was a good many years since any cattle had collected here, patiently waiting their turn to go into the milking parlour.

If further evidence was needed, the neat row of tubs, ranged along the front of the big, double doored barn, spilled over with cool blue pansies and vivid golden daffodils and would not have been in such good condition if they were within reach of the cows' eager tongues.

She turned towards the sturdy looking farmhouse with its tall Georgian style windows. Its somewhat austere exterior had been brightened up by a creeper which scrambled over most of the front and was just beginning to break out in its first flush of pale young leaves.

As she walked towards the stone porch, which was flanked by yet more colourful tubs, a volley of furious barking from the other side of the front door made her stop and want to turn and run. But before she could move, the front door shook as if it had just been thumped by something very large and very angry. She backed off, hoping the door was as strong as it looked.

She stayed a safe distance and waited for Mrs Russell to open the door. She must have heard the dog, even if she hadn't heard the car pull up. And, thanks to her dawdling by the gate, it was well after three by now, the time she was expected. So where was she?

She forced herself to approach the door once more and gave the iron knocker a couple of hard raps.

Still no sign of Mrs Russell, in spite

of the dog's frenzied barking. Jess looked across the yard, past the neatly trimmed hedges, the old stone barn with its high doors, the glimpse of an orchard beyond, until she found what she was looking for.

The Old Dairy was on the far side of the yard, a single storey building, with the paintwork almost the same shade of grey green as the lichen that spread across the stone lintel above the door. She gave a sigh of relief as she saw that the top half of the stable door that led into the cottage was open. Mrs Russell was obviously still getting the cottage ready.

She pushed open the door and let herself into a small but well fitted kitchen, that led into a sitting area. Much of the building's original features had been retained, from the raftered ceiling to the rough stone walls. It was charming but as cold and quiet as a winter churchyard.

There was also a faint smell of dampness in the air, as if the place had been unlived in for a long time. What was going on here? Jess shivered and pulled her coat closer to her.

'Hello?' she called into the unnatural stillness. 'Mrs Russell, are you there? Is anyone there?'

But the only response to her call was a renewed frenzy of barking from the farmhouse. Jess frowned and went to check out the bedrooms.

The first one was empty, the bed stripped back to its mattress, the furniture shrouded in dustsheets. She went into the second, expecting to see the same but stopped on the threshold and clapped her hand to her mouth to hold back a scream.

Stretched out on the floor beside the bed was an elderly lady, lying face down. And she was frighteningly still.

3

Jess knelt beside the old lady, who lay stretched out on the floor by the side of the bed. She was face down, one arm crumpled beneath her body. And by her head the carpet was stained by a small pool of blood.

Jess placed a tentative hand on her shoulder. The old lady stirred, moaned and began to move — and Jess began to breathe again. She was alive. Thank God.

'Don't try to move, Mrs Russell,' she said gently, not wanting to alarm her. 'I've called an ambulance and they'll be here soon.'

'Don't move?' The old lady lifted her head and looked at Jess, blinking hard as she did so. 'If you think I'm staying here like this for the time it takes an ambulance to come all the way out here, you can think again, young lady.

Who are you anyway?'

Jess's relief at discovering that the old lady, whom she took to be Mrs Russell, was not dead was short-lived as she watched her struggle to get up. 'Mrs Russell, please. I really don't think you should try and move.'

'The name's Elsie and will you please stop gawping at me, child, and help me at least get into a more comfortable position. I haven't broken anything, I assure you. I just can't get up and it gets me so damned frustrated. What's the time? Feels like I've been lying here for hours.'

'It's half past three. What time did you fall?'

'Just after twelve. Then I've been here — ' she shook her head. 'No. That can't be right. I've not been lying here for three hours.'

'You were unconscious — '

'Of course I wasn't. I was exhausted, that's all. Now, help me at least to sit up. I can — ' She stopped. Her face went grey and her eyes, that had been beginning to clear, appeared to swivel in her head as she sagged forward with a faint cry.

She'd fainted — or had she lapsed into unconsciousness? Jess cursed her lack of first aid knowledge and prayed for the ambulance to hurry. 'Mrs Russell? Elsie? Can you hear me?'

Elsie's eyelids fluttered, then opened. 'As a matter of fact,' she said through jaws clamped against the pain, 'I think I may have broken my wretched wrist. And the fact that I'm lying on it doesn't help. So please help me.'

'Of course.' Jess helped her turn on to her back. She brought pillows from the bed and put them behind her head, then covered her with a duvet. She suppressed a cry of dismay when she saw that her left wrist was, indeed, at a very strange angle to her arm and she made her as comfortable as she could with more pillows.

'You may well have broken it,' she said. 'Shall I get some ice?'

Jess shuddered at the thought of

braving the manic dog to get into the farmhouse kitchen. Would he even let her in? She doubted it and she was quite relieved when Elsie shook her head.

'What happened?' Jess asked, hoping that talking might take Elsie's mind of her pain.

'My own damn stupid fault,' Elsie said. 'I was trying to make the bed and overreached. Grabbed the end of the bed but wasn't quick enough. Went down like a blasted felled oak and landed on my wrist. And then, like the old fool that I am, with my wrist out of action I found I couldn't get up. Just lay here on the floor like some pathetic old biddie, calling for help.'

'You look as if you've taken a bit of a knock to the head as well,' Jess said, looking anxiously at the dried blood on her temple.

'Then perhaps that'll knock some sense in me,' Elsie smiled and Jess was relieved to see she was looking a bit better. Her eyes were clearer and it was good to see her smile.

'I'm so sorry,' Jess said, 'This is all my fault. I'm Jess Maybury. I phoned earlier about taking this place. If I hadn't pushed you into getting it ready — '

'My dear child, you don't know me very well. Nobody, but nobody makes me do anything I don't want to do.' Elsie spoke with such quiet determination that Jess believed her, although she still felt guilty about her part in her accident.

'Yes, but — '

'Now, child, there's something I need you to do. Urgently.'

'Of course,' Jess said, anxious to do what she could. 'What is it?'

'Cancel the ambulance. I hate hospitals. They're nasty, dangerous places where people catch all sorts of unpleasant things. And furthermore they interfere with the body's natural ability to heal itself and — '

Jess shook her head. 'I can't do that, I'm afraid. I think you'll probably have to go to hospital. I'm sorry. Your wrist needs to be seen to and there's that bang to your head. I'm sure when the paramedics see that, you'll be left with no choice.'

'But I can't leave poor old Benson.'

'Who's Benson? And is there anything I can do to help?' Jess eased the pillow at the back of Elsie's head to make her more comfortable. 'After all, it's my fault you're in this mess in the first place.'

'Benson's the dog,' Elsie said, 'He's been barking like that ever since I fell. The poor fellow's shut in the house and he knows something's wrong.'

'So, is there someone I can get in touch with? Your family?'

Elsie's face clouded. 'No one,' she said shortly.

'I'm sorry. Then friends, maybe? I mean, who looks after Benson when you're on holiday?'

'I never go away,' Elsie said. 'He hates to be left, you see. And I don't feel the need for holiday. If you won't cancel

38

the ambulance, then perhaps you'd stay here? You were going to anyway.'

'Here?' Jess gazed around the pretty, but too-long-empty room and shivered in the cold that was beginning to seep into her bones, making her wish she could share Elsie's duvet. Where was that wretched ambulance?

'No, of course not,' Elsie said. 'No one's stayed in here since last June.'

'Yet when I spoke to you on the phone this morning, you said you had guests that were waiting to leave today? What was that all about?'

Elsie's too pale face flushed. 'I'm afraid I was a bit . . . well, let's say creative with the truth there. The, um, guests I was referring to was a family of mice who'd taken up residence. It's all right, don't worry. They're gone now. I've been meaning to do it for ages and your phone call gave me the kick up the backside I needed.'

'A family of mice?' Jess tried to look shocked, but it was no good. The laughter broke through, sweeping away some of the tension that had built up since finding Elsie slumped on the floor. 'I was going to share my holiday with a family of mice?'

'No, of course not. They've been dealt with. But I'm sorry I lied to you. I was working up to tell you the truth on the phone when you said you'd pay premium rate and I'm afraid . . . ' She paused and looked away. 'I couldn't resist it. You see, I had this huge vet's bill to pay and, although Roger's very good and patient, it was becoming embarrassing. So you'll stay?'

'Here? With the mice?'

'Of course not. In the farmhouse. There's a room at the back of the house, with wonderful views of Glastonbury Tor and the Mendip Hills. It has full en suite facilities. You'll be very comfortable there, I promise you.'

'You're asking me to stay here? On my own?'

Elsie's face clouded. 'Oh, dear, I hadn't thought of that. Stupid me. It must be the bang on the head that's addled what little brains I have. Because you were so adamant about wanting a two bedroom cottage, I assumed you were with your husband or someone.'

'No. I'm on my own.' Jess swallowed hard, surprised at how difficult that was to say. *Better get used to it, girl*, she told herself firmly. *This is how it's going to be from now on.*

'I didn't mean to upset you,' Elsie said.

'You didn't. I just — '

'But someone has,' Elsie said quietly. 'I can see it in your eyes. Look, why don't you stay here anyway? This is a very special, healing place, you know. I know. It healed me when I first came here as a young bride. And don't worry about being on your own. You'll be perfectly safe here and Benson will look after you . . . '

'Benson? But I don't — '

But before Jess could tell Elsie that she had a bit of a problem with dogs and that she'd rather share a house with a family of mice than one big, barky dog, Elsie spoke across her.

'There's a casserole in the simmering oven,' she said. 'I was going to offer it to you anyway. So be sure you go ahead and have it, won't you?'

'But you can't leave me here, alone in your house. It wouldn't be right.' Jess was horrified at such trust. 'You don't know me. I could be the outrider for a gang of antique thieves who'll empty your house before you know what's happening.'

'Nonsense.' Elsie snorted. 'If your gang can find anything of value in there, they're welcome to it. And I do know you, child. I know people, especially people who are in trouble. As you are. You were sent here for a reason, you know.'

Jess felt uncomfortable at Elsie's sudden change of tone. Her eyes had become very bright and she spoke with almost feverish intensity. Jess looked at the dried blood on the side of her temple. Maybe the blow to the head had caused more damage than she or Elsie thought.

'You're thinking I've lost it, aren't you?' Elsie chuckled and as this was so close to what Jess had indeed been thinking she said nothing, merely shook her head.

'Okay, then tell me this,' Elsie went on, 'Do you usually subscribe to the magazine you saw my advert in?'

'Well, no but — '

'Then what were you doing with it?'

'Well, I'm not too sure . . . ' Jess was too embarrassed to own up to the truth of how the magazine came to be in her kitchen. That she'd been reading it in the dentist surgery and had liked the sound of a recipe for the salmon and asparagus quiche. She'd meant to copy the recipe and return the magazine. But, of course, she hadn't.

'You're feeling rejected and unhappy at the moment, but it will pass.' As Elsie spoke, she reached out to touch Jess's arm, but the movement made her cry out in pain and draw back against her pillows, her colour returned to the grey pallor that had so frightened Jess earlier.

'Why is the ambulance taking so long?' Jess muttered.

'Welcome to rural living,' Elsie said drily. 'Everything takes a long time here. Police, fire, ambulance. We're easy to forget out here in the sticks and not enough voters to make any politician, whatever their colour, bother about us. I despise them all so let's talk about something else while we're waiting. How about I tell you Benson's story?'

'The dog. Yes, well, the thing is — '

'It's a sad, but horribly familiar one,' Elsie said. 'He's a lovely dog, a complete hotchpotch. A bit of German Shepherd, some lab and goodness knows what else besides. The poor love had been abandoned when he was about six months old. His delightful owners took him for a drive in the middle of the night to the nearest motorway and tipped him out.'

Jess's heart lurched at the thought.

'What a terrible thing to do.'

'There's more,' Elsie said. 'Someone phoned the Police who came and caught him and took him to a nearby rescue centre. According to them, he was such a lovely natured dog that, in spite of what he'd been through, he didn't lose his faith in humans so he was ready for rehoming. He went to a young couple from the village down the road. They seemed the ideal family for him, until she became pregnant. She came here late on Friday night, saying that they had to go North — her mother was ill or something and could I look after him until they came back? Only they never did come back. Seems they'd skipped owing months of rent.'

'So the poor fellow was abandoned not once but twice.'

'You wouldn't believe people could be so heartless, would you? But at least these two had the gumption to leave him with someone they knew would look after him. Unfortunately, though, I'm pretty sure they used to beat him.

Certainly, he runs a mile if I pick up anything that looks even remotely like a stick.'

'How could people do that?'

'I have no idea. But I promise you, he'll be no trouble. He is inclined to be a bit stand-offish with strangers. But at least now you know why.'

'Look, I'll tell you what I'll do. 'Jess said. 'I'll go and find myself a hotel not too far away. I drove through Wells on the way here. That looks a lovely place and sure to have plenty of hotels. And then I'll come in every day and see to Benson for you. How about that?'

'It would be better for Benson if someone was in the house. I told you how the poor chap hates to be left alone.' Elsie winced as if the pain was becoming harder to bear. 'Better for you, too, child. Besides, there are the cats as well.'

Jess frowned. 'Cats?'

With her good hand, Elsie pointed towards the yard. 'On the other side of the big stone barn is the cattery.'

'A cattery? How many cats have you got in there, for goodness' sake?'

'There are only four at the moment. But they're no trouble, I promise. And there's a girl, Rachel, who comes up and helps out sometimes. Her mobile telephone number's on the notice board in the kitchen. You can't miss it.'

'Then why don't I ask her to come and see to the animals, all the animals, now?' Jess asked. She wasn't worried about the cats. She'd always loved them. But dogs were another matter. Her mother hated them because, she said, they were dirty, smelly and made a mess. Jess didn't exactly hate them, but certainly didn't feel comfortable around them.

'Because she won't be home from school yet,' Elsie said. 'She's hoping to be a veterinary nurse if she does well enough in her exams. And, as I keep telling you, you were sent here for a reason. Just like Benson was.'

'But I haven't been abandoned.'

'No? But, like him, you've been hurt

and you're running away. I can see it in your eyes. But, as I said, you've come to the right place. Can't you feel it? Can't you feel that this is a healing place? Please say you'll stay.'

Jess bit her lip. It was true, she had felt a kind of peace when she'd got out of the car, but that had more to do with the end of a long, tiring journey, with the sound of bird song and the promise of spring just around the corner, nothing to do with 'healing' or whatever. She'd never believed in all that mumbo jumbo, although her mother tried every self-help craze that came along.

Why, Jess wondered, could she never learn to say no? It had landed her in trouble before and was about to do so again. She was only here now because, without the story of a holiday, she'd have been unable to say no to her mother. And maybe if this morning she'd . . .

She broke off and looked at her watch, unable to believe that this time yesterday she'd been making chocolate mousse.

'Are you sure there's no one I should be contacting for you?' she asked. 'No family?'

For a moment, Jess thought Elsie was going to cry. She turned to Jess and was about to say something when she was interrupted by the sound of an ambulance turning in to the yard. A mud encrusted Land Rover pulled in behind it.

Jess showed the paramedics to the room where Elsie was. As she did so, the man in the Land Rover got out and she saw it was the angry farmer she'd met earlier. Without a word to Jess, he followed the paramedics into the cottage.

'Rob?' Elsie said. 'What on earth are you doing here?'

'Followed the ambulance down the lane,' he said, 'Then when I saw it turn in here, thought I'd better come and check if everything is okay. What's happened here?'

'Nothing at all,' Elsie said. 'It was Jess here, panicking over nothing. Rob, Jess is a — a distant relative on my mother's side. She's going to stay and look after Benson and the cats for me. Keep an eye on her, will you?'

She stopped as one of the paramedics went to move her arm. 'That hurt, love?' he asked. 'Just sit back now and try not to move. We'll have you up and out of here in no time.'

Jess went outside to give them room and also to give herself chance to simmer down. What was going on here? When had she agreed to stay? And what was all this about being a relative?

'You didn't say you were a relative of Elsie's?' Rob's voice unexpectedly behind her made her jump and she whirled round defensively.

'You didn't ask,' she hissed but before she could say anymore, the paramedics came out with Elsie on a stretcher, loaded her into the ambulance and drove away. She felt uncomfortable letting him believe Elsie's fib about them being related, but there was something about his bristly manner that brought out the contrariness in her.

'Elsie said I was to see you into the house and see if there is anything else you want,' he said, not meeting her eye.

Jess stood by the gate that led into the farmhouse, her heart thudding at the sound of the dog — Benson, she now knew he was called, although it didn't help — barking louder and fiercer than ever.

Rob walked ahead of her up towards the front door but Jess stayed firmly the other side of the gate.

'Are you coming?' he asked, frowning impatiently.

'I — I can't,' she said, backing away as she did so.

'Can't what?' Rob's dark brows darkened even more under his glare of disapproval. 'Are you telling me that Elsie got it wrong? That you're not staying after all? Because if that's the case — '

'No. I'm staying. I gave her my word.

And I'll do it — only, do you think you could do something about that dog?'

'Benson,' he shouted, 'Quiet boy. Now.'

Instantly, the dog stopped barking and the door stopped shaking. And Jess began to feel a little bit braver.

'It's just that — well, the thing is, I'm not very good with dogs, particularly big, hairy ones,' she said.

'How do you know he's big and hairy?'

'Because he has the sort of bark that goes with big and hairy.'

Rob laughed. 'You don't have to be scared of Benson. He's a pussy cat.'

'Sure. A pussy cat who's the size of a tiger, with a temperament to match, no doubt,' Jess said, although by this time she was standing behind Rob as he opened the door and let them in to the farmhouse.

The dog wasn't quite the size of a tiger but he was big and hairy. He had pointed ears, an intelligent face and the biggest paws Jess had ever seen.

'You have no reason to be scared of Benson,' Rob said, 'Despite the fact he's had a traumatic life, there isn't an ounce of malice in him. Although he is inclined to be a bit aloof with strangers, so I wouldn't be too upset if he doesn't greet you like a long lost friend.'

'I'll be more than happy to be ignored, I promise you,' Jess said as she followed Rob along the dark, narrow passageway.

'This is the kitchen,' Rob said. The door scraped along the floor with a discordant screech as he pushed it open.

He muttered something about fixing it for Elsie but Jess wasn't listening. Instead she had the most amazing sense of déjà vu as she walked into the big, airy kitchen. It was so like her grandmother's, it brought tears to her eyes. She hadn't thought of her for ages and yet, twice in one afternoon, she realised how very much she still missed her.

'An Aga,' she sighed, going across

and running her hands across the range's smooth, enamelled surface, which felt warm to her touch. 'My Gran had one of these and I always loved it. She used to make the most gorgeous drop scones on the hot plate. She used to — '

She broke off, her colour rising as she saw his smile and realised she was in danger of letting her enthusiasm run away with her again. It was, according to Matt, a very tiresome and childish trait and one she'd been working hard to eliminate.

'I'm sorry,' she said, 'Here am I prattling on and you must have one hundred and one things still to do. Not least, getting home to your wife. She must be wondering where you are,' she exclaimed as she glanced up at the large clock on the wall.

'I doubt that very much,' he said, his smile replaced by his more usual scowl. 'Seeing as she walked out on me three years ago next month.'

'Oh.' Jess felt her colour rise. 'I'm

sorry. That was stupid of me.'

He shrugged and turned to the Aga. 'You weren't to know. I take it you know how that thing works then, seeing as you're such a fan?'

'I've never used one, but yes, I can still remember what my gran taught me. Elsie said there was a casserole in the simmering oven.'

'Lucky you if you've one of Elsie's casseroles to look forward to. You're in for a treat. I'll just show you the rest of the house, explain how everything works then leave you to get on with things. I'd better give you my phone number as well. I promised Elsie I'd look out for you and, as I'm your nearest neighbour — my farm is another half mile down the lane — please call if you're concerned about anything.'

'That's very kind.' She looked at Benson, now stretched out in front of the Aga. Now he'd stopped barking, he didn't seem anything like as fierce. 'I'm sure everything will be okay and I can see Rachel's number from here, so I'll give her a ring.'

As soon as Rob left, Jess checked the casserole. He'd been right about that. It smelt delicious and she was suddenly ravenously hungry. So much for the Heartbreak Diet, she thought wryly.

Benson suddenly stood up and came towards her. For a moment, her heart leapt uncomfortably and she took a step backwards. Then he looked up at her, his eyes pleading and there was a faint flicker of his tail. And suddenly, the fear she'd felt of him melted away.

Why on earth had she thought she disliked dogs? Of course she didn't. In fact, when her grandmother had been alive, she'd had an elderly golden labrador called Honey, whom Jess had loved to distraction. It was her mother who hated dogs and who had passed that dislike on to her.

She looked down into Benson's beautiful, pleading eyes. How could she be scared of that?

'Ah, so now I know the way to your

heart, don't I? But this is not for you, sunshine,' she laughed and he turned his back on her with a noisy sigh. 'And before either of us get to eat, I'd better sort something out about Elsie's paying guests, don't you think?'

She picked up her phone and dialled the number on the board. 'Can I speak to Rachel please?'

'I'm sorry. She's not here at the moment.'

'Oh, dear.' This was unexpected. 'When will she be back?'

'I'm afraid she won't. Not until the weekend, that is. I'm her mother, Fiona. Can I help?'

Jess explained about Elsie's accident and how she'd agreed to see to the cattery for her. 'So, you see, when Elsie said Rachel could probably help out she obviously didn't know she was away.'

'Off on a field trip with the school. I'm sorry to hear about Elsie and I know our Rachel would have been only too glad to help out. Elsie's done such a lot for her over the years. But don't worry. I'll come up and help you. I've helped Rachel a few times when the cattery has been particularly full. How many cats are there now?'

'Only four.'

'Then that will be no trouble. It won't take very long at all.'

'That's so kind of you,' Jess felt a rush of gratitude.

'It's no trouble. Elsie has done such a lot for the whole family, not just Rachel. I'll be up in half an hour.'

Fiona was right. It took them no time at all to see to the cats. They were in a long, low building that, at one time, Jess supposed used to house cattle but was now sectioned off into a number of large runs. To one side was a small, spotlessly clean kitchen and, on a large whiteboard on the wall were very precise and detailed information about each cat's requirements, written in a bold, neat hand. She was able to reassure Fiona that she'd have no trouble dealing with the cats on her own from now on.

Jess finished her dinner — which was every bit as good as Rob had promised — and looked at her watch, surprised to see that it was only half past nine. She was completely exhausted. It had been a long day and she was ready for bed.

She'd already found the bedroom Elsie had suggested she use — and it was delightful. The bed looked very comfortable and she found herself looking forward to curling up in it.

'Benson?' She called the dog, still stretched out in front of the Aga. 'Are we friends yet, do you think?'

But he ignored her, giving only the faintest flick of his ears to show he'd heard her. A wave of intense loneliness washed over her. This time yesterday she'd been sitting chatting to Sophie about their day, their plans for tomorrow. Now she was talking to a dog who wouldn't even turn his head as she spoke.

But at least the dog wasn't planning

to steal her boyfriend.

'Enough,' she told herself firmly as she stood up. 'Sitting around feeling sorry for myself isn't going to help.'

She went out to the car to get her book. As she opened the front door, she stopped, unnerved for a second by the complete darkness. She'd lived in London for most of her life and was used to the fact that it never got completely dark. Unlike here where the darkness was so thick she could almost feel it pressing against her face.

But as she stood there, gradually she began to be able to make out the outlines of the buildings, of her car. She looked up and gasped as she saw the sky so full of stars it took her breath away. She'd never seen anything quite so wonderful.

And then she realised she was no longer afraid. Nor lonely. She turned back to the lighted house and there, down the hall watching her was Benson. He made no move to come any closer but, exactly as Elsie had said, he was watching out for her.

She went out to the car, got the bag that contained her book and went back into the house. As she did so, her phone began to ring.

'Jessica?' It was her mother again. 'Now, come along. You've made your point and I'm sorry if I wasn't a bit more sympathetic about Matt. But there really is little to be gained by sulking about it, you know. And I think — '

'Did you want something?' Jess said, wearily, 'Only I'm just about to go to bed. It's been a long, tiring day.'

'Want something?' Her mother sounded surprised at Jess's interruption. 'Well, yes. I want to know where you are, for a start.'

'I'm twenty-six years old and have lived away from home since I was eighteen. It's a little late to start worrying about where I am, don't you think? A little bit out of character, too.'

'Really, Jessica. I don't know what's got into you, really I don't. But, since you ask, I was calling for a reason. It's just — '

'Yes? Go on,' Jess prompted, as she heard her mother's voice begin to trail away.

'Well, to be honest, I'm getting in a bit of a state about these Americans your father insists on bringing home. I told you, they want proper, old fashioned English cooking and I thought you might — '

'Then try Marks and Spencer,' Jess said, tiredness making her snap. 'And while I'm thinking about it, please don't call me Jessica. You know how much I hate it. I prefer Jess.'

Her mother tutted. 'Now you really are being petulant. And I'm not going to start calling you Jess. If I'd wanted to name you after a sheepdog, I'd have called you Lassie. Good night, Jessica. I hope you're in a better mood by tomorrow.'

Jess switched the phone off and almost punched the air. She supposed she must have stood up to her mother at some time but it felt like the first time. And it felt good.

Maybe Elsie was right after all and there was something special in the air at Higher Neston.

She picked up her book and went to go to bed. She paused in the kitchen door and, as a gesture of rebellion to her mother, who'd have had a fit if she'd known, called the dog.

'You coming?' she asked but, once again, he turned his head away.

'Your loss, buster,' she laughed and went up to bed.

She was just about to get into bed when Benson started growling. 'Changed your mind, have you?' she asked, 'Well, tough. You had your chance. Now, settle down.'

But the dog didn't settle down. He kept on growling, a low threatening sound. Jess began to feel uneasy, then told herself not to be silly. The dog was probably hearing a fox or something outside in the field.

Then, she heard a noise that made

her freeze. A sound that carried, even above the loud thumping of her heart.

It was the sound of the kitchen door opening. There was no mistaking its discordant rasp. Someone was in the house.

4

Jess grabbed her dressing gown and pulled it tightly round her. She picked up her mobile phone and, thankful she'd brought her handbag upstairs with her, took out the scrap of paper with Rob's number on it.

He answered almost immediately. 'I — I think there's someone moving about downstairs,' she hissed.

'Jess? Is that you?'

'Yes. Sorry,' she whispered. 'Can you come?'

'I'll be right there. Stay where you are and don't confront him.'

From the room below, she could hear sounds of someone moving about and Benson's low growl turned into a warning bark. The next moment, she heard a loud curse and the dog's yelp of pain.

Without waiting for Rob, she took

her grandmother's ancient frying pan out of the box and crept downstairs. The kitchen door was open and she saw a tall, fair-haired man rifling through the drawers in the oak dresser.

She jumped as she felt something press against her hand but when she looked down, it was Benson, pressing his nose into her hand, his large body leaning into her leg.

'Who are you and what do you think you're doing?' she demanded, pleased at how steady her voice sounded.

The man whirled round, his eyes wide with shock. He closed the dresser drawer carefully then turned round to face Jess. Then, suddenly he relaxed and smiled, and as he did so she became aware of how she must look, in her Mickey Mouse nightie and dressing gown, clutching her grandmother's ancient frying pan.

'I might ask you the same question,' he said. 'Gran promised me she'd given up taking in paying guests. It's too much for her, you know. Look, I'm sorry I startled you. Although, it has to be said, you startled me even more. Er . . . would you like to put that . . . that frying pan down before you do some serious damage with it?'

'Did you say Gran? You mean Mrs Russell?'

'Elsie Russell is my grandmother. My name's Nick, by the way.' He shook his loose blonde hair from his eyes and held out his hand towards her. Jess put the frying pan on the table and looked at him suspiciously, not wanting to let him know she was alone in the house.

'Why did you kick the dog?' she asked. 'And why did Elsie tell me she had no family?'

'Firstly, I didn't kick the dog. I tripped over the damn thing. And I promise you, I'm Elsie's grandson. If you don't believe me, there are at least a dozen photographs of me in the other room, all in various stages of my education. As to why she told you she had no family — ' he shrugged. 'I guess she's the only one who can answer that.

Shall we call her?'

'No. You can't.'

He raised his eyebrow. 'I can't?'

'She's not here. I'm sorry you didn't know before. Your grandmother's in hospital. She had a fall this afternoon and has broken her wrist. They're probably going to keep her in for a few days, according to the paramedic.'

'Look, sorry. I don't mean this to sound rude,' he said with a frown, 'But who are you?'

'I'm — ' She was about to say she was just a paying guest, but stopped herself. 'I'm a friend of Elsie's,' she said. 'My Gran and her were friends from way back.'

Now why had she done that? It was something to do with the way he'd frowned when he said Elsie wasn't supposed to do Bed and Breakfast any more. The last thing she wanted to do was to make problems between Elsie and her family. It sounded as if they had enough of those already without her adding to them.

'I came down here to stay with her for a few days and found her on the floor in the Old Dairy,' she went on. 'She was worried about the cats, so I said I'd stay here and look after them for her. Just to put her mind at rest.'

'You're staying here to look after the cats?'

'Just until Rachel comes back,' Jess said. 'I don't mind at all. There's only four of them at the moment and they're no trouble.'

'No trouble?' Nick frowned. 'She told me she'd got rid of all her boarders. Something else she's forgotten, no doubt. After that last fiasco, with the law suit and all, she promised — '

Before she could ask him what he meant, there was a screech of tyres in the yard outside, a car door slammed and then pounding on the front door.

'Jess? Are you all right?'

Nick looked up at her quickly. 'What the devil — ?'

'It's the farmer from down the road. I thought — that is, when I heard you moving around down here, I thought you were a burglar or something and I sent for him.' As if to confirm this, Benson gave a bark of welcome and hurried to the door.

'Well, if it isn't the cavalry,' Nick drawled as Rob came in to the kitchen. 'I might have known it would be you.'

Rob ignored him and looked across at Jess. 'Are you all right?' he asked.

'Yes,' Jess felt her cheeks burn and wished, not for the first time she had a longer dressing gown — or better still, that she was fully dressed. 'I panicked, I'm afraid. Elsie didn't say — ' She was about to say that Elsie didn't say she had a grandson but the two men were looking at each other with barely disguised hostility and she didn't want to do or say anything that might make things worse. 'She didn't say her grandson might be looking in. I expect it slipped her mind, what with the accident and everything.'

Rob looked as if he was about to say something but Nick got in first.

'Obviously,' he said, 'Gran can be quite forgetful at times.'

'She's as sharp as you and I put together,' Rob glared at him. 'And well you know it.'

Nick returned Rob's glare and the two men stood, squaring up to each other like a pair of prize fighters. Benson must have been as aware as Jess was of the tension in the room, for he gave a low, warning growl and moved towards Nick, his hackles raised like a worn out toothbrush.

'Stay,' Rob said sharply and the dog obeyed without hesitation.

'Rob and I have known each other since forever,' Nick said, 'We started primary school together and I'd like to say we've been friends ever since. But, well,' he shrugged, 'You know how it is. We squabbled over who got to play with the toy train and we've been squabbling over everything ever since. Isn't that right, Rob?'

Jess felt very uncomfortable. Entertaining one strange man while wearing her Mickey Mouse nightdress was bad enough, but two of them — especially two who were looking like they'd like nothing better than to knock the other's teeth out — was simply too much.

'Look, Rob' she said, 'It was very kind of you to come rushing around here and I'm really sorry you've had a wasted journey. I feel a complete fool. But, if you don't mind, I'd prefer it if you left now. Both of you.' She turned to Nick, 'And Nick, perhaps you could come back tomorrow and search for whatever it was you were looking for? Or, better still, I'll mention it to Elsie and she'll no doubt be able to tell you where to look.'

'I'll be off then,' Rob said but only got as far as the door when he turned and asked Nick: 'What exactly were you looking for?'

'None of your damn business,' Nick snapped. 'Don't you have some cows to look after or something?'

Rob left, shutting the door carefully

behind him. Benson whined softly as he disappeared.

Nick smiled across at Jess. 'Poor Rob,' he said, 'He's not a bad bloke but I'm afraid he's jealous as hell of me. Always has been.'

'Elsie seems to think a lot of him,' Jess said.

'Just be careful, won't you? I'm sure if Gran had had more time with you, she'd have given you the same advice. He has his own agenda where she's concerned, you know. He'd dearly love to get his hands on some of her fields and barns. He wears the poor old girl down sometimes. I've had words with him about it, but, as you saw for yourself, one word from me, and it's red rag to a bull — or to a farmer, in his case, I suppose.'

His laughter broke the tension that had filled the room and Jess felt even more confused than ever.

'Look, I really don't understand what's going on here.' She dragged her hand through her hair. 'Why would

Elsie tell me she had no family?'

'Even Rob acknowledged that I was Elsie's grandson, didn't he? I'm afraid it's what I was trying to say before Rob bit my head off. Gran has been getting more and more confused lately. Forgets her name, who she is, thinks her husband is still alive, that sort of thing. We've been told, although we're trying hard not to believe it that it's the beginning of Alzheimers.'

'Oh, no. Surely not,' Jess protested. Yet when she thought about it there were a number of things that pointed to Elsie's confusion. The fact that she'd told Jess she had other guests staying, that she had no family and then claimed Jess as a distant relative. Was Nick right after all?

'You see,' Nick said gently. 'I've been watching your face and could read the doubt that was creeping in. It's heartbreaking, isn't it? Anyway, before I go, I'd better explain my reason for being here. I'm an Estate Agent and, in one of her more lucid moments, Gran instructed me to start making moves about putting the farm on the market.'

'Sell the farm? But that would break her heart, surely? It's so lovely here.'

'Lovely it may be, but it's far too isolated for someone of her age. Look what happened this afternoon. And once an elderly person has one fall, you know, there's always the risk of others. She's better off moving. In fact, I came round this evening to tell her that I've got some clients who'd like to come and view. They're not going to be happy about those cats though.'

Jess bit her lip. 'There are only four in the cattery at the moment but I see in the book there are a few more booked in for next week.'

'Look, best not say anything to Gran about all this at the moment. It's quite possible this place isn't what they're looking for at all. It's not going to be the easiest property to shift, I can assure you. I only thought I'd better tell you in case you were worried by the sight of strangers about the place.'

'That's thoughtful. And I really am sorry I thought you were a burglar.'

He smiled. It was a warm, boyish, attractive smile and there was something vaguely familiar about it.

'Forget it,' he said. 'I'm just happy you ask questions first and didn't hit me with that frying pan. Do you always take one of those to bed with you?'

'Of course not. I was just too tired to unpack.' She stifled a yawn. 'Now if you don't mind — '

'You're out on your feet. I can see that. I'll be off then.'

She followed him into the hall, said goodnight, then, feeling a bit melodramatic, drew the heavy bolt across the front door behind him. She turned out the lights in the kitchen and went up to bed. As she did so, she was surprised to hear the tap of the dog's claws on the floorboards as Benson followed her upstairs.

He wouldn't come in to the bedroom though, but positioned himself with a heavy sigh outside the bedroom door.

For the first time since she'd met him, Jess felt herself warming to him and beginning to understand what people liked about dogs. There was something very comforting about having something big and scary-looking guarding your door and Jess knew she would sleep sounder for the knowledge.

'We have more in common than you realise,' she said to him as she went to turn off the light. 'We both have to learn to trust people again.'

But Benson turned his head away and Jess realised she still had a long way to go towards winning him over.

5

Early the next morning Jess had only just finished dealing with the cattery and come back through to the cottage when the phone rang. It was Fiona calling to check everything was okay.

'I hope I didn't wake you,' she said. 'I'm just calling to check if you need help with the cats this morning. I meant to phone earlier but we've had a bit of a to-do in the lambing shed this morning and — '

'I'm fine. I told you last night I could manage. I've already seen to the cats. They're all fed, watered and cleaned and are snoozing quietly as we speak. I'm glad you phoned though. I'd like to go and see Elsie today, to reassure her about the cats and Benson and everything but have no idea which hospital she's in. Nor do I have any idea how to get there.'

Fiona's instructions were clear and concise. 'When are you going in?'

'I thought this afternoon. How long will it take to get there from here?'

'About 40 minutes, although if you catch it wrong in the hospital, it'll take you that much time again to find a parking spot. It's a nightmare.'

As Jess was leaving the house to drive to the hospital to see Elsie, Benson jumped up and followed her to the door.

'What is it, boy?' she asked. 'What do you want?'

She remembered Elsie telling her how Benson hated to be left alone. But that was when he was with Elsie, surely. He acted as if he couldn't bear to be in the same room as Jess, so surely he'd be only too pleased to have the place to himself for a while. But no, he followed her out to the car and when she opened the door, he'd jumped in and settled himself on the back seat before she could move.

Once there, she didn't have the heart

to turf him out again. So she shrugged, started the car and took one last glance at Fiona's instructions.

They were spot on. So, too, her warning about the time it took to park the car. Elsie was delighted to see her and, although still pale, she looked a lot better than when she'd been put in the ambulance, in spite of the colourful bruise on her left temple.

'How are you feeling?' Jess asked. 'I understand it's a broken wrist.'

'Yes. Nothing to worry about at all. I shouldn't be in here, you know. I feel a complete fraud to tell the truth.'

'It's as well to have these things checked out.'

'And I behaved so ungraciously towards you yesterday,' Elsie said, her eyes clouded with remorse.

'You were in a great deal of pain. Besides, if I hadn't insisted on having the cottage, none of this would have happened.'

'I don't want to hear any more of that nonsense,' Elsie said sharply. 'But I'm glad you came today. I was going to get hold of the telephone trolley otherwise and call you. I've been lying here all morning fretting about the disgraceful way I took advantage of you yesterday. What must you think of me? Blame it on the bump on the head. I don't usually take such shameful advantage of kind-hearted strangers. I thought afterwards that it was quite a thing I was asking of you, not just looking after the cats, but staying in the house all on your own.'

'But I wasn't on my own,' Jess smiled, 'As you so rightly pointed out, I had Benson with me and we — ' she paused, 'I can't say we're best friends, although he did sleep outside my bedroom door last night, after — ' She stopped, remembering just in time she wasn't going to mention Nick's visit — nor her panicky phone call that brought Rob running. 'Benson's beginning to thaw, I think, and he insisted on coming here in the car with me, although he still won't acknowledge me when I speak to him.'

'It takes time to learn to trust again,' Elsie said softly. 'And the same for you, my dear. But already your eyes have lost that haunted look.'

Jess flushed and steered the conversation back to the safer topic of the animals. 'When I was doing the cats this morning — '

'Wait a moment — you were doing the cats? But where's Rachel?'

'Away on a school field trip. Won't be back until the weekend, but you're not to worry. Her mother, Fiona, came up and showed me what to do last night. I love cats and am happy to help out for the rest of the week. Fiona offered to come up and help, which was very good of her. But as they're busy lambing at the moment, I told her not to.'

'She's a dear girl — and you must try her Farm Shop. She's doing really well with it now it's getting established. She started it when they were trying to rebuild after the Foot and Mouth outbreak and realised they could no longer afford to rely on farming as their sole source of income. They began the shop just to sell their own lamb, but they sell all sorts of things now.'

'Sounds like my sort of place,' Jess said. 'I'll certainly check it out. Now, there's something I have to ask you about yesterday.'

'Ask away.'

'Why did you tell Rob that you and I were related?'

Elsie gave a shamefaced grin. 'That's someone else I have to apologise for. Rob's a good neighbour and a dear and trusted friend. But I knew if he thought I was letting a stranger stay in my house, he'd worry. He doesn't know you like I do, you see.'

'But you don't know me,' Jess protested.

'Now, we're not going into all that again, are we? I told you, I know people and I know you are trustworthy. Haven't you just proved that? I'm sorry about Rob — that young man really has got to learn to lighten up and start trusting people again. I hope he hasn't given you a hard time?'

'As he was showing me around, he quizzed me quite hard about which branch of the family tree I came from and as I'm not a very good liar and just mumbled something vague, I got the distinct impression he didn't believe a word I said.'

Elsie's smile faded. 'Oh, my dear, I am so very sorry. What can I say? I'm feeling terrible now. In fact — ' she broke off, her face screwed in pain.

'What is it?' Jess asked quickly, 'Do you want me to call a nurse?'

'No. It's passing. It's only when I move quickly.'

'I'll go off and leave you in peace then, so you can get some rest. I'll come in and see you again tomorrow.'

'No. You mustn't do that. You're supposed to be on holiday. You should be out and about, seeing the sights, not stuck in here listening to me droning on.'

'You don't drone — and I've enjoyed

today. It's such a lovely drive here, across the Somerset Levels. And that reminds me, I love your kitchen — would you mind if I used your cooker? My Gran had one just like it and I'm itching to get my hands on it.'

'Of course — you shouldn't even have asked.'

Jess left, promising Elsie she'd bring in some home made cakes the next day and promising herself she'd call in at the Farm Shop that Elsie had recommended.

* * *

'Can I help you? Oh, hi, it's you. Perfect timing.' Fiona gave a welcoming smile as Jess walked into the Farm Shop. 'I've just phoned to see how Elsie is but you know what hospitals are like. Tell you nothing except they're comfortable, which, knowing Elsie and her hatred of being stuck indoors at the best of times, least of all on a lovely day like today, she'll be anything but comfortable.'

'Apart from her broken wrist and the fact that she's still a bit woozy from the anaesthetic, she's fine.'

'Did they say when she'd be coming home?'

Jess shook her head. 'Too soon to tell,' she said. 'Elsie mentioned something about tests, which seemed to bother her a bit so I didn't push her for information.'

'Well, don't worry about the cats. Rachel's home later today and I'll send her round tonight.'

'No. Not this evening, she'll be tired after her trip. I can manage, I promise now that I know where everything is.'

'Are you sure?'

Jess nodded. 'Elsie told me how hectic things get for you during lambing time. You really shouldn't have come up last night, you know.'

'I told you, we owe Elsie, as a family. She's been so good to us over the years. So, did you say you were related to Elsie?'

'No. Not at all.' It was a relief to be able to tell the truth. 'I'd just booked up for a few days in her holiday cottage and said I'd stay on to help out. She only told that little fib for Rob's benefit — afraid he would worry unnecessarily or something.'

'He's certainly very protective towards her, that's for sure.'

Jess looked approvingly around the old stone barn that had been converted into a light, bright shop. 'Elsie suggested I come here and I'm so glad she did. This is wonderful. I'd no idea you carried such a range. I don't know what to choose.'

The Farm Shop was every bit as good as Elsie had said. In addition to the locally produced meat there was a mouth-watering assortment of cakes, fresh vegetables, local cider and wines. It reminded Jess of the stalls at London's famous Borough Market, where she and Matt loved to browse. Correction: used to love to browse.

'Is this all local produce?' she asked.

'Oh, yes,' Fiona said. 'Well, apart from the tinned stuff, of course. I stock that sort of thing for my customers who've run out and don't want to drive in to the supermarket. So, if you want lamb, then that's ours. But if it's beef you're after, then that comes from Neston Manor. You're lucky we've got some in at the moment. Most of it is snapped up in London now. But Rob always keeps some back for my customers, seeing as we were the first to 'discover' him as it were.'

While Jess was still trying to decide between lamb or beef the phone rang and Fiona excused herself.

'I'm sorry,' Jess heard her say, 'I don't have any pies at all. My pie lady's let me down, I'm afraid. She told me last week she won't be doing it any more. I'm trying to find a replacement but it's not easy, seeing as we're up to our ears in lambing at the moment.'

'Excuse me,' Jess said quickly before she had too much time to think about it and maybe change her mind, 'I make pies. That's what I'm buying this meat for. Would you like me to make you one to try? And you don't have to buy if you don't like them, I promise you. But in my last business they were without doubt our best selling line.'

'Your last business?'

'My — ' She'd been about to say my friend, checked herself and went on, 'A colleague and I ran a catering company. Dinner parties, board room lunches, that sort of thing. She did the admin and I did the cooking. And my pies are — were — without doubt the most popular thing on the menu.'

'Well, I don't want to put you to any trouble . . . '

'And you don't want to embarrass me by saying no,' Jess grinned. 'I won't be offended, I promise. Forget about supplying the shop. Let me make you one as a thank you for helping me out with the cats last night.'

'You don't have to do that.'

'Yes, I do. But think about it,' Jess said, eyes shining as her enthusiasm mounted. 'Locally produced pies, cooked in an Aga, using produce from this shop. I'll even use some of that lovely sounding organic flour you've got on sale there. Is that local too?'

'It certainly is. Just a couple of miles down the road, in the next village. And if this thing works, you can buy your flour direct from the miller. I shouldn't be saying this, of course, doing myself out of a sale, but it's much cheaper. And then I've got this person who produces the most wonderful mushrooms, another one who does organic vegetables. We could — '

Jess realised as she spoke that she'd sold herself too well. She'd only meant to offer to supply Fiona with pies to tide her over until she'd found a new supplier. But it sounded as if Fiona was thinking she was applying to be that supplier permanently.

'Look, I think — ' she got no further in her attempts to put things right because the phone rang, then a group of customers arrived, so in the end, Jess paid for her purchases and went back to Higher Neston, her head teeming with ideas for all sorts of sweet and savoury pies.

As she set to work in the kitchen at Higher Neston, Jess suddenly realised she felt happy. But how was that possible? This time yesterday, she'd had her heart broken, and yet here she was now, dicing meat and vegetables, making pastry and feeling a kind of quiet contentment she hadn't felt for years — if ever.

Was Elsie right when she spoke of Higher Neston being a healing place? But could a place have that kind of power?

Certainly Jess felt a sense of home-coming, of belonging, that she'd never felt anywhere else before — at least certainly not since her grandmother had died. And it was so untrue that country people were stand-offish. Every-one she'd met since arriving in Somerset had been so friendly. Except Rob who, like Benson, still regarded her with sus-picion.

She'd just taken a lamb and leek pie out of the oven when her mobile rang. She placed the pie carefully on the table to cool, wagged a warning finger at Benson and picked up the phone. But her sunny mood disappeared as she saw her mother's number in the display window.

'Well, have you had enough of mouldering in the countryside now and come to your senses?' her mother demanded, jumping, as she so often did, straight into attack mode.

'I'm well, Mother, thank you very much. And you?'

'In a state, if you must know. When are you coming home?'

'Usually you don't want to know me, let alone insist on me staying.'

'Of course I do. I worry about you. You must know that. Besides — '

'Besides, you've got this group of Americans coming to dinner. I know. Well, go to M and S, like I suggested.'

'Your father doesn't like the idea.'

'Then don't tell him.'

'At least tell me where you are.'

'Why? It's never bothered you before.' Jess surprised herself at how calm she felt. Usually her mother could browbeat her into doing whatever she wanted. But not today. Something had happened to her today. She could feel it.

At that moment, the house phone rang, giving Jess the chance to finish the call before she said something to her mother that she'd later regret.

'Jess? It's Nick here. I've got some rather worrying news, I'm afraid.'

Jess's heart skipped a beat as she remembered Elsie's unease about the tests. 'It's not Elsie, is it? She was concerned about the tests when I saw her this afternoon but I hoped it was just the hospital being ultra cautious.'

'Tests? No, nothing like that. I've just had a call from the Council and it's bad, I'm afraid. Gran's been operating a cattery illegally. Apparently, you have to have a licence. They'll be charging us to breathe next, no doubt. Anyway, I explained to the guy that she's an old lady, inclined to get muddled about things and that she's not here anyway. He was very sympathetic and understanding really. Says that, provided all the cats are gone by the weekend, he'll turn a blind eye.'

'But surely they'll allow her to apply for a licence.'

'Shouldn't think so. Not after what happened last time.'

'Last time?'

Nick hesitated. 'Look, there's something you ought to know. Gran can and does play the sweet old lady, but there's another side to her, I'm afraid.'

'In what way?' Jess asked, uneasy at the seriousness of Nick's voice.

'There was a very unpleasant incident a while back. A cat died and the owners threatened to sue for neglect. In the end, they settled out of court. Gran of course won't speak about it. In fact, she's blanked it out and it's like it never happened. But the upshot was, she was banned from running a cattery ever again. It was one of the conditions.'

'That's terrible.'

'So you'll see that all the cats have gone by the weekend, will you? All you have to do is phone their owners and tell them to come and get them. There's a very good cattery not five miles from here. I've already been in touch with the owner and she says that any cats that can't be collected by Saturday can go there.'

'But Elsie will be so upset.'

'She'll be even more upset if she gets taken to court. I promise you, Jess, you want to help her? Then this is the only way. The cats have got to go. The sooner the better.'

6

As soon as Jess walked into the ward, she knew something was wrong. Elsie was sitting in the chair by her bed, her damaged arm resting on a pillow placed across her lap, her head bent. She didn't even look up as Jess approached the bed. Jess stood for a moment, uncertain what to do. She'd looked so well yesterday, in spite of the obvious pain she was in. But today she looked small and lost and Jess's heart sank as once again she remembered the tests.

Had she been given the results? Was it bad news? Whatever it was had obviously hit Elsie hard.

'Elsie?' she asked gently, 'Are you all right?'

Elsie's head jerked up. She'd obviously not heard Jess's approaching footsteps. Her eyes were red rimmed, her mouth trembling as she struggled to regain her self control.

'I've brought you some daffodils and forsythia from your garden,' Jess said, wanting to give her chance to recover her composure, 'I'll see if I can find you a vase.'

When she came back, Elsie was looking more like herself and her voice held only a slight hint of a tremor. 'They're beautiful,' she said, 'Thank you for such a thoughtful gesture. But what are you doing here? I told you not to come in any more but to be off enjoying your holiday. It's bad enough you have to take the time to look after the cats for me. Is Rachel back yet?'

'This morning. And I'm here because I want to be. Besides, I've brought you this.' Jess took out a plastic container with some home made biscuits in it and placed it on the locker. 'You're not on a special diet are you?'

Elsie shook her head but before she could say any more, the movement of her head dislodged a couple of tears which rolled down her cheeks. She brushed them away with an impatient hand.

'Silly old fool. What must you think of me?'

'I think you're someone who's been given some bad news,' Jess said softly, 'Would you like to share it with me? Is it the tests?'

'It's nothing like that. It's . . . it's just . . .' Elsie took a deep breath then looked up, her eyes brimming, 'I've had this foolish young slip of a girl in here, social worker or some such nonsense, I think she said. And she tells me — tells me I can't go home. That I'm to go into a nursing home.'

'What?' This was the last thing Jess expected to hear. 'But surely they can't force you to do something like that. Not if you don't want to.'

'She said, although I had the impression she was reading from a carefully prepared script and that the decision wasn't hers alone, that because I'm — because of my age and the fact that I live alone in a fairly isolated area,

I have to go to a nursing home to convalesce. Did you ever hear anything so ridiculous? And when I told her I'd no intention of ending up in one of those ghastly places where they play bingo and everyone treats you as if you are a rather dense child, she implied that I'd have very little choice in the matter. I'm afraid I lost it a bit then and said things that I probably shouldn't have.'

'Good for you,' Jess murmured, incensed on her behalf.

'I got a ticking off from the ward sister because of it,' Elsie said, looking decidedly unrepentant. 'But she made me so mad. She wouldn't listen. Every time I tried to get my point across, she just ploughed on, saying the same thing over and over again, as if she was some sort of mad parrot.'

'But would a couple of weeks there be so bad?' Jess said soothingly. 'Just until you regained your strength and mobility?'

'You bet your life it would. If I go

into one of those places, I'll never come out again and that's a fact.'

'But what about your grandson, Nick? He seems very anxious about you. Couldn't he help?'

'Nick?' Elsie's head shot up. 'You've met Nick? When?'

'The night you were brought in he came round to the farm to see you. I explained who I was and what had happened to you and he was very concerned. No doubt he'll be in to see you soon.'

'Nick came round to see me?' Elsie frowned and her lips compressed in a tight thin line. 'What did he want?'

'To see how you were, I expect. He was very upset about your accident.'

'Really? He was upset, was he? This is Nicholas, my grandson, we're both talking about, isn't it? Tall, with floppy fair hair and a smile that would melt butter?'

Jess grinned as she remembered Nick's attractive smile. 'Melts butter, you say? Yes, I'd say it's the same man all right. He seems very nice — and obviously thinks the world of you. I don't understand why you told me you had no relatives.'

'I have my reasons,' Elsie snapped, her cheeks burning hot pink. 'And they're not something I care to discuss right now.'

'Oh, Lord. I'm so sorry.' Jess's hand flew to her mouth, her eyes wide with remorse. 'I'm such a fool. Matt always says I'm a clumsy fool, that as soon as I open my mouth, I put my foot in it. Please, Elsie, don't be upset. I'm sorry.'

'Nonsense. I'm the one who should be sorry,' With her good hand, Elsie patted Jess's arm. 'I'm the one who should be overcome with remorse. Not you. And if you ever quote that oaf again — '

'Oaf?'

'The idiot who called you a clumsy fool. You're nothing of the kind. You're kind and sensitive and don't you dare let anyone tell you otherwise. You had every right to ask about my relationship with my grandson. After all, I'd let you believe I had no immediate family, although that was not an intentional deceit on my part. Just something I find difficult to talk about.'

'Then don't,' Jess said as she mentally filed away her questions about the cattery and its licence for another time. 'I've been thinking. There might be a way you can come home to convalesce.'

'What? Nick's going to come and look after me, is he?' Elsie gave a bitter laugh.

Jess felt uncomfortable about hearing Elsie being so critical about Nick, in view of the trouble he'd gone to on her behalf to sort out the problems of the cattery and its licence. Something was obviously very wrong between Elsie and Nick but it was obvious Elsie didn't want to talk about it.

'No,' she said. 'But — '

'Not in a million years, he wouldn't. He's far too busy. He's like his mother in temperament, which is really odd, because he's so much like his grandfather in looks that sometimes it actually hurts to see him.'

'Your husband?' Jess prompted, feeling that this was safer emotional ground for Elsie today.

'His name was George and he had the same easy good looks that Nick has. We met at a dance in the village — I was down here visiting a cousin and thought I was much too grand and sophisticated to find anything exciting about a dance in a village hall, for goodness' sake. It was in 1940. I didn't want to stay in the country and I sure as hell had no intention of marrying a farmer's son. But the first time I saw George Russell, well, that was it for me.'

'I take it you did marry this particular farmer's son?'

'Within six months. Much to the dismay of our mutual parents. Mine because they thought the country was the back of beyond and his because they'd wanted him to marry a farmer's daughter, someone who'd been born into the hard work that being a farmer's wife involved, particularly back in those days.'

'How long were you married?'

Elsie drew a long, deep breath. 'Not long enough,' she said. 'In 1942, George signed up for the RAF. He didn't have to, of course. Farming was a reserved occupation and farmers were working flat out to meet the War agricultural requirements for food production at the time.' She shook her head. 'They were hard times . . . sad ones too . . . his parents blamed me, but it was as much a shock to me as it was to them, I can promise you. I didn't want to him go off fighting.'

'But he did?'

'Oh, yes. And, like so many of those brave young men, he never came back. He was killed two days after our daughter Sandra's first birthday. His plane was shot down in only the third operation he went on. Sandra and I stayed on the farm and in time I got on very well with his father and took over the running of the farm eventually, when it became too much for him. But his mother never forgave me. Always felt I should have done more to keep George home. But how could I?' She blinked hard. 'What sort of fool must you think me?

'I think you're a very brave lady to whom life handed a pretty raw deal,' Jess said softly. 'It makes my problems seem insignificant now.'

'If your problems have anything to do with the idiot who's given you such a low sense of self esteem, then you're well rid, if you ask me.'

Jess had always been a very self-contained, private person who never shared her problems. And yet, perhaps as a result of Elsie's frankness about her own life, before she realised she was doing it, Jess found herself telling Elsie how she'd been a constant disappointment to her parents.

'My father's a lawyer,' she explained, 'And they always wanted me to do something high powered and academic, preferably follow him into law. But that wasn't me. I did okay at school. Nothing outstanding but good enough. I'd always loved cooking but when I chose to do a catering course, rather than something more academic, my father was quietly disappointed, while my mother would have disowned me if she could.'

Elsie tutted, took a biscuit from the box and motioned Jess to carry on.

'That's about it, really. My mother thought if I couldn't make the grade through my own efforts, then my only hope was to marry someone who'd do it for me. So she fixed me up with a series of eager young career men, mostly from Dad's office, each one more disastrous than the last. Until Matt, came along, that is.'

'He sounds the biggest disaster of the lot,' Elsie said through a mouth full of crumbs. 'By the way, this biscuit is delicious.'

'Thank you. Your Aga is a real delight

to cook with so I simply couldn't resist it. I usually serve them to use for dunking into a chocolate mousse. Not that I'll be making chocolate mousse for a while, that's for sure.'

And then, sitting in the dreary hospital ward, with the late afternoon sun picking out the gold of the forsythia, Jess did what she never thought she'd be able to do. She told someone how, in one short, shocking moment, she lost her boyfriend, her job, her best friend and her home in one fell swoop.

'Or rather, one swirl of chocolate mousse,' she said, and then, unable to resist it, she went into detail; much greater detail than she'd intended, about the sight that had greeted her in Matt's kitchen.

'And do you know the thing that hurt most of all?' she said, as the entire episode slipped seamlessly from tragedy into comedy. 'The thing I was most angry about was that, because she'd forgotten the cream, which I'd whipped up so carefully, there, on top of the mounds of my lovely chocolate mousse, arranged so artistically, on my ex-boyfriend's chest, was a dollop of squirty cream. Sacrilege. And I'll never be able to eat chocolate mousse again as long as I live.'

Elsie and Jess were laughing so hard by this time that a nurse put her head around the door and raised an eyebrow.

'Oh, dear,' Jess said, 'I'm going to get thrown out of here in a minute.'

'I wish I could,' Elsie said, still wiping her eyes. 'Oh, thank you for that. That's the best laugh I've had in ages.'

'Me, too.' Jess agreed and meant it. In fact now she'd been able to see the funny side of it, she wondered why she'd been so upset about it.

'Elsie, there's something I want to discuss with you. It's about your convalescence when they let you out of hospital.'

'Hmm. You know how to poop a party, don't you?'

'No, listen, let me finish. What about

if you come back to the farm — and I look after you?'

The hope that flared in Elsie's eyes quickly died. 'You can't do that,' she said. 'You have your life in London to get back to.'

'But that's it. I'm not going back.' As Jess said this, it felt as if a bank of storm clouds had just rolled away. 'I'm never going back to London. I don't know what I'm going to do with my life, but whatever it is, it'll be around here, or somewhere very like it. I can't explain the feeling of homecoming I've experienced since I've been here. Certainly, it's very like the area my grandmother used to live in. But I feel at home here as I've never felt in London. And people with cooking skills are always in demand. I'll be able to get a job, I'm sure. So, what do you say? I mean, if you want references — '

'References?' Elsie's eyes sparkled with tears, but this time, at least Jess hoped, they were tears of happiness, or at least of relief. 'Of course I don't need references.'

'Great. I'll go and have a word with the powers that be, shall I?'

'Are you sure you wouldn't like time to think about this?'

Jess shook her head. 'I have never been so sure about anything.'

'Do you know, child, I would really like to meet your parents,' Elsie said.

'Oh?' Jess flushed. How was she going to tell Elsie tactfully that her parents, her mother in particular, probably wouldn't want to meet her? 'Well, they're really busy, you know, and my mother has an aversion to green fields, but perhaps — '

'I'd like to tell them what complete idiots they are not to realise and appreciate what a quite exceptional daughter they have,' she said.

'Oh. Right.' Elsie's comment was so far from what Jess had been expecting and she didn't know what to say. She looked down at her hands, her cheeks reddening.

'Now I've made you uncomfortable, haven't I? I see one of the things I'm going to have to teach you is how to accept compliments gracefully. And, in return, you can teach me how you make these lovely biscuits — unless, of course, they're a secret recipe and you'll have to kill me if you tell me.'

'Nothing so desperate.'

'You know, I'd really like you and Rob to — '

'No, please.' Jess's cheeks flamed scarlet. 'Please don't say you'd like me and Rob to get together,' she said, her voice low. 'That's what my mother always does. Why can't people believe I'm actually capable of finding my own men? At least I would be if I was given the chance.'

'Good for you,' Elsie grinned. 'But I wasn't thinking about you and him dating, although now you mention it, he's quite good looking in an under-stated way and is available — '

'I've done it again, haven't I? Jumped in with both feet? I suppose you were going to say he could fix my car or supply me with eggs?'

'No. You did right to choke me off. But I'm not trying to matchmake, I promise you. I'm fond of Rob and, like you, he's been hurt very badly. I know he can be a bit prickly at times. And living on his own has done nothing for his social graces, but in many ways he reminds me so much of my George.'

'Look, I'd better go,' Jess said uncomfortably. Whatever Elsie might say about not matchmaking, it sounded horribly familiar. 'I'll call in at the nurse's station on the way out and tell them about our arrangement. Rachel said she'd do the cats this evening but I'd like to be back in time to help her if I could, which means getting out of here before the traffic builds up. I'll see you tomorrow, then.'

⋆ ⋆ ⋆

Jess stopped the car by an open gate on the way home to let Benson stretch his legs in the empty field. She leaned on the gate and watched with a smile as the dog chased a couple of rooks across the field.

But her good mood only lasted a few seconds as the peace of the afternoon was broken by the arrival of a Land Rover coming up the lane towards her. It could only be Rob's and, sure enough, he pulled up beside her car and got out.

'The gate was open,' she said defensively. 'He's not doing any harm, I promise you.'

She felt uncomfortable meeting him again, after making such a fool of herself the night Nick turned up at Higher Neston. She called the dog back, but he was too busy sniffing out rabbit holes to respond.

'I'm sorry,' she said, picking up the dog's lead, 'I'll go and fetch him.'

'Don't bother. He's not doing any harm, providing he stays in this field, of course. I've had a lot of trouble with sheep worrying this year and lost a couple of my best ewes as a result of it.'

'I'm sorry. That's awful.'

He nodded. 'It's not just the money,' he said. 'The insurance coughs up for that. I've spent years building up my breeding stock and had high hopes of this year's lambs. And contrary to what people may think, I happen to care very much about the welfare of my livestock and it grieves me to think of the poor creatures frightened out of their wits because someone's family pet, who wouldn't say boo to a goose, suddenly reverts to wolf when left on his own in a field full of sheep.'

'Yes. I can see that,' Jess said, keeping an anxious eye on Benson, who was still nosing around the rabbit holes. 'I'll make sure he doesn't leave this field, I promise.'

'Okay. But that isn't why I stopped. I called in at Fiona's Farm Shop just now and she offered me a piece of one of your pies. I just wanted to say how delicious it was.'

'Oh. Right. It was — ' Jess was about

to say it was nothing when she remembered Elsie's comment about learning to take compliments gracefully. 'Thank you,' she said as the colour flooded her cheeks. 'Which one did you try?'

'Both, of course. And whilst I enjoyed the lamb and leek, I thought the beef and mushroom was amazing,' he said, his face transformed by a sudden smile. 'Although I must admit to a slight prejudice there when Fiona told me you'd used my beef.'

'My pies work because I only use the best ingredients and your beef is without doubt the best I've tasted in a long time. Fiona tells me you sell in London now?'

'As much as I can produce,' he said, 'It's the way forward for farmers. Top quality organic food, produced slowly and carefully. All my animals have a good quality of life and it shows. I couldn't do it any other way.'

He looked at Jess and gave a sheepish grin. 'Sorry,' he said 'When I get on my soap box, there's no stopping me.'

'I'm glad. It's . . . organic foods are a passion of mine as well,' she said as she returned his smile. 'And look, about the other night. I'd like to explain — '

'Nothing to explain,' he said gruffly. 'I'm glad you felt you could call on me and relieved that it was nothing serious.'

'Thanks, but — '

'Fiona told me what you're doing for Elsie,' he said suddenly. 'It's really good of you and — '

'There's something you should know,' Jess said, cutting across him as they both started speaking at the same time. 'I'm not related to Elsie at all.'

'I know.'

'And I'm really sorry I let you — ' She broke off and stared at him. 'What did you say?'

'I said I know. I know you're not related to Elsie.'

'But how?'

He shrugged. 'One of the advantages, or should I say, penalties for living in a place like this. Everyone knows everyone else's business. I've known Elsie all my life and I know she has no relations, distant or otherwise, on her mother's side.'

'She said that because you're such a worry-wart where she's concerned. Her words not mine.'

'Oh does she?' he growled, then smiled. 'Yeah, well, I suppose she's not wrong there. I do worry about her.'

'And I'm sorry I panicked. If I'd known it was Elsie's grandson moving about in the kitchen I wouldn't have bothered you.'

'How did he get in?'

'He had a key, I suppose. Elsie must have given it to him.'

He shook his head. 'I think that's very unlikely. What did he want?'

'To see how she was? He seemed very concerned when I told him she was in hospital and — ' She stopped as she remembered something. 'He was looking for something.'

'Did he say what?'

'No. He was rummaging around in the drawers of the oak dresser and when I asked him what it was and should I ask Elsie, he said, no, that it didn't matter. He left soon after you.' But not before he'd warned me about you, she added silently to herself. 'And of course,' she added with a rush, her cheeks burning as if he could read her thoughts. 'He also said about bringing some clients to look around the farm.'

'To look round the farm?' Rob's dark brows drew together in an angry frown. 'You didn't tell Elsie this, did you?'

Jess's heart lurched as she wished she could have pressed the rewind button. Nick had made a point of asking her not to tell anyone and what had she done? Only told the one man who had a very close interest in Elsie's land. The man he'd warned her against.

She shook her head. 'No. To be truthful, what with everything else that's been going on, I forgot about it until now. And he said the viewing would have to be put off until he'd resolved the cattery thing. Which, needless to say, I haven't said anything to Elsie about either. At least not until she's feeling a bit stronger.'

'The cattery thing?'

'The problem with Elsie's license. It appears she doesn't have one.'

Rob frowned harder than ever. 'That sounds most unlike Elsie,' he said. 'But I'm more concerned about Nick and his so-called clients at the moment. You know what he plans to do with Higher Neston as soon as he gets his hands on the place, don't you?'

Jess shook her head.

'I've heard he's got this deal lined up with a firm of property developers. They're going to pull down the buildings and build one of these holiday complexes on the site.'

'No, I'm sorry. I can't believe that. Nick really cares about his grandmother. He'd never do anything that would hurt her like that.'

'You know him that well, do you?' Rob's hard angry look had returned.

'That guy's trouble. Always has been, always will be. Where Nick's concerned, what you see is most definitely not what you get. You'd do well to steer well clear of him. I'm only saying this for your own good.'

This was so exactly the words that her mother would use when she was trying to get Jess to do something she didn't want to do, that Jess's rising sense of unease spilled out into anger.

'When are people going to stop telling me what I can and can't do with my life?' she fumed. 'I am a fully fledged adult, you know. I do not need someone like you telling me what to do. Benson. Come on, boy.'

To her surprise and relief, the dog came bounding towards her. She clipped his lead on and walked him to the car, leaving Rob staring after her, with a face as black as the storm clouds above him.

7

Apart from a lingering regret at having spoken so sharply to Rob, the next two days passed fairly peacefully and happily for Jess. She'd talked it through with Fiona and Rachel who agreed with Rob that the license thing sounded totally out of character for Elsie and, as for the neglect charge, absolute rubbish.

So they agreed to do nothing about the cats until Elsie was back home. The hospital were happy for her to come home after the weekend and Jess was in a baking frenzy trying to fulfil the orders that Fiona kept sending, as well as getting the house ready for Elsie.

Friday morning she awoke to a day of glorious spring sunshine. Lovely to be out and about in but not the weather to leave dogs shut up in cars.

'I'm sorry, boy,' she said as Benson began to follow her out to the car, 'This is one time when you're better off at home. You stay.'

He looked so pathetic that, without stopping to think what she was doing, she knelt down beside him, hugged him and kissed him lightly between his soft, pointed ears. To her surprise and delight, he wagged his tail and licked her hand enthusiastically.

'Sorry. All the soft soap in the world isn't going to make me change my mind, but I'll be back soon,' she said, but inside she was delighted, feeling that she had gained the dog's trust at last.

When she got to the hospital, she was surprised and pleased to see Elsie looking so well and full of plans for coming home on Monday.

'If the weather stays this good I'll be able to get out in the garden.'

'You do realise the garden is strictly for sitting in at the moment, don't you?' Jess said anxiously.

'Nonsense. I've only broken my wrist, you know. Not my legs. I can still get about. They wouldn't have kept me in here so long if it hadn't been for those blasted tests. Just because I had a touch of angina a few years ago. But it's fine now and I can't wait to get home and see Benson. How is he?'

'Thawing fast,' Jess said, scarcely able to believe that she was thinking so fondly of the dog who'd scared her half to death a few days ago. Their relationship had come a long way in a short time.

Jess spent a very pleasant hour chatting to Elsie, then left to have a look around the town. Fiona had recommended a herbal shop she wanted to have a look at but as she got to the car park, she saw Rob coming towards her.

Her heart gave an uncomfortable lurch as she remembered how she'd snapped at him the last time they met.

'Elsie told me you'd already been in to see her this morning,' she said.

'I had,' he said, 'And I've just popped into town to get her a book I'd promised her. The bookshop rang just as I was leaving to say it was in and Elsie, being Elsie, wanted it straight away and didn't want to wait.'

Jess laughed. 'She's certainly a lot better today.'

'Almost back to her normal bossy self, I'd say,' Rob said, then looked at her closely. 'Jess, I'm really sorry I went on at you like that yesterday. You were quite right to choke me off.'

'No, it was my fault. I shouldn't be so touchy,' she said hastily, then changed the subject. 'Elsie's really looking forward to coming home.'

'She certainly is. Thanks to you,' he said. He stepped towards her and for a moment Jess thought he was going to take her hand.

'Oh, well — ' she mumbled awkwardly, 'It was nothing, really.'

'It was anything but nothing. It was a very kind, generous thing to do. To give up your holiday like that.'

'It's not really a holiday. I'm in between jobs as it were and so a few weeks here or there won't really make much difference to me. And I am enjoying myself here. Elsie's right when she says Higher Neston is a very special place. I've even made friends with Benson today. He actually allowed me to kiss the top of his head.'

Rob laughed. 'And if you make friends with me, I'll allow you to kiss the top of my head too, if you like.'

Jess blushed and looked away. 'Look,' she said, 'About what I said — I really am sorry I snapped. I shouldn't have — '

'Yes you should. It was my own fault for speaking first, thinking later. I'm always doing it.'

'You are? Me too,' she said wryly, thinking how many times Matt had accused her of doing just that. 'So that probably makes us quits, then?'

'I guess it does. Look, I've just got to drop this book off to Elsie then I was wondering if you'd like to join me for lunch? I know a very good pub on the way back home where they serve a mean ploughmans.'

'That sounds — '

'Jess. I'm so sorry I'm late. The traffic was awful, I was so afraid I'd missed you.'

At the sound of Nick's voice, Rob's smile changed to a scowl. 'You've made other arrangements, obviously. Some other time perhaps,' he said as he strode away.

'Sorry. Did I come at a bad time?' Nick asked.

'No. But what's all this about being late? We hadn't made any arrangements to meet.'

'We didn't? But I left a message for you on Gran's answerphone. About meeting up for lunch. I assumed when I saw you here that you'd got my message and — ' Nick stopped short before adding, 'Oh, Lord, I hope I didn't spoil a moment between you and Rob?'

Jess shook her head. 'Of course you didn't,' she said quickly. 'Look, I feel really bad about this, Nick, but I wasn't planning on staying in town for lunch. I've left Benson on his own for the first time and I really must get back to him. Usually I bring him with me, but I had to leave him behind because I was worried he'd get too hot in the car.'

'He's in the best place and come on now, you've got to eat sometime. Look, I know a really nice bar just across from here. It hasn't been open very long and they do the most wonderful crispy duck rolls. Come on, please?'

'Aren't you on your way in to see your grandmother?'

'She'll be having lunch now, so it's better I come back later. Come and eat with me and you can tell me how she is and everything.'

He was so persistent that Jess gave in and allowed herself to be led to the bar that, being one of a large chain was identical to the one a few yards from her London flat. As she looked at the trendy menu she thought wistfully of the country pub that served a 'mean ploughmans'.

Nick placed Jess's drink in front of her and Jess sipped the sparkling mineral water, her appetite suddenly deserted her.

'I'm so glad I bumped into you,' he said, 'I called round this morning and was disappointed to find you were out. Then I realised that you'd be here which is when I had my idea about meeting for lunch. That was really lucky.'

'Lucky indeed,' she murmured.

'So, are you enjoying your stay at Higher Neston?' he asked.

'It's lovely. The peace and quiet — I just love it.'

'Sure. It's okay for a short break but after a while you must miss the bright lights. I know I do. This part of the country needs to be dragged kicking and screaming into the twenty-first century. I mean, this place is okay, but the rest of the town looks as if it's stuck in a time warp.'

'Oh, I don't know,' Jess murmured as she recalled uneasily Rob telling her that Nick had plans to redevelop the lovely old farm house and buildings at Higher Neston. Knowing the bad blood between the two men, she hadn't really believed Rob at the time and thought he was just saying that to put Nick in a bad light.

But now, listening to Nick enthusing about the advantages of modern architecture, she wasn't so sure.

'So how did you find the old witch today?' he asked.

'I'm sorry?' Jess looked up, startled, from the menu she was studying, as she tried in vain to find something that appealed.

'Gran — the Witch of the West, that's what we call her. With her herbs and her crystals and her healing. It's all just so much hocus pocus.'

'She seems fine,' Jess said, uncomfortable with his disrespectful tone.

'I hope she's in a better mood today. I hear she wasn't too pleased yesterday at the thought of going to a nursing home for a few weeks convalescence.

She does make such a fuss. Can't bear any sort of change. Typical old people, eh?'

'But she's not going to a nursing home.'

'What?' He knocked a spoon to the floor.

'She's coming home — back to Higher Neston. On Monday. And she's so excited, you can see how much she's looking forward to it. It's done her the power of good.'

'But she can't go home. She has a hard enough time looking after herself as it is, without trying to do it with a broken wrist,' Nick said'

'It's all right. You needn't worry about her. She won't be on her own. I'm going to stay on and look after her.'

'You? How long are you planning on staying?'

And it was in that moment that Jess realised that whatever happened in the future, she would never leave this part of Somerset. Even when Elsie had recovered fully, and didn't need her any more, she'd find somewhere to live and work that wasn't too far away.

130

She glanced at her watch. 'Look, I'm sorry. I really don't have time for lunch. I must go. Thank you for the drink.'

'Are you sure?' He looked so disappointed, she felt guilty. 'What about tonight then? There's a new Thai restaurant in town I think you'd like.'

She hesitated. She didn't really want to go out as she had a stack of things to do that evening.

'How about you come to Higher Neston and I cook you dinner?' she said. 'I'm doing a batch of lamb and apricot pies for the Farm Shop. I could try one out on you, if you're prepared to take the chance?'

'You've just got yourself a guinea pig,' he said with a grin. 'Will seven-thirty be all right?'

*　*　*

As soon as she opened the front door, she could hear the house phone ringing. It was Fiona.

'Great news, Jess,' she said. 'I've been

giving people tastings as they come in to the shop and I've got a list of orders for your pies as long as your arm. If you can do them, that is?'

'Oh, wow! Yes, I'd love to. But I'm not sure . . . '

'Now, don't worry about the cats. You just concentrate on the pies. Rachel will do the rest, she says, as well as take Benson for a walk.'

'Benson! Oh, my God, Benson.' It wasn't until that moment she realised what was missing in the kitchen.

'Are you all right?' Fiona asked.

'No! Oh, Lord, Fiona, I can't see Benson anywhere and — oh, no, the back door's open. I must have left it open when I went out. And yet I'm sure I remember closing it.'

'He'll turn up. Don't worry. That dog knows what side his bread's buttered on. But I'll tell Rachel to keep an eye out for him.'

But as Jess went to put the phone down, her eye was caught by the sudden movement of sheep in the field outside the kitchen window.

The animals were scattering in panic as a large brown and black dog ran between them, his head thrust forward in an aggressive pose.

8

Jess's hands were shaking so much, she could hardly punch out Rob's number. 'Hurry, please hurry,' she begged, when after several rings he still hadn't answered. She groaned as the call went in to voice mail.

'Please, Rob. Hurry,' she said. 'There's a dog chasing your sheep — or someone's sheep in the field at the back of the farmhouse. And I'm very much afraid it might be Benson. I'm so sorry.'

She put the phone in her pocket and raced out into the back garden, hoping there would be a way out into the field. But there wasn't, just a high stone wall. Without stopping to think she clambered on to the wall then over into the field, narrowly missing a line of barbed wire fencing. She landed with such a thud that for a moment it knocked the breath out of her body.

The dog had chased the sheep into the far corner of the field and without stopping to think Jess ran towards them, calling the dog's name as she went. The sheep scattered, panic stricken, their lambs pushed and jostled and crying piteously as they didn't know who they feared most, the dog or this mad woman running towards them.

To her relief and frustration she saw the dog slip through the hedge and into the field beyond, where he was soon lost to her sight. Relief because as soon as he'd gone, the sheep calmed down, but frustration because she'd been unable to catch him and bring him back to the farmhouse before he caused any more damage.

She found to her dismay that the wall was much higher on the field side than on the garden side, thanks to a ditch that ran alongside, and realised there was no way she could get back the way she came. She'd have to use the field gate and come back along the lane.

As she did so, she took out her phone and called Rob again. Still there was no answer.

'Rob. It's Jess again. Look, I've managed to chase Benson off, but I'm afraid I couldn't catch him. The sheep and lambs seem okay but it would be better if you, or somebody, checked them over.' She paused to blink away the tears that filled her eyes. 'Look, I'm really sorry about all this. I can't think how he got out. I suppose I didn't shut the back door properly. If . . . if you find him, you won't . . . well, you know. I mean, I know you'll be angry with him and of course, you've every right to be. But . . . well, Elsie's so terribly fond of him. And he really is just a great big pussy cat. I'm sure he didn't mean to hurt them.'

Jess had heard awful stories about dogs savaging sheep and how the farmers were within their rights to shoot them. But she couldn't bear that to happen to Benson. And who would tell poor Elsie? It would break her heart.

As Jess got back to the farmhouse, a sleek, black BMW had just pulled into the yard and a tall elegant woman climbed out, dressed in the kind of clothes that wouldn't look out of place at a Buckingham Palace Garden party. Her high heels clicked on the concrete as she came towards Jess, her nose wrinkled in disgust at imaginary farmyard smells.

'I'm sorry,' Jess said, 'I should have taken the sign down. I'm afraid we're not doing Bed and Breakfast at the moment.'

'Do I look as if I'd stay in this hole?' the woman snapped, her dark eyes sweeping dismissively around the yard.

'Then what can I do for you?' Jess said, bristling at such rudeness.

'Let's go into the house,' the woman said brusquely, 'We need to talk. About my mother.'

'Your mother?' Jess frowned and then realised why the woman had looked vaguely familiar. There was a photograph of her on the piano in Elsie's front room. Although she looked younger — and happier — then. 'I'm so sorry. You're Elsie's daughter, Sandra, aren't you? It's good to meet you, but I'm sorry — '

'Do you have a key?' Sandra stood at the front door, one expensively-shod foot tapping impatiently on the step.

'Er . . . no . . . I . . . that is, I went out the back way. I was in a bit of a hurry. You see, I heard the sheep — '

But before Jess could complete her explanation, Sandra had stormed off around the back of the house and in through the back door.

'Do you make a habit of leaving my mother's house wide open to all and sundry?' she demanded angrily. 'When Mum told me she was letting a complete stranger stay alone in her house, I was furious with her. Still am, of course. But furious with you as well. How dare you take advantage of a confused old lady. What sort of game do you think you're playing at?'

'Nothing. I'm not — '

'Mum says you've offered to stay here and look after her when she comes out of hospital. So, I'll ask you again. What's your game?'

'I have no game, as you put it,' Jess said, feeling more and more resentful of Sandra's increasingly aggressive tone.

'What do you think you are doing, interfering in my family's affairs?'

'I'm not interfering in your family's affairs. But whatever arrangements Elsie and I have made are between me and her, surely?'

'They most certainly are not,' Sandra hissed. 'Do you know how long I've tried to persuade my mother she'd be better off in a residential home?'

'Oh, no, surely not. From what I've seen, she's perfectly capable of looking after herself.'

'Oh, really? And what about that fall? I understand you were the one who found her. If you hadn't come along, she'd probably still be there now.'

'We all have accidents,' Jess said, making a huge effort to keep her voice level, her tone reasonable. It would be oh-so easy to descend into a slanging match with this woman but that wouldn't help Elsie at all. 'Look, if your mother wants to stay in her own home, that's up to her, surely?'

'But that's just the point. It's not her own home.' Sandra prowled around the kitchen, her gaze flicking dismissively over the cosy room. 'I don't know why I'm telling you this, because, goodness knows, I don't make a habit of discussing private family matters with complete strangers. But the farmhouse doesn't belong to my mother, but to my son, Nicholas. Mum signed it over to him years back and we have the documents to prove it.'

'But why would she do that?' Jess said. 'That doesn't make any sense. Elsie loves this place so much and was only saying yesterday how she — '

'Do you have any idea how much nursing home fees are these days?'

'No, not really. But as Elsie isn't going in one, I don't see what that's got to do with anything.'

'It has everything to do with it. She's going to have to go in one sooner or later. She can't live with me because she and my husband don't get on and I'm not there often enough to keep the peace between them. So as soon as that happens, social services will insist on her selling this place to pay the fees, which, let me tell you, are currently in the region of over well two and a half thousand pounds a month. How long do you think her capital would last? You do the maths.'

'But I don't get it.' Jess shook her head. 'If they're so expensive, why are you so keen for her to go in one?'

'Because now she's signed over the house to Nicholas she has no assets and it would be social services picking up the tab and not her.'

'But that sounds — ' Jess stopped herself. She'd been going to say that it sounded less than honest but realised that, in one respect at least, Sandra was right. It was none of Jess's business.

Nevertheless, she found the whole thing difficult to reconcile with the Elsie she'd come to know.

Except, of course, Nick had already told her about his plans for Higher Neston. But were they Nick's plans? Now that she'd met his mother, she was beginning to see what must have happened. Sandra must have persuaded poor Elsie to sign over the house to Nick. Which Elsie would have done, thinking that she was ensuring it would be kept in the family. Instead of which, it had simply ensured that the place would be sold for redevelopment while Elsie was still around. It would break her heart.

'So, I told Mother I would tell you myself.' Sandra said.

'I'm sorry?' Jess flushed, as she realised she'd completely missed whatever Sandra had been saying. 'I didn't quite catch that.'

'I told Mother that I've already fixed up a nice convalescent home for her to go to on Monday, so you can pack up your things and go back to wherever it is you came from. And she agrees. So she asked me to tell you. She actually feels quite awkward about the whole thing and would rather not face you again.'

'I'm sorry but I'm not going anywhere.' Jess said firmly. 'At least not until I've talked to your mother about it. I don't believe for a single moment that Elsie would do such a thing.'

'I told you,' Sandra's voice rose shrilly, causing Benson to look up with a low growl. 'This is my house — or rather, my son's house — and I'm telling you on his behalf to pack up your things and get out. Now.'

'As charming as ever I see, Sandra?' Rob's voice, coming from the open back door made both women jump.

'I was just telling her not to poke her nose into other people's business,' Sandra said, her face turning deep crimson.

'She also says that Elsie is now quite happy to go to the convalescent home on Monday,' Jess said, her voice shaking with anger. 'And that she doesn't want me at Higher Neston any more.'

'Really?' Rob's dark eyebrows raised. 'That's funny, because when I saw Elsie only just this afternoon, she was saying how pleased she was that Jess was staying on and how much she was looking forward to coming back to her own home. Not a word about going into a convalescent home. Least of all anything about Jess leaving. Quite the opposite in fact.'

Jess waited for Sandra to point out that Higher Neston was not, in fact, Elsie's home but Nick's. But she didn't. Instead, she glared at him.

'You're just as bad, Rob Carrington,' she spat, looking like a woman on the verge of completely losing control. 'Sticking your nose in where it's not wanted, minding other people's business when you should have been looking out for your own. No wonder you couldn't hang on to your wife. Nick did her a big favour, taking her away from you. It was only a matter of time. I knew she'd never stick with a boring stick in the mud like you.'

'I think you'd better leave, Sandra, don't you?' Rob said quietly, his face white as a sheet.

As Sandra left, she slammed the front door so hard, a picture fell off the wall. Jess picked it up. Her hand was shaking as she reached up to hang it back up again.

'How can a lovely lady like Elsie have a daughter like that?' she murmured sadly.

Rob shrugged. 'I'm sorry you had to hear that,' he said. 'Sandra and I have never got on, ever since I knocked two of Nick's front teeth out when we were five years old.'

Jess felt uncomfortable. If what Sandra had said was true, about Nick stealing Rob's wife, no wonder there was no love lost between the two men.

'What must you think of me?' she said suddenly. 'Sandra's rudeness sort of pushed everything else to the back of my mind for a moment. How are the sheep? Have you checked them over?'

'They're fine,' Rob said. 'You chased him off before he could do any real damage.'

Jess's knees went weak with relief. 'But Benson — I'm so very sorry. I still can't understand how he got out. Or where he is now. Unless . . . ' Her throat went dry and she had a bad feeling in her stomach. 'Oh, no, you've found him, haven't you?'

He nodded. 'I have indeed, the old rogue,' he said sternly.

Jess's mouth went dry. 'Oh, no. You haven't shot him, have you? I'm sure it was just a one off, you know. He's not a vicious dog. He wouldn't have meant them any harm. He's a pussy cat really.'

'That's not what you said a couple of days ago.'

'I know, but that was before . . . ' She stopped. She'd been about to say before he'd started sleeping at the foot of her bed, before he'd put his wet nose into her hand when she thought Nick was a burglar, before he let her cuddle him this morning. Before she'd allowed herself to get fond of him.

'Come outside,' Rob said and went into the yard, where his Land Rover was parked. And there, in the back, sat a very sorry looking Benson, his head down. He wagged his tail sheepishly at her.

Jess's relief was overwhelming. 'Where did you find him?' she asked.

'I'll tell you where I found the old reprobate,' Rob said, 'One of my collies is on heat. That's where this old villain has been. He hasn't been chasing sheep at all — but my bitch.'

'Oh, thank God,' Jess said.

Rob looked pained. 'You might well say that,' he said, 'But my dog has a pedigree as long as your arm and I was going to mate her, not this season but the next. And with another pedigree border collie, not this old mongrel here. I had high hopes of her pups.'

He opened the car door and Benson jumped out and went straight into the kitchen, where he flopped down in front of the Aga.

'Oh, look, Rob, he's worn out,' Jess laughed and the dog turned his head away, looking deeply offended at being laughed at. 'But did you find the dog that was worrying the sheep?'

'He's safely locked up in one of my barns,' he said. 'He, too, was after my bitch and came right into the farmyard. The poor chap looks as if he hasn't had a decent meal in months, so it was easy to entice him in there with food. I'll get on to the Dog Rescue people and see what they can do for him. Contrary to what you might think, I don't go around shooting dogs, you know. I happen to be very fond of them. Even that old rogue there.'

'So am I,' Jess said, 'Which really surprises me because until I met Benson, I thought I didn't. Would you like a cup of tea while you're here?'

'Great. Thanks.'

'Come on, Benson,' she said. 'I know you're worn out after all that philandering but you'll have to move out the way so I can get to the kettle.'

As she stepped over the dog, something clicked in her mind. She remembered someone else stepping over the dog. Nick. The night she came in to the kitchen and found him rummaging in the dresser drawers.

'I've just remembered. Nick was looking for something,' she said suddenly. 'Remember the night he came in and I called you because I thought he was a burglar?'

'The idea of Nick paying his grandmother a call to see how she was never did ring true. That he'd come here looking for something would make sense, knowing Nick. Do you have any idea what it was?'

'He wouldn't say. And when I said that, if he told me what he was looking for, I'd ask Elsie about it, he told me not to bother and then changed the subject.'

'He would have been up to no good, that's for sure.'

'But Sandra was talking about a bit

of paper Elsie had signed, making the farmhouse over to Nick. Do you think it would be that?'

'She did what?' Rob looked astonished. 'I can't believe that. I think that's something Sandra made up to put you at a disadvantage.'

'I hope so. Sandra said it was to ensure that Social Services wouldn't force Elsie to sell the farmhouse to pay for her nursing home fees.'

Rob shook his head. 'That doesn't sound a bit like Elsie to me. As for letting Nick get his hands on Higher Neston — ' He shook his head. 'It makes no sense, no sense at all. She knows as well as I do what he would do to the place if he got the chance.'

'And something else has occurred to me too,' Jess went on, 'When I saw Nick outside the hospital today, he let slip something about having been here earlier this morning. I think he came back when he knew I'd be out, to have a better look for whatever it is he's looking for. I think, too, he was the one who left the back door open and let Benson out. Because the more I think about it, the more convinced I am that I remember shutting it.'

'I'm sure you did. And knowing Nick, I'm willing to bet he left that door open deliberately.'

'Well, I'm not sure about that.' Jess said.

'You still don't get it about him, do you?' Rob snapped suddenly. 'I've told you before, he's not to be trusted.'

'I know you two have . . . ' she hesitated, trying hard to choose the right words. 'Have issues between you but I don't think he's the villain you're making him out to be.'

'You don't know him very well. That man would sell his own grandmother if he could,' Rob said.

'Not his grandmother, but perhaps her house,' Jess murmured as she remembered Nick telling her that he had clients lined up to buy Higher Neston. 'Do you have any idea where Elsie would keep important papers?'

she asked Rob. 'I'd ask her myself only I don't want to worry her about this, in case I'm wrong.'

'Wrong about what?'

'About Nick's plans to sell Higher Neston,' she said.

'There's an old walnut writing box. She keeps it hidden in an old blanket chest on the top landing. I know that because she got it out once to show me some of the pedigrees of her dogs. She used to breed German Shepherds, you know. If I know Elsie, she'd keep anything valuable there.'

'Will you come with me and we'll look together? I don't feel comfortable about rooting through her personal things, particularly not valuable ones. It's just that my father's a solicitor and, if we find this paper, I'd like to fax him a copy so that he can see if it's legally binding.'

'Elsie doesn't have a fax but I do.' Rob said as they went up to the top landing. The box was where Rob had said it would be and it looked as if it had lain there undisturbed for some time.

Rob opened the box, looked through several pieces, then drew out a paper. 'Would this be it?' he said, his face darkening with anger as he read it. 'The slimy little toad. This was signed last February, the time when, if I remember right, poor Elsie had a particularly rotten dose of flu. He must have got her to sign it then.'

'So maybe we can prove she signed it under duress or something.' Jess said. 'Look, I'll give you my father's fax number and I'll phone him to let him know you're going to fax something through.'

Rob looked at her, his eyes warm. 'You really care about Elsie, don't you?' he said.

Jess nodded. 'I think she's brave and clever and she deserves to live in her own home for as long as she wants, without being hounded out.'

'I think it's great that you're going to stay on and look after her.'

Jess blushed. 'It's an excuse for me to stay here a bit longer,' she said.

'Do you need an excuse?' he said quietly.

'Yes. No. I'm not sure.' She felt and sounded flustered, aware of how very close he was, of how he smelt of the outdoors, of how attractive he was when he smiled. 'I've got such a large order for pies for Fiona, I'll be up all night doing them if I don't get on.'

'They'll go well. The one I had was superb.'

'They had superb ingredients,' Jess said, trying to pass off the compliment. She'd never been very good at accepting compliments gracefully, partly, she thought ruefully, because she'd never had much chance to practise.

'Look,' Rob said suddenly. 'Would you like to have dinner with me this evening? Like you, I've got a hundred things to do today.'

'I'm sorry.' Jess's regret was genuine as she bitterly regretted agreeing to cook dinner for Nick that evening. 'I've got things to do tonight. I'd love to another time perhaps?'

She crossed her fingers as she said this, hoping that he would suggest another time but instead he shrugged, his eyes went cold as he turned back into the aloof stranger she'd first met.

'I'd better get this sent off,' he said as he turned to go. 'And you'd better phone your father.'

9

Jess sighed as the door closed behind Rob. She hesitated as she picked up the phone, finding it harder than she'd have thought possible. The memory of her mother's words floated back to her. For as long as she could remember, her father had been a hero in her eyes. And to find out that he had been living a lie was almost more than she could bear.

Since she'd found out, she'd been tempted several times to call him up and give him a piece of her mind, but she'd held back, figuring that how her parents chose to conduct their marriage was their concern, not hers.

She thought of the piece of paper that meant so much to Elsie and her way of life and that feeling over rode everything else. She took a deep breath and picked up the phone.

'Dad?' she got through on his private number.

'Jess? For heaven's sake, child, where are you? Your mother has been going out of her head with worry — and driving me mad into the bargain, I can tell you.'

'I told her, I'm staying in Somerset, with an . . . an old friend,' she said, consoling herself that it wasn't exactly a lie. She'd like to think she and Elsie had become friends and was sure that, in this instance, Elsie would forgive her for calling her old.

'So, how are you?' he said. 'And when are you coming home? We do miss you, Kitten.'

'You mean your dinner guests miss my cooking,' she snapped, her voice sharper than she'd intended in her determination not to succumb to the concern in his voice.

'No,' he said quietly. 'I mean we missed you. I'm worried about you and was very sorry to hear about you and Matt splitting up.'

'Well, I'm so sorry if it's caused you embarrassment in the office. No doubt you think, like Mother, that I should have put up with it, turned a blind eye to the fact that my boyfriend was cheating on me, said boys will be boys, or something like that.'

'No, of course I don't.' He sounded bewildered. 'I happen to think that trust is the cement in any relationship and when that's gone — '

'I'm sorry, Dad, but I hardly think you're in a position to lecture me about relationships, with or without the cement.' She forced herself to stay angry with him. There was no way she was going to let him off the hook because of a few fine words. He was a lawyer and words were his stock in trade. He had a way with them and could always talk her round. But not this time.

'Mother told me,' she blurted out, ignoring the small voice of reason in her head that was cautioning her to think about what she was going to say.

'Told you what?'

'About your — your floozies,' she said, using the first word that came into her head and instantly regretting it.

'My what?' To her fury, she could hear a catch of laughter in his voice. 'Darling girl, what on earth are you talking about?'

'Mother told me how you've been unfaithful to her for most of your married life,' Jess said, 'Something she says she's prepared to put up with. Well, let me tell you, I think that's terrible. Quite terrible. How could you?'

'She thinks I am still having affairs?' There was no laughter in his voice now. 'I can't believe it. — '

'You thought she didn't know, didn't you? That you'd got away with it? But she's known all along.'

'But it's not true. Listen, Kitten, I swear on anything you want me to swear on, I am not cheating on your mother. Yes, for my sins and to my everlasting shame, I did once. But it was just that one time. A brief fling with one of my secretaries. It never meant a thing.'

'That makes it worse somehow,' Jess said.

'I know. And like I said, I'm bitterly ashamed. But in my defence, it never meant anything to her either. It was a moment's madness on both sides and it was years ago, when you were a small baby. I thought . . . I can't believe your mother thought . . . I mean, I know I've been working late a lot recently but work is exactly what I have been doing. I wouldn't hurt your mother again like that for the world. Do you honestly mean to tell me that for all these years, she's thought . . . ? I can't believe she thinks that.'

'Then tell her, Dad,' Jess urged as his voice trailed away. 'Tell her, not me. Leave work early tonight, pick up a bunch of flowers and a nice bottle of wine and tell her.'

'You believe me, don't you?' he said.

'Of course I do,' she said, relieved to discover that she meant it. 'I dare say

Mother does too. You know what she's like about making a drama out of a crisis. I dare say she's even forgotten she said it to me.'

'I will, of course. And, well, I suppose I should say thank you, although it seems a strange thing to thank your own daughter for. I still can't believe it.'

'Talk to her. You'll never sort anything out if you don't talk.'

'And neither will you, Kitten,' he said softly. 'Why don't you call her and tell her where you are? She's genuinely worried about you, you know.'

'I doubt that. But I'll call her tomorrow, I promise,' she said. 'Although she's not going to make me change my mind about coming back to London. Meanwhile, I've got a hundred and one things to do today. Including, I hope, sorting out a piece of paper that someone is supposed to be faxing through to you. If you wouldn't mind having a look at it for me. It's really important. It concerns a very dear friend who, I've got a horrible feeling, is being conned out of her home.'

'Of course I will. I'll call you back when it comes through. Oh, no, hang on a minute. That was quick. Sara's just come in with your fax. Let me see,' There was a pause as her father read the paper carefully, not speaking until he had carefully considered his answer. He was always like this. Her mother always teased him that he gave the same focussed attention to a shopping list as to a legal contract.

'Well?' Jess could stand the silence no longer. 'Is it legally binding?'

'Of course it's not,' he said. 'Has nothing of what I do for a living rubbed off on you over the years? There are two signatures, but they're not even witnessed, so whoever tried to enforce it would have a pretty hard time trying to doing so.'

'Dad, you're an angel,' Jess breathed.

'That's better than the devil incarnate you had me pegged out for just now,' he said with a laugh. 'Well, I'm neither. Just a mere mortal, trying to do my best and not always succeeding.'

'Point taken,' she smiled, glad to be back to their former easy going relationship. 'How did the dinner party go, by the way?'

'Don't ask.' She could feel her father's shudder down the phone line. 'Why your mother didn't do as I suggested and get something from M and S, I'll never know. Still, the clients seemed happy enough and that's the main thing. Sadly, the same cannot be said for your mother. She's still recovering from the trauma.'

'I can well believe that. But you will sit down and talk to her tonight, won't you? Promise? Oh, and don't forget the flowers.'

As soon as she put the phone down, it rang again.

'Oh, Jess, thank goodness I've got you at last. I've been trying for absolutely ages. Please, please don't hang up on me. I wouldn't blame you if you did, of course. But I really am in the most terrible mess.'

'Sophie?' Her ex-business partner sounded as if she was on the edge of total melt down and it was a measure of how much Jess had changed since coming to Higher Neston that she didn't bang the phone down on her but asked instead, 'What's wrong?'

'Everything!' Sophie, ever the drama queen exclaimed. 'It's all going horribly wrong, and yes, I know you probably think I'm getting nothing more than I deserve and I don't blame you for that. But I've got this really desperate situation and — and I really miss you, you know.'

'You should have thought of that before,' Jess couldn't resist a dig.

'Oh, God, I'm so sorry. We didn't mean to hurt you, nor for you to find out the way you did. I really love Matt, you know.'

Jess was about to snap, *And I didn't?* but pulled back. She bit her thumb and stared out of the farmhouse window. But had she ever loved Matt? What would she do if he walked in the door that moment, went down on his knees and begged him to forgive her? Would she take him back, or throw the first thing that came to hand — in this case a tray of eggs that she'd picked up from the Farm Shop earlier?

Then the weirdest thing happened. As she was thinking of Matt — the man she'd been in love with for the last six months and who'd broken her heart just days ago — instead of his face coming to her mind, she saw Rob's. The warm, friendly version, that is, the way he'd been just now when he'd asked her to dinner and before he retreated into that damn prickly shell when she'd had to tell him she had other plans.

'Hello? Jess? Are you still there?'

She forced her thoughts back to Sophie and her 'desperate situation'. Whatever it was it must be pretty serious to make Sophie call her, knowing the way her ex-friend hated confrontation of any sort and would usually go to any lengths to avoid it.

'What's the problem?' Jess asked.

'Remember the Targusta Group? The guys who really went for your spicy lamb pies? Well, they're insisting on having them for their next lunch, otherwise I lose the contract.'

'So what is it you want from me? I hope you don't expect me to give you the recipe?' Jess had worked hard on that particular recipe. It was one of her signature dishes and she had no intention of simply giving it away, least of all to Sophie.

'God, no. I don't have time to shop around for a pastry cook. The one I've got is okay but she's not in your league. No, I was hoping maybe you could make them for me. The lunch is next Tuesday. I'll pay you whatever you want. You can name your price. Like I said, I'm desperate.'

Jess was about to say no, when she realised that, in fact, she bore Sophie little ill will and to turn down a good business deal would be crazy.

'I could do them,' she said. 'But I'm

not coming up to London. I'll cook them here and deliver them to you by courier.'

'You will? That's brilliant. Jess, you're an angel.'

'Like father, like daughter then,' Jess murmured, recalling how a few moments earlier she'd called her father the same thing.

'Sorry?'

'Nothing. Just wait until you see my bill.' She laughed as she said it, but Jess was only partly joking. 'You might not think me quite so angelic then.'

She needed to call Rob to let him know what her father had said before turning her attention to the preparation of dinner. Her heart sank at the prospect of entertaining Nick. Why had she agreed to this? Why did she feel she had to give him one last chance?

Saying yes to Nick had seemed the easiest thing to do and she'd thought she could use the opportunity, while he was mellow with her special lamb and apricot pie to persuade him to give up his plans for Higher Neston and to let Elsie live in peace. Having now met his shrew of a mother, she was pretty sure Sandra was the one who'd really had all these wicked plans for Higher Neston.

She was convinced Nick's fondness for his grandmother was genuine. Of course, it was also quite possible that he, too, would tell Jess to mind her own business and to keep her nose out of family affairs, but that was a chance she was willing to take. She was fairly confident she could talk Nick round, in which case Elsie's future would be safe.

As she dialled Rob's number, she cursed as his answerphone cut in. 'Hi, Rob, it's me, Jess. Just to say I've heard from Dad — '

'I'm here,' his voice suddenly cut in, startling her. Her heart was thudding so loudly it was almost difficult to speak.

'Right. Good,' she stammered, as her mind went blank. 'I — I was just leaving you a message — '

'So I heard.'

'Yes, well. It was to say — ' she

stopped. What was going on here? What was she going to say? Who'd sneaked in and filled her brain with cotton wool when she wasn't looking? Why had she suddenly started acting like a star struck teenager over a man she hardly knew? A man who, moreover, she seemed to manage to annoy almost every time they met. But a man who, when he smiled, made you think the sun had just come out.

'You were saying? Something about your father?' Rob prompted.

'Yes. Yes. Of course. Sorry. She forced her thoughts back to saner ground. 'Dad said the paper wasn't legally binding and that I should have known that for myself, of course. If I'd just stopped to think for a moment . . . '

'As indeed did Elsie.'

'Sorry? What did you just say?'

'I've just been talking to Elsie on the phone. She knew the paper Nick persuaded her to sign wasn't legally binding.'

Jess couldn't believe what she was

169

hearing and could only echo his words, while her brain tried to work out what on earth was going on. 'She knew the paper was worthless?'

'One of her cat owners is a solicitor. Elsie had her check it over although of course she didn't tell Nick that.'

'I don't understand.' Jess was beginning to feel very hurt. 'Why didn't you tell me that? Why let me phone my father and . . . ?'

'Because I've only just found out. But Elsie said to go ahead and let you do it anyway. She really is a manipulative old witch, you know. I tell her so to her face on numerous occasions.' There was a smile in his voice as he spoke which robbed his words of offence, even though they were the same words Nick had used and which had made Jess so annoyed. 'She told me how unhappy you were about the rift between you and your father and how you needed to talk to him. She also said — and I completely agree with her — that you're an unbelievably kind and generous person and your desire to help her would override your reluctance to speak to your father.'

For a second, she was tempted to become angry, to complain at Elsie and Rob for daring to interfere in her private family matters — until she realised that that was exactly what she'd been about to do with Nick. Besides, there was something about the way Rob had talked of her being warm and generous that was giving her a very pleasant glow.

'Well,' Rob said gently. 'Was she right?'

'I suppose,' she said, 'Although she had no right.'

'Of course she didn't. But, where Elsie's concerned, it's easier to go with the flow. Something I found out ages ago,' he said.

'And, of course, the end justifies the means,' she said, thinking of her forthcoming evening with Nick. Only now, she realised, there was no need to go through with it. If Elsie was still the legal owner of Higher Neston, then Nick's plans for the place were totally irrelevant.

But when she tried to phone him, in the hope of putting him off, she couldn't get any reply from his number. She shrugged. Just as well really, she thought. It was a pretty rotten thing to do, to cancel at the last minute.

10

She was part way through preparing the sweet she planned to serve that evening, when she heard Benson give the low, warning growl that meant someone was in the yard. She went to the front door in time to see Nick getting out of his car. She took a deep breath and forced a smile.

'Nick, you're early,' she said.

'I couldn't keep away,' he gave her another of his long, lingering smiles and she realised with a jolt what it was that seemed familiar to her. It was the same smile as Matt's.

He reached back into the car and brought out a bunch of flowers — half a dozen perfect roses, their deep pink accentuated by the lacework of gypsophila around them.

'Oh, Nick, they're beautiful,' she said, 'But you shouldn't have. I'll put them in water and then place them here on the hall table so that they'll be the first thing Elsie sees on Monday when she comes home.'

Nick had been walking ahead of her into the kitchen but he stopped so suddenly, she almost cannoned into him.

'She's coming home?' he said.

'Yes, isn't it great? I knew you'd be pleased because I know how you've been worrying about her. The hospital said she can come home on Monday, after she's seen the doctor and provided he says she's fit enough, so fingers crossed.'

'But I thought it was all fixed up that she was going to go to a nursing home for convalescence. My mother went to endless trouble to sort it. Are they mad? Sending a frail old lady out here in the sticks to fend for herself?'

'But she won't be fending for herself,' Jess was touched by his concern and was anxious to reassure him. 'I'll be here. I managed to convince the powers that be that I'm a fit and proper person to look after her,' she added with a grin.

But her smile faded at the sight of Nick's face. It was like looking at the face of a stranger. Furthermore, a furiously angry, about to lose control stranger. She took an instinctive step backwards.

'Nick? What's wrong?' she asked. 'I thought you'd be pleased. Your mother was furious and, I must say, incredibly rude. She told me to keep my nose out of her family's affairs in no uncertain terms. But I thought you would be pleased, knowing how you worry about your grandmother. Poor Elsie is being stifled in that place. She's such a free spirit. She needs — '

'She needs? How would you know what she needs?' he snarled, his face, which she'd once thought so attractive, now contorted with rage. 'Suddenly, you're a medical expert, are you?'

'No, of course not. But Elsie is — '

'My mother was right,' He spat the words out. 'You're nothing but an interfering busy-body. What do you think is in it for you? Do you think Elsie is loaded, is that it?'

'No. Of course not!'

'Well, let me tell you,' Jess took another step backward and put the width of the table between them as he lunged towards her. 'She hasn't got a bean. She doesn't even own this wreck of a house — I do. And I want you out of here by tomorrow. I'll sort the hospital out, say there was a misunderstanding. But you're out of here, get it?'

Jess was furious. 'I'm going nowhere. I'll stay here as long as Elsie needs me. As for the house being yours, you must know as well as I do, seeing the line of business you're in, that the paper you coerced your grandmother into signing isn't worth a damn thing. You were simply using it as a lever against her, thinking she'd believe it, didn't you? Well, let me tell you, she didn't fall for it, not for a single moment.'

'You reckon?' he glared at her defiantly. 'That was what you came back for, wasn't it? That first night when I came down and found you rifling through the drawers.'

'So, what if it was?'

'And it was you, wasn't it?' Jess said as realisation came to her.

'What?'

'When I saw you outside the hospital earlier, you let slip something about having been at Higher Neston this morning. It was you who left the back door open, wasn't it? You who let Benson out? How could you have been so stupid? When I saw the sheep running . . .'

Nick grinned. 'So he's a sheep worrier, is he? Well, that's the trouble with Gran taking in all these strays, isn't it?' His contemptuous glance told Jess that he included her in that number. 'You never know when bad blood will out, do you?'

'You did it deliberately, didn't you?' Suddenly Jess was more angry than she'd ever been in her life. 'You let Benson out, hoping that he'd have a go at the sheep, didn't you?'

'I did better than that,' he grinned, 'I made sure he'd go in the field. I threw his ball and the mutt chased after it, scattering the stupid sheep as he did so.'

Jess remembered the way the lambs had bleated in terror as they'd become separated from their mothers.

'Get out!' She picked up the first thing that came to hand which happened to be Elsie's heavy old wooden rolling pin and took a step towards him, her arm raised. 'Get out now before I do something I regret.'

'There's no need to be like that,' Nick muttered and, as he stepped back, he tripped over Benson who was stretched out in his usual place in front of the Aga. The dog yelped more from surprise than pain and Nick fell heavily.

Jess had to bite her lip hard to stop herself from laughing. 'Serves you right,' she muttered.

'Wretched dog,' Nick fumed. 'Fancy letting him lie there. It's unhygienic for a start.'

As he stood up, Jess noticed something on the floor that must have fallen from his pocket during the fall. 'Here, you've dropped something,' she said as she reached to pick it up. But when she saw what it was, her anger returned even stronger.

'That's Elsie's silver snuff box,' she said. 'The one on the hall table. 'You were stealing it!'

'It's not stealing,' he said. 'It'll all be mine one day anyway. She has so many little knick knacks about the place, she'd never miss it. And besides, now the deal with the farmhouse has fallen through, I need the cash. Desperately. I owe money to some very impatient people.'

'That's your problem.'

'You think Gran will enjoy reading about how her grandson has been beaten to a pulp over a measly few hundred quid? Come on, Jess, what do you say?' His voice had softened to a low, wheedling tone. 'There's loads of these little bits of silver lying around and I know someone who'll give me a good price. What do you say? Fifty-fifty?'

'I say if you get out now, I'll pretend this conversation never happened,' Jess said and, brandishing the rolling pin, hustled him to the door.

As soon as she heard the sound of Nick's car being driven away at high speed, she dialled Rob's number.

He listened without interruption, apart from a quiet intake of breath, as she told him what had happened with Nick.

'Look,' she said quickly before her nerve failed her. 'There's something I want to talk over with you. I know I said I wasn't free this evening, but, well, that was because I had arranged to see Nick because I thought I could talk him into doing the right thing for Elsie.'

'Why didn't you say?'

'Because I figured if you thought that's what I was doing; you'd have tried to stop me.'

'Too damn right I would have,' he growled.

78/4945

DUCTION TO

THE ENGLISH NOVEL

VOLUME I

English Literature

Editor

PROFESSOR JOHN LAWLOR

MA

Professor of English Language and
Literature in the University of Keele

By the same author

An Introduction to the English Novel

VOLUME II: HENRY JAMES TO
1950

AN INTRODUCTION TO
THE ENGLISH NOVEL

VOLUME I
TO GEORGE ELIOT

Arnold Kettle

Professor of Literature at the Open
University, Milton Keynes

HUTCHINSON OF LONDON

HUTCHINSON & CO (Publishers) LTD
3 Fitzroy Square, London W1

London Melbourne Sydney Auckland
Wellington Johannesburg Cape Town
and agencies throughout the world

First published November 1951
Reprinted 1954, 1957, 1959
1961, 1963, 1965
Second edition 1967
Reprinted 1969, 1972, 1974, 1976, 1977

Printed in Great Britain by The Anchor Press Ltd,
and bound by Wm. Brendon & Son Ltd,
both of Tiptree, Essex

ISBN 0 09 031603 7 (cased)
ISBN 0 09 031604 5 (paper)

CONTENTS

6   Contents

PREFACE

The purpose of this book and its successor (which will bring the story up to the present day) is not to attempt a history of the English novel. But because the novel, like every other literary form, is a product of history, I have tried, in the first two Parts, to indicate something of the historical development of fiction and to face—if not to answer satisfactorily—the essential questions: why did the novel arise at all, and why should it have arisen when it did?

The third part of the book makes even less claim to exhaustiveness. I have taken nine well-known nineteenth-century novels (of which six are included in the present volume) and tried to bring out in analysis certain critical questions which emerge from a study of each. Three reasons in particular have led me to adopt this method: (1) the field, by the nineteenth century, has become so wide that an exhaustive treatment would be in any event impossible, (2) novels tend to be rather long and for any course of study in this subject it is useful to concentrate on a reading list that is both short and accessible, and (3) critics of the novel appear to have shirked, with a few honourable exceptions, the business of analysis and of disciplined critical evaluation. Although I would not for a moment claim to have said the last word about any of the books treated here I have consistently tried to get to the heart of each novel, to pose the questions: what *kind* of a novel is this? What is it about? It is not enough to consider a novel, any more than a poem or a play, simply in terms of plot-construction and characters. We have to see each novel whole before we can attempt to assess the parts or even to decide the criteria relevant to our judgments.

Of course the choice of my novels is somewhat arbitrary. I do not claim that they are the nine best nineteenth-century novels. I have left out plenty of books I would have liked to have included and I feel a particular pang in having represented Dickens, the greatest of the English novelists, by a book which is by no stretch of the imagination his best, though I believe it is underrated. My only claim for my chosen books is that they are all good novels (though not equally good), all readily accessible, and that they happen to raise a variety of critical problems which have a general interest and significance.

The original plan of this book meant stopping, with Conrad, at the beginning of the present century. And yet to leave off there was clearly unsatisfactory. Everything would be left in the air; to raise and yet not to attempt to answer any of the problems of our own contemporary fiction would seem irritating and somewhat cowardly. And so it was decided to bring the whole survey (it should not really be given so portentous a name) up to date and to divide it into two volumes. The present volume ends with *Middlemarch*. It is not an inappropriate break, for George Eliot's great novel is in a number of respects the culminating point of Victorian fiction. The volume that is to follow will begin with the consideration of novels by Henry James and Samuel Butler (very unalike and yet both somehow distinctly nearer to our own century than George Eliot) and go on to examine some of the tendencies and experiments in the fiction of the twentieth century.

I should like to thank many friends who, through their advice and conversation, have helped in the writing of this book; particularly Professor Bonamy Dobrée, Mr Douglas Jefferson, Mr Edward Thompson, Mr Alick West and Professor Basil Willey. My sense of gratitude to them is equalled only by my concern that they should not be associated with the book's many imperfections or with judgments (there are many) which they do not share. There is another debt too which I would not wish to be ambiguous or at least more ambiguous than all such debts are. I have used throughout the book to describe a particular kind of novel the term 'moral fable'. The phrase, so far as I know, is Defoe's, but it has been used and, so to speak, developed in recent years by Dr F. R. Leavis. I hope that in using the term, as I believe I have, in a sense rather more narrow than his habitual use of it I have not compromised a critic to whom anyone who has done any serious thinking about the English novel must owe a particular debt.

A. K.

PART I
Introductory

I

LIFE AND PATTERN

Catching the very note and trick, the strange irregular rhythm of life, that is the attempt whose strenuous effort keeps Fiction on her feet. HENRY JAMES

We might as well start—when we have finished our preliminaries— with Bunyan and Defoe. The starting-point is neither original nor inevitable, but it is convenient. For Bunyan and Defoe are both great figures in their own right, the first writers whom no consideration of the English novel could possibly leave out, and they also happen to belong to two separate lines in the development of prose fiction which make useful, though by no means water-tight, categories.

This business of 'lines' and 'categories' is, we should realise, extremely dangerous. If it were not that its opposite—the refusal to differentiate, to recognise that, say, *Pride and Prejudice* and *Wuthering Heights* are as different in kind as *The Duchess of Malfi* and *Major Barbara*—has been one of the banes of novel criticism, one would be tempted to try to dispense with it altogether.

It is always dangerous to take a work of art apart and to abstract from it particular qualities. Once one has pigeon-holed a book or dissected it there is the danger that one may never again see it whole. Moreover, one aspect of a book is always closely connected, if not interwoven with another. You cannot really separate, say, 'character' from 'plot', 'narrative' from 'background'.

People often talk of these things [wrote Henry James] as if they had a kind of internecine distinctness, instead of melting into each other at every breath, and being intimately connected parts of one general effort of expression. I cannot imagine composition existing in a series of blocks, nor conceive, in any novel worth discussing at all, of a passage of description that is not in its intention narrative, a passage of dialogue that is not in its intention description, a touch of truth of any sort that does not partake of the nature of incident, or an incident that derives its interest from any other source than the general and only source of the success of a work of art—that of being illustrative. *A novel is a living thing, all one and continuous, like any other organism, and in proportion as it lives will it be found, I think, that in each of the parts there is something of the other parts.*[1]

This is well said, definitively said perhaps, and chastening. It cannot be too often insisted that criticism, analytical or historical (and the terms themselves are not mutually exclusive), the tracing of lines of development, the setting of a book in its historical background, is useless and misleading unless it brings us to a fuller, richer, more complete view of the book we are considering. It may be to the purpose of the historian, the sociologist, the psychologist, to abstract from particular novels factors which illustrate and enrich his own study; it may even be to the purpose of the literary critic, in so far as he too is necessarily concerned with history, with placing and elucidating literary developments, thus to abstract. But we must always remember that the ultimate concern of the study of literature is evaluation, the passing of judgment on each particular work of art.

Yet it is impossible to evaluate literature in the abstract; a book is neither produced nor read in a vacuum and the very word 'value' involves right away criteria which are not just 'literary'. Literature is a part of life and can be judged only in its relevance to life. Life is not static but moving and changing. Thus we have to see both literature and ourselves in history, not as abstract entities. 'Criticism', as the nineteenth-century Russian critic Belinsky put it, 'is aesthetics in motion.' Though we must see each novel as a part of history and its value as the quality of its contribution to the achievement of man's freedom, yet it is important to remember that it is the book *itself* we are judging, not its intention, nor the amount of 'social significance' to be got out of it, nor even its importance as a measurable historical influence.

Uncle Tom's Cabin has been, in this last sense, a more important book than *Wuthering Heights*; but it is not a better book. For whereas *Uncle Tom's Cabin* can bring to the reader's attention facts he had previously ignored and has pricked men's consciences and urged them into action on behalf of what they knew to be just and necessary, *Wuthering Heights* has that within it which can *change*

---

[1] Superior figures refer to Notes and References, pp. 179-81.

men's consciousness and make them aware of what previously they had not even guessed. *Uncle Tom's Cabin* may enlarge the realm of our knowledge, *Wuthering Heights* enlarges that of our imagination.

Uncle Tom's Cabin's contribution to human freedom (which, heaven knows, one doesn't wish to undervalue) is in a sense fortuitous. Someone else might have written something else which had roughly the same effect. It was an act of courage rather than an act of art (and if an American Negro tells me it is worth more to him than *Wuthering Heights* I cannot argue). But no one else could have—or at any rate has—written anything very like *Wuthering Heights*, and no reader who has responded fully to *Wuthering Heights* is ever, whether he realises it or not, quite the same again.

This said, it may be permissible to suggest that there are in all novels which are successful works of art two elements, emphatically not separate and yet to some extent separable. These are the elements of life and pattern. Art, as T. E. Hulme has put it, is life-communicating; it must give us a sense that what is being conveyed across to us by the words on the page is life or, at any rate, has something of the quality of life. Novels which do not give us this sense of life, which we do not respond to with a certain quickening of our faculties, which we do not feel—in Keats' famous but never-bettered phrase—'upon our pulses', such novels may be worth an inquest but not a second edition. At the same time the good novel does not simply convey life; it says something about life. It reveals some kind of pattern in life. It brings significance.

It must be emphasised that the two elements—life and pattern— are not separate. If we ask of any particular novel that 'lives' the question, 'what is it that gives it vitality?' we shall find that the vitality is inseparable from the novelist's view of life, which is what decides what he puts into every sentence and what he leaves out.

In that wonderful first chapter of *Pride and Prejudice*, which 'comes alive' so immediately and gives so sharp and yet so subtle a sense of life, so that we know at once so much about the Bennet family, this 'life' would not be there but for Jane Austen's tone, her ironical opening generalisation, her choice of words, her italics, her decision at each point and moment as to just how and where her reader's attention shall be directed. Even a photograph involves choice—of subject, composition, light—which reveals something of the photographer's mind; with the writer—even the most apparently photographic in technique—the issue is infinitely wider because every word he uses involves a choice, a choice dependent (though he may not be aware of it) on the kind of man he is, on his view of life, on the significance he attaches to what he sees.

And yet, despite all this, it will be generally agreed that in some novels 'life' is more obviously there than 'pattern'. There are writers, and great ones, whose books have more vividness than wisdom, more vitality than significance. *David Copperfield* is such a book. It is a novel almost completely lacking what I mean by pattern. The earlier parts, perhaps, have a kind of pattern, the pattern of David's struggles (passive as they tend to be) against the forces of darkness—Murdstone and the London factory; but once these struggles have been obliterated (not solved) by a *dea ex machina*, Betsy Trotwood, pattern disappears altogether and is replaced only by plot, anecdote, contrivance and an insistence on 'characters' (the inverted commas are inevitable) like the Micawbers.

The result is that though *David Copperfield* conveys something of life it tells us very little about life. It is hard to say what it is about, except that it is about David Copperfield, and there again David's life is not presented to us in a way that can reasonably be called significant. He is born, has a bad stepfather and a kind aunt, goes through a number of adventures, marries twice (the problems of the first, unsatisfactory marriage being conveniently shelved by Dora's death), gets to know a good many people including some delightful ones, and it is all (or most of it) quite interesting and frequently very amusing; but that is all. There is no pattern.

Pattern is not something narrowly 'aesthetic', something which critics like Clive Bell used to talk about as 'form' (as opposed to life or content). Pattern is the quality in a book which gives it wholeness and meaning, makes the reading of it a complete and satisfying experience. This is a matter partly, but only partly, discussable in terms used by the devotees of 'form'. Sometimes the pattern of a book does have a geometrical quality. Mr E. M. Forster has discussed Henry James's *The Ambassadors* in such terms;[2] *The Spoils of Poynton* has an even more strongly marked formal pattern. An early example of pattern of this kind is Congreve's *Incognita*, a pretty little story in which two pairs of lovers intrigue, pirouette and exchange partners with the kind of grace and precision one associates with a formal aristocratic dance of the eighteenth century.

The value of this kind of geometrical 'form' is an interesting question. In general we should, I think, treat it with some suspicion because of the tendency to use such forms for their own sake, that is to say for no good reason. To give your story the pattern of a figure of eight is only worth while in so far as that pattern has a significance relevant to what you are saying. Abstract geometrical patterns do in fact have some significance in relation to life. So do such formal patterns as are evolved in dances which clearly have a direct relationship to courtship or harvest rituals.

Again, many mental processes have their fairly precise formal equivalents: the 'shape' of *The Ambassadors* which Mr Forster compares to an hour-glass is, in effect, the formal equivalent of what the Greeks called *peripeteia*, that reversal of a situation from which, as Aristotle noted, so much both of irony and tragedy has sprung. This, I think, is the point. 'Form' is important only in so far as it enhances significance; and it will enhance significance just in so far as it bears a real relation to, that is to say symbolises or clarifies, the aspect of life that is being conveyed. But form is not *in itself* significant; the central core of any novel is what it has to say about life.

When we say, then, that a novel has more life than pattern we are in fact making a criticism of the quality of perception of life which the novelist is conveying. For the pattern which the writer imposes is the very essence of his vision of whatever in life he is dealing with. To say of *David Copperfield* that it is of the kind of novel that has more vividness than wisdom, more vitality than significance, is to say something which, though not meaningless, has (unless we are quite conscious of the way we are using words) many misleading overtones. For such a statement might well imply an actual separation of vitality and significance, a suggestion that significance or pattern is something to be spread like marmalade on a given surface of 'life'; whereas it is actually out of the writer's very perception of life that the significance emerges.

The vitality of *David Copperfield* is in fact limited by Dickens's failure to master and organise significantly the raw material of his novel. Mr Murdstone is more vital than Agnes precisely because Dickens's perception of him is more profound, morally and aesthetically (you cannot separate the two). The last half of the book is—except for odd snatches of idiosyncratic observation—a bore precisely because it lacks a convincing conflict, that is to say, moral significance, to give it pattern.

What, then, is the point of labouring this admittedly rather artificial distinction between life and pattern? Simply that a great many writers have, in practice, tended to separate the two and almost all have approached the business of novel-writing with a bias towards one or the other direction. They have either begun with a pattern that seemed to them valid and tried to inject life into it, or they have begun with a fairly undefined concern with 'life' and tried to make a pattern emerge out of it. One would not for a moment suggest, of course, that this is anything but a crude simplification of the infinitely subtle and complicated question of the springs of artistic creation.

Exactly how an individual novel, or any work of art, comes into being is a fascinating problem far outside the scope of this book. What one would here stress is that there is one line in the development of the novel in the eighteenth century—a line which includes, for example, *Gulliver's Travels* and *Jonathan Wild*—in which pattern is clearly the novelist's supreme and prior consideration. In this kind of novel it is not unfair to say that the author starts with his pattern, his moral vision, and that the various elements of the novel, character and plot in particular, are continuously subordinated to and in a special sense derived from the pattern. Gulliver, for instance, though he is a convincing enough figure for Swift's purposes, has no existence of his own. We do not feel any temptation to abstract him from the story in the way that we might abstract, say, Mr Dick from *David Copperfield*.

The type of novel I am referring to has been excellently described as a 'moral fable'. Now the author of the moral fable is not necessarily more concerned with morals than other novelists. Joseph Conrad, for instance, whose novels certainly do not come within this category, saw the essential feature of a story as its 'moral discovery'. The distinction—an important one—is that in the moral fable the central discovery seems to have been made by the author prior to his conception of the book. In other words, the fable-writer starts off with his vision, his moral 'truth', and, so to speak, tries to blow life into it. In the course of this process the original 'truth' will no doubt be deepened and enriched, made living instead of abstract; but the original abstract concept will have its effect on the book.

All good novels, like all other good works of art, are concrete, not abstract, but to describe the original concept of a novel as abstract is not necessarily to condemn either the concept or the novel. A writer has to start somewhere and there is no obvious reason why the germ of his novel should not be an abstracted 'truth' capable of generalised expression. That the subject of *Candide* is the fallacy of the belief that 'all is for the best in the best of all possible worlds' does not invalidate Voltaire's novel, though it does determine the kind of novel it is. But it is clear that, if the tendency of the novelist who begins, as I think Dickens does in

David Copperfield, with 'life' will be to write books that are amorphous and unorganised, that of the writer of moral fables will be towards a certain rigidity.

If you start with an abstract 'truth', even a profound one, it is difficult to avoid the temptation to mould life to your vision. That is why a book like *Candide* has, for all its brilliance, a certain brittle quality. The reader cannot help feeling that any facets of life which happened not to fit in with Voltaire's thesis would stand a poor chance of gaining admission. This is not to say that there is no vitality in *Candide*; it has all the vitality of the author's fearless, incisive view of the world: but it is the vitality of Voltaire rather than of the world that comes across.

It is perhaps to get to the heart and the difficulty of the moral fable to say that it illustrates an idea about life. The idea may be a precept (as in the stories of Mrs Hannah More 'wholly holy, hale and wholly wholesome') or it may be something a good deal vaguer—a view of life (as in *Gulliver's Travels*). The key-word is 'illustrates'. Now, an illustration may be a work of art, it may enrich that which gives rise to it and stand in its own right as a successful expression. But the danger is that it will be limited in an unfortunate way by having to illustrate something else rather than develop freely by its own laws of growth. The illustration, by its nature, must never get out of hand. The purpose behind it must never be lost sight of, otherwise it will become not an illustration but something else.[3]

The danger, so far as the moral fable is concerned, is all the greater if what it must illustrate is a fairly precisely framed abstract idea; for abstract ideas—and particularly abstract precepts ('it's never too late to mend') have a way of being over-simplifications of life, useful enough no doubt for their purpose of the moment, but not bearing over-much probing. And good art, including the good illustration, must probe. If we begin probing the precept 'It's never too late to mend,' we find, alas, that it is sometimes not true. An illustration of it (Charles Reade's novel for instance), is very likely therefore to give us the sense not of facing all the issues of life it evokes, but of avoiding a good many of them.

One of the limitations of the moral fable is likely to be, then, the limitation inherent in an over-simplified or dishonest philosophy of life. This is indeed the limitation of Hannah More or Mr Aldous Huxley. The successful and enduring fable avoids this kind of weakness in one of two ways: either the 'truth' that it succeeds in adequately illustrating happens to be in itself so profound, so full of the stuff of life that it can bear deep probing (Fielding's parable of bourgeois society, *Jonathan Wild*, survives, despite weaknesses, for this sort of reason), or else the writer in the telling of the fable, in the very act of illustration, so fills his creation with the breath and tensions of life that the fable transcends the idea which evoked it. *Gulliver's Travels* seems to me a book of this sort. It is a fable (or series of fables) obviously and insistently expressing Swift's moral criticism of his world. The fantasy is continually directed to this end so that there is no question of our 'losing ourselves' in the book. The whole effect depends on the degree and quality of the moral feeling involved. And yet when we ask, in terms of a precise philosophy, what Swift is saying, what moral values he is recommending, we find it impossible to give (on the evidence of the book itself) an answer adequate to the kind of experience the book has been.

Is man really the kind of creature Swift has evoked? What positive statement about life, what philosophy has been conveyed? The questions raise nothing but a hollow echo. The truth is that hardly anybody, and certainly no normal person either today or in the eighteenth century, agrees with Swift's philosophy (such as it is), or thinks the view of man he is expressing adequate. The kernel of the fable is maggot-ridden. Yet the fable remains; and its enormous moral force remains.

Swift's opinions (taken as a serious positive judgment about the nature of man) may not be acceptable to us; but his sense of life, of actual reality, is so profound and passionate that the inadequacy of his opinions does not matter. The sterility of his philosophy is negated by the vitality of his observation. That is why, in the great fourth book, as Dr Leavis has pointed out, 'The Houyhnhnms may have all the reason, but the Yahoos have all the life.'⁴ The Yahoos may not tell us much about Man, but they tell us a deal about men, the men Swift knew, which the complacent and privileged would sooner forget or turn to favour and prettiness and falsity.*

Those who would like to preserve the illusion of eighteenth-century society as a whole world of elegant refinement and rational, even if aristocratic, beneficence, are forced to carry Swift off to the psycho-analyst's consulting-room. He has, we are assured, all the

---

* It would be an oversimplification to equate crudely the Houyhnhnms with the eighteenth-century aristocracy, polite, 'enlightened', rational, and the Yahoos with the masses in their gin-soaked squalor; but the contrast is there and the dissatisfaction we feel with the Houyhnhnms whose wisdom is always slightly off the mark matches precisely the human inadequacy, for all its 'enlightenment', of eighteenth-century rationalism.

symptoms of the anal-erotic, and this explains everything.[5] It is not rare or new, this concern

> to mock with the aspersion of Madness
> Cast on the Inspired by the tame high finisher of paltry Blots
> Indefinite, or paltry Rhymes, or paltry Harmonies. . . .

and, as Blake well knew, it is among the most effective of the manacles which the minds of certain men have forged for their own purposes. But it does not explain away *Gulliver's Travels* because it does not begin to explain the quality of the indignation which brings Swift's fable to life. *Gulliver's Travels* does not need twentieth-century psychiatry for its interpretation; if we find it hard to understand (and there is no good reason why we should), Hogarth's pictures and Fielding's novels will give us more hints than Freud.

But my immediate point is that *Gulliver's Travels* succeeds as a moral fable despite the weaknesses of Swift's positive philosophy. It succeeds entirely on account of the quality of Swift's indignation, which is what brings the fable to life and stirs our imagination. It is this life-stirring quality, the sense of the degradation of man in Swift's world, which makes *Gulliver's Travels* a great book and renders unimportant the inadequacy of Swift's positive philosophy. There is an anger in *Gulliver's Travels*, a bitter anger at what man has made of man, which springs not from an abstract idea nor from a neurotic sensibility, but from a courageous realism, an ability to look the facts of eighteenth-century society in the face, an un-flinching sense of life. And it is this that Swift has breathed into his fable and into his prose.

Literary critics who think that style in writing is a pretty accom-plishment, like arranging the flowers, often tell you that Swift's prose style is a model to be copied by those who want to write well. But you will only write like Swift if you feel as Swift felt and see life as he saw it.

The moral fable, then, is one kind of novel, one line of develop-ment which we shall trace in the eighteenth century, from Bunyan onwards. It does not, of course, originate with Bunyan. Its roots are in the parables of the Bible, the Morality plays of the Middle Ages, the sermons which for centuries the common people had listened to every Sunday in every village and town throughout the land. It is a part of that great allegorical tradition which had eaten so deep into the consciousness of medieval man. We have already noticed that its pattern derives from and illustrates some kind of generalised moral concept or attitude. And we shall see that this insistence on pattern is its strength, but can easily, if the pattern is inadequate, become its weakness.

There is also, in contrast to the moral fable, another line of English fiction which springs from an opposite kind of interest in life. Nashe and Defoe and Smollett deal, in varying degrees, with moral issues, but the germ of their books is never an idea, never an abstract concept. They are not in any sense allegorists. They are less consciously concerned with the moral significance of life than with its surface texture. Their talent is devoted first and foremost to getting life on to the page, to conveying across to their readers the sense of what life as their characters live it really feels like. If any pattern emerges from their books it is not the kind of pattern that is imposed upon the material by the writer's conscious philosophy, but one which somehow or other springs out of the 'sense of life' in the particular book.

If the moral fable grew out of the 'morality' literature of the Middle Ages and is a development of the allegory, the new non-allegorical story was a direct product of the breakdown of the medieval world. It is associated in particular with such developments as the growth of science and the beginnings of journalism. It is not by chance that both Nashe and Defoe were journalists and pamphleteers, caught up in the topical issues of their day less through any passionate moral partisanship than through a lively concern with the exciting business of living and making a living. Their dominant interest was in what has come to be called in a debased currency 'human interest'.

Now, 'human interest' implies today a concern with life which is not a generalised moral interest and is certainly the very opposite of allegorical. 'Human interest stories' in our papers, in so far as they are not entirely trivial or sensational, are the bits and pieces of life, the odd corners of experience, sometimes bizarre, sometimes typical, but never, by an essential rule, 'significant'; that is to say, you are never expected to draw any conclusion from them except the vague overall conclusion: well, life's like that.

The atom bomb is dropped on Hiroshima and the event of it is front-page news, 'dramatic', 'sensational', 'of far-reaching consequences' according to taste. The political and moral implications are examined, with whatever inadequacy, in the leading articles. And then, gradually, there creep in the 'human interest stories': what it felt like to be in Hiroshima when the bomb fell, what it felt like to pull the lever that dropped the bomb, the kind of life the pilot led when he wasn't dropping atom bombs, how long the trams stopped running, how Mr Mitsuoto made his miraculous escape. It is precisely the fact that the 'human interest story' in our newspapers is nearly always presented from a morally neutral standpoint, without significance, that makes it so often rather disgusting. A concern with the texture of life which is not accompanied by an attempt to evaluate the experiences recorded is bound to be in the end irresponsible. And this is the danger of the novelist who thinks he can ignore pattern.

It would not be fair to Nashe—and even less fair to Defoe—to couple them with the debased qualities of modern sensational journalism. Their human interest (humanism is perhaps a juster word) is not that of the Sunday papers. But it has nevertheless some important implications. What made their novels possible was the new attitude to the world brought about by the decadence of feudal society. Nashe and Defoe, separated as they are by more than a century, are both bourgeois writers, anti-romantic in their attitudes, inspired (though in different ways) by the confidence, the optimism, the enterprise of the class which acquired its wealth and culture through commerce—especially the wool-trade—and lived by the exploitation of paid employees.

Defoe, as we shall see, accepts the Puritan morality of his class, and is at pains to establish his moral bona fides. Yet these writers are not basically concerned with morals but with a curiosity about life, which one might describe as amoral were it not that every action and response has its moral implications, however unconscious of them the individual concerned may be.

The point is that such writers *accept* bourgeois morality (still unconventional and imperfectly formulated in Nashe's time, more respectable by Defoe's), and, having accepted it, are no longer interested in it. Their eyes are on what men and women do; they spend far less time in judging and valuing than in observing and recording, with interest and gusto. And their vitality comes from this gusto, this unprejudiced curiosity about the facts of life, the curiosity of the scientist rather than the moralist, a curiosity that has not yet degenerated into sensationalism—though already in Nashe there are elements of that—but has still the sense of liberation, freedom from feudal fetters.

It is not fortuitous that this non-allegorical line in fiction to which I am referring sprang from the picaresque stories which originated in fifteenth-century Spain and quickly spread to France and England. The *picaro* or rogue was the social outcast, the man rejected by, and rejecting, feudal society and its morality. But if he was spewed out by the feudal order he was also fostered by it, particularly in the days of its decay. The *picaro* might be a younger son of a good family gone to the dogs, more likely he was a bastard, or he might be a nobody, a hanger-on.

Even in its heyday feudal society (partly because of the system of primogeniture) had always thrown up a considerable number of such adventurers, who could not be absorbed in the normal feudal world. They became, among other things, the recruiting material for the crusades. With the growth of trade, the tendency towards centralised monarchies, the invention of gunpowder, and—in England—the enclosures, their number greatly increased. The less fortunate dwindled into beggars (those grim skeletons in the Elizabethan cupboard); many became soldiers. The feudal kings needed mercenaries to fight their wars.

The best illustration in English literature of the social pheno-menon which gave rise to the picaresque novel is the Falstaff section of *Henry IV*. (Poins would have made an admirable picaresque hero with his vitality and resource and lack of morals.) Falstaff and his cronies are of varying social origin; but they are all the rejects of feudalism, and they belong to the Elizabethan rather than to the fifteenth-century world. In another sense they do not 'belong' to any society at all. They are without roots. They have no fixed abode. They live on their wits. They have no morals except the good new rule of each for himself and the devil take the hindmost. And they mock every sanctity of the feudal world—chivalry, honour, filial piety, allegiance, even kingship.

It was with just such people that the picaresque novelists dealt. They got on to the page the sense of life of the Poinses and Bar-dolphs and Pistols of all Europe. And life for these folk was not something organised and serene. The qualities that emerge from the picaresque novels, from the *Lazarillo de Tormes*,[6] from *The Rogue*,[7] from *The Unfortunate Traveller*,[8] are violence and adven-ture, vividness and variety. These stories are all (despite the occasional romantic episode) realistic; the attitudes behind them range from the mischievous to the cynical; they have in them nothing of the spirit of feudal literature. And they are without pattern. Like Falstaff himself they deal with life without principle and so are ultimately at the mercy of life itself.

It was natural that Nashe, a writer responding fully in his sensi-bility to the new world, but not yet fully conscious of what it meant to be a bourgeois, should write a book like *The Unfortunate Traveller*, perhaps the most remarkable picaresque story in our language. *The Unfortunate Traveller* is a hotch-potch; it has no central core to it. It is the story of the adventures of a young man, Jack Wilton, who has almost all the characteristics of the outcast rogue. He is the servant of a nobleman and therefore has a certain place in society, but in no sense does he 'belong' to that society or feel himself in any way morally bound to its standards. The sense of 'not belonging' is increased by sending him to the Continent for all his adventures. I emphasise this point because it is what determines the form of the picaresque novel, its casual shapelessness. It is a series of incidents held together by no informing plan, by nothing save the presence of the hero, who is himself a vagabond whose life has no centre and no pattern.

Behind *The Unfortunate Traveller* there is no consistent moral attitude beyond a concern in getting out of awkward situations and a rather superficial anti-Catholicism; but there is a powerful curiosity (vigorous rather than consistent) about the sixteenth-century world and a remarkable attempt to get the physical 'feel' of that world on to paper.

It is not surprising that the early picaresque stories lacked a consistent moral standpoint which might have given them pattern, for the social outcasts with whom they dealt were not yet a conscious class with a conscious ethic. Nashe's Jack Wilton, like Rabelais' Panurge, is an utterly irresponsible character who gets his vitality from his irrepressible determination to hold his own in a world for which he has no respect. But until bourgeois man had a clearer idea both of what he stood for and of what he was up against his social and literary adventures were bound to be a series of disconnected skirmishes lacking a central significance.

I shall have more to say in the next Part about Defoe and the picaresque novel. The point I want to make here is that, just as the moral fable fails unless the writer imbues his original moral concept with the stuff of life, so will the non-allegorical novel, which begins with the writer's undefined 'sense of life', fail unless he gives his 'slice of life' a moral significance, a satisfying pattern. That is why the two categories I have discussed in this section only have a limited usefulness. They serve to distinguish between two methods of approach, that is all. With the truly successful novels they have little relevance, for the greatest novels are satisfying precisely because their pattern is adequate to their sense of life and vice versa. Nor is the distinction between the tradition of the moral fable and the picaresque tradition the distinction between writers who have a philosophy of life and those who have none. Every writer has a philosophy. The distinction is, rather, between those who are quite conscious of their philosophy and those who do not formulate their sense of life in generalised terms.

The history of the novel is, in this sense, the history of the novelists' search for an adequate philosophy of life. This is not to say that the novel *is* philosophy. A writer may hold a very profound conscious philosophy and yet be no artist (though the chances are that if his philosophy is truly profound in its human understanding his writing will achieve something of the quality of art); and a great artist may not be able to formulate his view of life satisfactorily in philosophical terms. But the view of life is nevertheless there, illuminating every word he writes, and it is his view of life which will determine the nature and the profundity of the pattern of his book. Life and pattern are not, in truth, separable. Pattern is the way life develops.

2

REALISM AND ROMANCE

The moment we found ourselves, a few pages back, asking, by implication, the question, 'Why were the first novels written?' we had to begin thinking in terms of history, and it is essential that we should not run away from history. The rise and development of the English novel, like any other phenomenon in literature, can only be understood as a part of history.

History is not just something in a book; history is men's actions. History is life going on, changing, developing. We, too, are characters in history. Men make history. Every action of every man, consciously or not, is directed, satisfactorily or not, towards the solving of the myriad problems, gigantic and trivial, complex and random, first of keeping alive and then of 'living', with all that the word, after centuries of experience, implies. Living alters. It alters according to the degree to which man masters his problems, wins new battles with nature, solves the countless difficulties and possibilities of existing alongside other men. History is the process of change in living.

It is not by chance that the English novel dates from the eighteenth century. This does not mean, of course, that nothing like a novel existed before the year 1700 and then someone—Defoe presumably —waved a wand and there it was. We have already taken a glance at some of the writing on which the eighteenth-century novelists could draw. Nothing will come of nothing, and even the most original artist starts off from what has gone before.

The eighteenth-century novelists had on the one hand the medieval romance and its successors, the courtly novels of Italy and

France, and the English stories which in the sixteenth and seventeenth centuries had grown out of these two main sources: Lyly's
Euphues, Sidney's *Arcadia*, Greene's *Menaphon*, Ford's *Ornatus
and Artesia*, Congreve's *Incognita*, the stories of Mrs Aphra Behn,
to mention only a few of the best known. And they had on the
other hand the 'rogue' novels, the picaresque tradition which we
have already briefly noticed. They had also translations from the
classics (not to mention their originals) like *Daphnis and Chloe* and
the *Golden Ass* and the *Satyricon* of Petronius. They had Boccaccio.
They had Rabelais (Urquhart and Motteux' translation appearing
between 1653 and 1694). They had the Authorised Version of the
Bible. They had Cervantes. They had Bunyan.

It may appear pedantic to try to decide which of these writers
should be called novelists. Certainly from many points of view it
is of no importance what they are called, and certainly one does not
wish to fall into a formalistic approach, than which there is little
more futile. And yet, to avoid unnecessary confusion of terms, one
or two definitions are inevitable.

The novel—as I use the term in this book—is a realistic prose
fiction, complete in itself and of a certain length. Any such definition of a term so loosely and variously used over a long period is
bound to be somewhat arbitrary. The question of length I leave,
deliberately, vague. The point, I think, is that the novel is more
than an anecdote and more than the exploration of one particular,
more or less isolated, episode. Peacock's *Nightmare Abbey*, for
instance, I take to be a novel, though a short one, while Conrad's
Heart of Darkness, which is a little longer, I would class as a long
short story; but such borderline problems are not really important.

The adjective 'realistic' is likely to need more justification. The
words 'realism' and 'realistic' are used throughout this book in a
very broad sense, to indicate 'relevant to real life' as opposed to
'romance' and 'romantic', by which are indicated escapism, wishful
thinking, unrealism. The distinction is not, it must be insisted,
between the photographic on the one hand and the fantastic and
imaginative on the other. All art involves fantasy. A highly fantastic and superficially unlifelike story like *Gulliver's Travels* I class
as realistic because it has to do with the actual problems and values
of life. Mrs Radcliffe's *Udolpho* or P. C. Wren's *Beau Geste*,
although presented as lifelike, are romance.

Clearly in both categories degree is important. Mrs Radcliffe's
stories have more relevance to life than Mr Wren's, and it is not
implied that a romance can have *no* serious value, merely that in

it unrealism predominates. Similarly, nearly all fundamentally realistic novels have their romantic tint; some—like *Jane Eyre* and *Adam Bede*—are so shot through with romantic colouring as almost to cease to be serious works of art at all.

I do not pretend that either word is fully satisfactory: realism or romance. Realism has too many suggestions of mere photographic naturalism: Zola, Arnold Bennett and James T. Farrell. Romance is an even more dangerous word, on the one hand because of its connections with Romance (as opposed to Teutonic or Slav or Celtic) languages, on the other because of all the associations of the Romantic Movement, the fashionable denigrations of which one would not wish to support. But unfortunately no happier terms suggest themselves, and I therefore use realism and romance in the way I have indicated, conscious of the dangers involved, yet conscious also of the real and essential distinction underlying the terms.

If a novel is a realistic prose fiction, complete in itself and of a certain length, none of the books that have been mentioned as the store upon which the eighteenth-century writer had to draw—the fund of experience with which he began—is, with the exception of *Don Quixote* and, with certain reservations, *The Pilgrim's Progress*, a novel.

Apart from the picaresque stories, the *Satyricon*, Rabelais and the Bible, none of them is, in the sense I have indicated, realistic, though a number have realistic elements. While of the realistic stories none has the self-completeness, the unity of organisation and the length which we shall find to be characteristic of the novel. *The Unfortunate Traveller* is a series of episodes, a diary almost, with no beginning and no end. The *Satyricon*, as it has come down to us, is fragmentary. The Bible is only partially, in such books as *Esther*, *Ruth* and *Job*, written in the terms we are discussing. And even *Gargantua and Pantagruel*, superb, incredible masterpiece that it is, is less a novel than a gigantic chunk of novel-matter, the clay of half a dozen never quite organised novels.

Only Cervantes—the case of Bunyan is rather different—of all the prose writers to whom Defoe and Fielding and Richardson had access, was, in the sense we have come to give the term, a novelist. And Cervantes is indeed, with Rabelais, the great genius and architect of the modern novel. We shall see how direct and yet how subtle was his influence on Fielding and we shall see what it was that gave that influence its potency. But we cannot, in a book of this length, deal, even if we should wish to, with the question of formal 'influences'. The time has come to pose explicitly our first essential problem: why did the modern novel arise at all?

The answer can be put in a number of ways. The novel, we may say, arose as a realistic reaction to the medieval romance and its courtly descendants of the sixteenth and seventeenth centuries; the great eighteenth-century novels are nearly all anti-romances. Or the novel, we may say, arose with the growth for the first time of a large, widely distributed reading public; with the increase of literacy the demand for reading material naturally rose and the demand was greatest among well-to-do women who were the insatiable novel-readers of the time. For such a public, spread all over England in country houses, the theatre was not a feasible form of entertainment, but the novel was perfection. Hence the length of the novels (for their readers had only too much time on their hands), hence their tone, hence their number, hence (by the end of the eighteenth century) the circulating libraries. Or the novel, we may say, grew with the middle class, a new art-form based not on aristocratic patronage but on commercial publishing, an art-form written by and for the now-powerful commercial bourgeoisie.

These answers are all a part of the truth, but they are less than the whole of it. The whole answer cannot be condensed into a sentence and is as hard to grasp as history itself. We shall not understand the rise of the English novel unless we understand the meaning and importance of the English revolution of the seventeenth century.

Great revolutions in human society change men's consciousness and revolutionise not only their social relationships, but their outlook, their philosophy and their art. Feudalism, the society of the Middle Ages, had as its principal characteristic a peculiar rigidity of human relationships and ideas which sprang inevitably from the social structure.

The basic activity of feudal society was agriculture, the basic social unit the feudal estate or manor. Towns, though they gradually grew in importance, were the exception, not the rule. The governing class, that small minority who alone had the leisure, the education, the wherewithal to develop a sophisticated art (as opposed to the unwritten folk-culture of the unlettered), owed their social superiority to their ownership of the land and their virtual ownership of their serfs. Their chief concern, inevitably, was to maintain that ownership. Since their wealth and power did not depend on technical advances, they could have no deep interest in scientific experiment or widespread education. On the contrary, their whole interest, their very existence as the kind of people they were, demanded the preservation (with whatever sanctions, spiritual and physical, that might be necessary) of the *status quo*.

All summaries and simplifications inevitably do violence to the infinitely rich and complex processes of social and cultural change. One cannot hope to do justice in a few sentences to the whole vast complicated medieval culture. What one would emphasise here (without suggesting for a moment that there is no more to be said) is the social rigidity and intellectual conservatism of the feudal order. Such an order was bound to produce art of a particular kind and its characteristic product in the realm of prose literature was the romance.

Romance* was the non-realistic, aristocratic literature of feudalism. It was non-realistic in the sense that its underlying purpose was not to help people cope in a positive way with the business of living but to transport them to a world different, idealised, *nicer* than their own. It was aristocratic because the attitudes it expressed and recommended were precisely the attitudes the ruling class wished (no doubt usually unconsciously) to encourage in order that their privileged position might be perpetuated. And romance performed, as it performs to this day, the double function of entertainment through titillation and the conveying in palatable form of a particular kind of philosophy of life.

Romance grew in popularity in the Middle Ages as social relationships and class differences under feudalism became increasingly rigid. The connection between the emergence of a leisured ruling class and the growth of romance is very significant. It is not, of course, that only the leisured read or listen to romantic literature; on the contrary its quality of 'substitute-living' (the evocation of a kinder, more glamorous world) especially recommends it to the unleisured, those who most need the consolations of an escape from a cruel or humdrum reality.

The important point is that as division of labour increases and classes become as a consequence more stratified the rulers come to adopt a way of life very different from that of the majority. They have long, by virtue of their ownership, lived better; now they come to live differently. The ruling-class men no longer actually till their own fields and sell their own chattels at market, but pay someone else (not necessarily in money) to do it. The ruling-class

---

* I should make quite clear that I am not referring to the great medieval epics—such as the *Niebelungenlied* or the *Chanson de Roland*—which are not romance in the sense I use the word.

women, in particular, become less and less like the women of the people in activity and even in appearance. And so the ideas and attitudes of the ruling class inevitably become different. Their culture, in all its many forms, changes.

The directions in which it changes—as far as literature is concerned—all lead away from realism, the frank and uninhibited representation and consideration of the experiences and potentialities of the community as a whole.[9] For how can such complete frankness exist? Not only do the rulers have their own way of life and therefore their own standards and values which the people do not, cannot—except in their dreams and fantasies—share; the rulers also have their secrets, secrets they are not prepared to share with the people or even to express quite frankly and openly to themselves. And what now primarily interests the ruling class is not the people's way of life (the word 'vulgar', originally connoting simply 'of the people' takes on new overtones), but the achievement of a culture which not merely pleases but actually strengthens and defends their class. Such a culture relies, is bound to rely, not on realism (even though the occasional realistic and—to that extent—revolutionary artist, like Chaucer, appears) but on romance.

Romance, in the first place, delights and entertains the rulers without bringing them face to face with realities they would sooner put behind them. The wimpled lady of the feudal court and her modern counterpart who steps out of her limousine to ask the attendant at the circulating library for a 'nice book' are one and the same. In the second place it builds, for the edification and pleasure of those unfortunate enough to find themselves outside the privileged *élite*, a fantasy, a pseudo-world, seductive or sad, delightful or horrible, which has one unfailing quality: that, however remote it may be from reality, the values and attitudes it incorporates are such as are least likely to undermine the theories and practice of class society.

Closely connected with, indeed inseparable from, the escapist nature of romance is its function as a form of titillation, a function that has had a profound influence on the modern novel. The bulk of medieval romances did not enlarge the consciousness of their audience in any helpful way, neither does *The Blue Lagoon*; but they did give their audience a kick, so does *The Postman Always Rings Twice*. The aim of such literature is not to sum up experience, not to enlarge the imagination, and not merely to provide an escape from the sordid (in many modern cases it is rather an escape *to* the sordid), but to provide sensation for sensation's sake. It thrives on the boredom and cynicism, the blasé and jaded unfulfilment of people who have too little to do or too little purpose and satisfaction in what they do do. Its crudest form is pornography: but it has many other forms less crude though scarcely more desirable.

The world to which medieval romance transported its audience was a world of chivalry and exciting adventures, of gallant men and charming women, of bad magicians and Christian gentlemen *sans peur et sans reproche*, above all of idealised love. It is not sufficient to label this world escapist and imagine one has explained it away. All art is, in an important sense, an escape. Nor is it enough to refer to romance's idealised picture of the world as though idealisation were a form of original sin and needed no more explicit condemnation. There is a sense in which the capacity to escape from his present experience, to use his accumulated consciousness of the past to project a vision of the future, is man's greatest and distinguishing ability. We must not forget the force of Aristotle's argument that poetry is valuable precisely because it shows men not simply as they are, but as they ought to be or (in terms more sympathetic to us today) as they are capable of becoming. This fantastic quality of art, that it takes us out of the real world so that, as Shelley put it, it 'awakens and enlarges the mind itself by rendering it the receptacle of a thousand unapprehended combinations of thought', this quality is not a trivial or accidental by-product but the very essence of the value of art. If art did in fact—as the ultra-naturalistic school tends to assume—merely paint a picture of what is, it would be a much less valuable form of human activity, for it would not alter men's consciousness but merely confirm it.

What we should remember, then, about romance, is not that it involves an escape, but a particular kind of escape. Medieval romance makes no attempt to give an impression of life in the lands and times it is dealing with, but it does attempt 'to use its subject matter as a means of conveying a new philosophy'. Dr Vinaver, in the Introduction to his monumental edition of *The Works of Thomas Malory*, writes: 'Whatever the subject of the narrative (of the courtly romance) its primary function . . . was to serve as the expression of the thoughts and emotions inspired by courtly idealism, to translate in terms of actions and characters the subtle varieties of courtly sentiment and the highly sophisticated code of courtly behaviour.'[10] And this is as true of the seventeenth-century prose romances like *Ornatus and Artesia* as it is of the twelfth- and thirteenth-century poets to whom Dr Vinaver is here referring.

The didactic element in romance is important. The picture of gallant knights and their ladies (usually married to somebody else) told a story which not merely elevated the feudal idea of chivalry, but as often as not had a religious sanction too. One of the principal results of the Christian world-picture in medieval romance (a world-picture generally superimposed upon an older, pagan mythology) was to emphasise a tendency to the over-simplification of ethical questions. Life becomes a battle between Good and Evil. Characters, instead of being realistic, that is to say human, that is to say neither wholly good nor wholly bad, tend to become entirely black or white. This is the effect of imposing a static, idealist moral code upon the actual movement and complexity of human behaviour. A static pattern imposed upon a changing, developing object is bound to be inadequate. The best of the romances, of course (much of Malory for instance), avoid these crudities and come thereby that much nearer realism and life.

The impulse towards realism in prose literature was part and parcel of the breakdown of feudalism and of the revolution that transformed the feudal world. Because today the term bourgeois is connected in our minds with people well-established, comfortable, conservative, it is not easy for us to think of the bourgeoisie as a revolutionary class. But we must recall that this was the very class which in seventeenth-century England organised the remarkable, democratic New Model Army, cut off the King's head and established the republican Commonwealth. The commercial bourgeoisie were revolutionaries against the feudal order because the feudal order denied them freedom. It denied them freedom, physically, legally, spiritually, to do what they wanted to do, to develop the way they needs must develop.

The feudal world, based on static property-relationships, exalting an unchanging, God-ordained hierarchy in Church and State, was a prison to the rising commercial class and to their artists and thinkers. Freedom to trade, freedom to explore, freedom to investigate, freedom to invent, freedom to evolve an adequate philosophy, these were the supreme, undeniable needs of the men of the new society, and for them they were prepared, as men always must be for their necessary freedoms, to die. They were prepared to risk death on the high seas or on the battlefields; they were prepared, in full consciousness and with the black horror of the medieval hell as the reward of error, to go to the block or to the fire. And the bourgeois writers, exalted by their vision of

> a world of profit and delight,
> Of power and honour and omnipotence,

were revolutionaries too, prepared like Faustus to play for the very highest and most desperate stakes in their task of forging a new literature adequate and helpful to the revolutionary consciousness of their age.

In the late sixteenth and the seventeenth centuries, the critical period of revolutionary transformation, the main emphasis and achievement in literature was in poetry. In the eighteenth century it is in prose. The shift corresponds to the changing needs and spirit of society.

Most of us tend to assume, until we think more carefully about it, that prose is simpler, more 'natural' and therefore probably older than poetry. But we now know from anthropologists that poetry is almost certainly a more primitive and historically an earlier development than prose. Because early literature is oral and not written down it is hard to get to know very much about it, and only slowly are we beginning to delve into the fascinating problems of the origins of literature. Such a study is not, however, an academic one in the narrow sense, indeed it is one from which the pedants tend to sheer off because it brings them up against too many inconvenient questions (the whole issue is therefore too often shelved on the grounds that we have not sufficient objective material).

The basic questions involved are: what is the *purpose* of poetry and prose? What functions do they perform in primitive society and why therefore do they arise? Clearly in the light of such questions many of the stock 'theories' of literature, that it is 'self-expression', that it gives delight, that it has something to do with the eternal verities, are hopelessly inadequate. Obviously literature expresses the self of the author (though when we recall that in primitive art there is often no one 'author' the problem becomes less simple); obviously it gives delight (or no one would like reading it); obviously it has something to do with long-term truths (or we would get nothing out of Homer today); the important questions are, why? In what way? How does literature work?

It seems reasonably certain that while the earliest poetry in primitive society is connected with ritual and work and is, in Christopher Caudwell's words, 'the language of collective speech

and public emotion',[11] prose or non-rhythmical speech is the
language of private persuasion. Poetry arises before prose not only
because (in a period when writing is not yet practised) it is easier
to remember and hand on (that is a consequence rather than a
cause), but because it helps the people in their necessary common
rituals through which they achieve their collective ability to master
nature. The primitive affinity of poetry is with magic.

Prose arises later as science gradually supersedes magic and
conscious control replaces instinctive emotion. Prose is a later,
more sophisticated use of language than primitive poetry precisely
because it presupposes a more objective, controlled and conscious
view of reality. Stories—'images of men's changing lives organised
in time'—can only come into existence as men become conscious,
however imperfectly, of social processes and man's complicated,
unending struggle against nature. This *objective* quality of prose,
that it makes coherent some facet of outer reality already apprehended, is very significant. It explains, for instance, why it is more
possible to translate a novel than a poem. And it explains why in
eighteenth-century England there should have been a particular
impulse towards prose-writing. For literature to the bourgeois
writers of this period was, above all, a means of taking stock of the
new society. A medium which could express a realistic and objective curiosity about man and his world, this was what they were
after. It was the search for such a medium that led Fielding to
describe *Joseph Andrews* as a 'comic epic poem in prose'. Their task
was not so much to adapt themselves to a revolutionary situation as
to cull and examine what that revolution had produced. They were
themselves revolutionaries only in the sense that they participated
in the consequences of a revolution; they were more free and therefore more realistic than their predecessors to just the extent and in
just those ways that the English bourgeois revolution involved in
fact an increase in human freedom.

We must not push too far this distinction between prose and
poetry because in practice the two interpenetrate and it would be
disastrous to underestimate the degree to which *all* modern novelists
use language poetically. But we will do well, nevertheless, to bear
in mind some of the fundamental problems involved in this difficult
subject. Two points in particular are worth emphasising.

In the first place I think it is as well to approach the study of a
great body of prose literature, such as the English novel, with the
realisation that prose is not just poetry's plain sister, a haphazard,
prosaic (how significant the word is!), inferior, easy alternative to

verse, but that it is a great and wonderful field of human activity and experiment. I think it is good to realise that the development of prose-writing is not a mean or humdrum part of man's history, but that it is linked close to his continuous, infinitely rich and various struggle to control his world and transform it, to evolve a philosophy adequate to his necessities and a society adequate to his desires. And particularly it is worth bearing in mind that prose is an advanced, subtle, precise form of human expression, pre-supposing a formidable self-consciousness, a delicacy of control which it has taken human beings untold centuries to acquire.

Secondly, I believe even this superficial glance at the origins of literature gives us a clue to our question: why did the novel arise when it did? Why did the medieval romance not continue to satisfy the needs of the men and women of the bourgeois revolution?

The answer, at bottom, is that the bourgeoisie, in order to win its freedom from the feudal order, had to tear the veil of romance from the face of feudalism. To the bourgeois man, as we have seen, feudal society was not satisfying but frustrating. And so he felt no impulse to defend that society and no sympathy with a literature designed to recommend its values and conceal its limitations. On the contrary his every need and instinct urged him to expose and undermine feudal standards and sanctities. Unlike the feudal ruling class he did not feel himself immediately threatened by revelations of the truth about the world and so he was not afraid of realism.

The first revolutionary bourgeois writers, like Rabelais, were by no means conscious of being bourgeois or, in any political sense, revolutionary. Rabelais is soaked in the learning and tradition of the Middle Ages; no book tells us so well as his what medieval France was like. And yet Rabelais, in his full-blooded assertion of the glory of physical living, in his colossal irreverence, in his profound and daring inventiveness, in the realism which underlies his most fantastic flights and images, is utterly anti-romantic. His exuberance and his laughter shatter every pretence of the world of chivalry. No idealised picture of genteel womanhood could be proof against the irrepressible obscenity of a Panurge.

Gargantua and Pantagruel enlarged the scope and potentialities of prose literature both through Rabelais' view of life (the content of the book) and his language (its form). And, as always, the form and content are inseparable. The hilarious verbal experiments, the incredible lists, the inventive energy of the style cannot be isolated from what Rabelais had to say: the flights of fantasy, the delight in science, the confidence in human reason, the respect for the human creature in all its absurdity, the refusal to be bamboozled about mankind.

And because Rabelais' book was carried over into English by translators of genius who understood precisely what he was saying, he enriched the English language too and gave to English prose-writers (as we shall see particularly when we come to mention Sterne) a sense of the variety and potentiality of their medium. Rabelais' use of language is to a large extent poetic, that is to say words are used for their own associative values, and rhythms originate not simply from an attempt to record accurately the actual values of speech, but from an attempt to use, weight and give new significance to those values.

In Rabelais, then, we find a revolutionary impulse towards realism in a still essentially medieval man, but when, half a century later, in 1605, the first part of *Don Quixote* appeared, the revolt against medieval standards had become fully conscious. Cervantes' novel is sometimes regarded as essentially a burlesque. One might as well describe *Macbeth* as a play about witchcraft. Certainly Cervantes' purpose is to a high degree satirical—'the Fall and Destruction of that monstrous Heap of ill-contrived Romances, which, though abhorr'd by many, have so strangely infatuated the greater part of Mankind'—but romance is satirised not for its own sake but because it hinders the writer from telling the truth about life in all its aspects. To over-emphasise the negative side of *Don Quixote* is to reduce it to the stature of a *Cold Comfort Farm*; whereas Cervantes' tremendous achievement is that, quite apart from the intrinsic value of his own rich creation, he re-asserted in story-telling the tradition of the realistic epic.

The fantasy of romance carries away the reader in order that he need not face life, the fantasy of *Don Quixote* quickens his sense of life, involves him in a critical questioning of values and attitudes, imposes a pattern on experience which deepens its meaning. Cervantes knew quite well that the destruction of romance was a necessary act in the freeing of the world from the chains of feudalism. And he closes his book with the words:

As for me, I must esteem myself happy, to have been the first that render'd those fabulous, nonsensical stories of Knight-Errantry, the object of the public Aversion. They are already going down, and I do not doubt but they will drop and fall altogether in good Earnest, never to rise again. *Adieu.*

PART II

The Eighteenth Century

I

INTRODUCTION

The eighteenth-century writers created the English novel. Sometimes they worked in the allegorical tradition of the moral fable; sometimes they concentrated on the apparently non-moral approach of the picaresque tradition. The greatest of them—Defoe, Richardson, Fielding, Sterne—attempted, not always consciously, not always successfully, to bring the two traditions together, to achieve in their books both realism and significance, to equate life and pattern.

The writers whom today, looking back, we see specifically as novelists were not, of course, alone in building up the novel tradition. The studies of the *Tatler* and *Spectator*, the polemics of the pamphleteers, the habit of diary and journal-keeping, the growth of historical writing, the increasing popularity of travel-books all contributed, along with other even more general influences, towards the production of novels. Defoe's *Journal of the Plague Year* and Swift's *Tale of a Tub* are, obviously, near-novels; Boswell's *Journal* and Gibbon's *Autobiography* are not even near-novels, but they would have a place in an exhaustive history of the growth of fiction.

2

THE MORAL FABLE

Almost every household in eighteenth-century England in which any member was literate must have possessed a copy of *The Pilgrim's Progress*. Lady Wishfort in *The Way of the World* might be cynical about Bunyan but her cynicism was in itself a tribute to the universality of his book, even apparently among that small, fashionable section of London society that had arrogated to itself the title of the 'world'.

The quality in *The Pilgrim's Progress* and *Mr Badman* that gives such force and solidity to their allegory and makes them a part of the tradition of the English novel is what we have already defined as realism, a concern with the actual, unimaginary problems of living besetting the average man and woman of the time. And the realism emerges not only from the unsuspecting detail (like Mr By-ends' great-grandfather, merely a waterman 'looking one way and rowing another') but from the very texture of Bunyan's prose. This prose has too often been described simply as 'biblical'. Obviously the influence of the Bible is there and the Authorised Version itself was no dead work of academic translation; but to over-emphasise Bunyan's debt to the Bible may easily lead to an underestimation of his debt to his own ear.

> *Christian:* And what did you say to him?
> *Faithful:* Say! I could not tell what to say at first.

The tone of that 'Say!' is not the tone of the Bible. Nor is it sufficient to attach the label 'biblical' to this conversation between Faithful and Talkative:

Faith: . . . for what things so worthy of the use of the tongue and mouth of men on Earth, as are the things of the God of Heaven?

Talk: I like you wonderful well, for your saying is full of conviction; and I will add, what thing is so pleasant, and what so profitable, as to talk of the things of God?

What things so pleasant? (that is, if a man hath any delight in things that are wonderful) for instance? If a man doth delight to talk of the History, or the Mystery of things; or if a man doth love to talk of Miracles, Wonders, or Signs, where shall he find things recorded so delightful, and so sweetly penned, as in the holy Scripture?

Faith: That's true: but to be profited by such things in our talk should be that which we design.

Talk: That is it that I said; for to talk of such things is most profitable, for by so doing, a man may get knowledge of many things; as of the vanity of earthly things, and the benefit of things above: (thus in general) but more particularly, By this a man may learn the necessity of the New birth, the insufficiency of our works, the need of Christ's righteousness, &c. Besides, by this a man may learn, what it is to repent, to believe, to pray, to suffer, or the like: by this also a man may learn what are the great promises and consolations of the Gospel, to his own comfort. Further, by this a man may learn to refute false opinions, to vindicate the truth, and also to instruct the ignorant.

Faith: All this is true, and glad am I to hear these things from you.

Talk: Alas, the want of this is the cause that so few understand the need of faith, and the necessity of a (work) of Grace in their Soul, in order to eternal life; but ignorantly live in the works of the Law, by which a man can by no means obtain the Kingdom of Heaven.[1]

What brings this little scene so splendidly to life is the way Bunyan captures the colloquial note of the speech around him, so that Talkative becomes not a dim personification, not a stock figure of allegory, but a genuine flesh-and-blood person, a real next-door-neighbour. It is a very subtle passage not because Talkative is a subtle character or his shallowness hard to see through, but because the precise nature of that shallowness is revealed to us with a remarkable economy of words and without any extraneous comment. The difference between his view of 'profit', for instance, and Faithful's could not be more effectively conveyed, nor could the quality of his interest in 'the History, or the Mystery of things'. Even the glib near-rhyme has its contribution to make.

The Pilgrim's Progress is allegory. Bunyan himself significantly calls it a Dream. It is an allegorical representation of the individual Christian's struggle to achieve salvation. He abandons life (including his unfortunate wife and family) and seeks death. But the

desire for death in *The Pilgrim's Progress* has little in common with
the death-wish of later literature. Christian's aim is not to cease upon
the midnight with no pain. On the contrary his progress is one of
constant struggle and conflict and the words 'Life, Life, Eternal
Life' are on his lips. True this identification of life with death leaves
Bunyan with some unsolved problems, some loose ends to his
pattern—Christian's wife in the first part, her children in the second
—and to the modern reader the picture of Mr Greatheart and Mr
Valiant playing for joy upon the well-tuned cymbal and harp while
the children weep is inadequate and indeed repulsive. But the
essential point is that, though he cannot wholly evade the consequences of a world-picture which sees death as more important
than life and salvation as a matter concerning the individual as an
isolated entity, in spite of this basically life-denying philosophy
Bunyan manages to infuse a living breath into his fable. As Mr Jack
Lindsay has put it:

> The impression conveyed by the allegory is the exact opposite of
> what it literally professes. The phantasms of good and evil become the
> real world; and in encountering them the Pilgrim lives through the life
> that Bunyan had known in definite place and time. The pattern of his
> experience, the fall and resolute rising-up, the loss and the finding, the
> resistance and the overcoming, the despair and the joy, the dark moaning
> valleys and the singing in the places of the flowers—it is the pattern of
> Bunyan's strenuous life. There are comrades and enemies, stout-hearts
> and cravens, men who care only for the goal of fellowship and men of
> greed and fear; and these are the men of contemporary England. The
> Celestial City is the dream of all England, all the world, united in
> Fellowship . . .[2]

I think Mr Lindsay is wrong to identify in too facile a way
Bunyan's Celestial City with the modern man's goal of fellowship.
Bunyan believed in a life after death and there is no point in in-
sinuating that, had he known better, he would have believed in
something else. What is important is that the positive quality of
Bunyan's belief in a life after death and the actual tensions of mortal
struggle which (as Mr Lindsay excellently brings out) give the
prose its muscular, colloquial vitality, these qualities go far to
negate the anti-humanist, defeatist character of the myth itself. And
the power to transform the myth in this way into something
positive and vital comes from Bunyan's profound and disciplined
participation not only in the folk-mythology of his day, which he

made new, but in the life of his time—he the jailed dissenting tinker —and in the actual problems which racked seventeenth-century England.

The Pilgrim's Progress, at once allegorical and colloquial, is the link between the medieval allegory and the moral fable of the eighteenth century. The austere yet unsophisticated (though by no means unsubtle) Puritan morality of Bunyan may have little that is obviously in common with the worldly and bitter satire of Swift, but essentially *The Pilgrim's Progress* and *Gulliver's Travels* are of the same genre.

The difference in tone springs to a large degree from the differences in background of the authors. Whereas from every page of Bunyan's book there emerge the attitudes and hardships of the humble but independent 'small-man', the honest, upright, morally desperate journeyman, the tone of *Gulliver* is that of the supremely intelligent and sensitive member of the ruling class who has behind him, despite his lack of 'politeness', all the sophistication of a polite society in which, on one level at least, he is very much at home. His very capacity to shock his world comes from Swift's own inclusion in it. So does the lack of good advice. Unlike Bunyan he is not addressing an audience desperately desiring to know how to cope with their crushing burdens. And so his shock-tactics, though not less intense, are entirely different. Above all he is concerned to tell his readers that their world is not in the least like what they think it is. Not wickeder but worse. It is not the Puritan soul seeking salvation but England in the reign of Queen Anne that is Swift's subject, and his weapon is his human indignation.

It is Fielding's weapon, too, in *Jonathan Wild* which is sometimes referred to as a picaresque novel because the chief character happens to be a rogue, but which is in fact a moral fable. For there is no doubt about Fielding's moral intention or the moral pattern which shapes the book: indeed it may well be argued that this moral pattern is *too* insistent; certainly the story cannot be said to have that haphazard quality which we have seen to be typical of the picaresque tradition. It is all most carefully planned and controlled.*

The theme of *Jonathan Wild* is the antithesis between greatness and goodness. 'No two things can possibly be more distinct from

---

* I do not think that the fact that *Jonathan Wild* is based on a real person (a criminal hanged in 1725) and actual events should effect our attitude to it as fiction any more than the knowledge that most of Henry James's novels were suggested by true anecdotes.

each other, for greatness consists in bringing all manner of mischief
on mankind and goodness in removing it from them.'

It is this abstract antithesis that informs the whole novel and
makes it into the kind of thing it is, and unless the reader quickly
realises the kind of book he is dealing with his reactions to it are
likely to be always a shade off-centre, his criticisms a trifle irrelevant. *Jonathan Wild* is not a psychological study nor even an
exposure of criminality.* The characters are all relevant to the
basic pattern of the book, the antithesis already mentioned. It is
not Wild himself, in glorious isolation, that interests Fielding, not
simply Wild the super-criminal who lives by exploiting other
criminals, but Wild as a representative symbol. The chief pro-
tagonists of the contending camps, the great and the good, are
Wild and Heartfree, the innocent jeweller; but the novel is not
about Wild and Heartfree, it is about eighteenth-century society.
The great are the successes of that society, not just the Wilds but
the Robert Walpoles, the politicians, the rulers, the exploiters; the
good are not just the Heartfrees but all those who put human
values, the values of the heart, above such success.

Because the generalised moral intention of such a book as
Jonathan Wild is so basic to it, does this mean that it is by its intention, by the truth of the generalised moral, that it should be
judged? Certainly not. The test of a moral fable is not whether the
moral is true but whether the fable convinces. Clearly it will not
convince unless it *is* true (so we cannot dismiss the truth behind it
as irrelevant); but we must be particularly careful in the case of the
moral fable not to confuse performance with intention. Because in
analysing such a book as *Jonathan Wild* one is bound willynilly to
be dealing in general moral principles it is tempting to judge the
principles rather than the novel.

Fielding makes quite clear the nature of his intention in *Jonathan
Wild*. It is no part of his method to leave us in any doubt as to
what his story is about. When Bagshot the highwayman innocently
expects a half-share in the booty he has by his own efforts obtained

* Perhaps a useful comparison is with the early plays of Bernard Shaw (e.g.
Widowers' Houses; *Mrs Warren's Profession*) or with Chaplin's *Monsieur Verdoux*.
Mrs Warren and Verdoux are seen not as individual 'cases', but as symbols of and
participants in a social situation rotten at the very foundations. Unlike most 'socially-
conscious' literature the object here is not to expose to our pity what frightful things
a bad society does to individual people. We are not invited to pity but to think. It is
the implications of Mrs Warren's profession, not merely its existence, that must give
us pause. Fielding is not so consciously radical as Shaw or Chaplin (in a very real
sense he is perfectly at home in his society and feels no urge to look beyond it), but
his method is similar.

(Wild's only part has been to tip him off as to the traveller worth robbing) Wild philosophises on the relation of rulers and ruled:

'It is well said of us, the higher order of mortals, that we are born only to devour the fruits of the earth; and it may well be said of the lower class that they are born only to produce them for us. Is not the battle gained by the sweat and danger of the common soldier? Are not the honour and fruits of the victory the general's who laid the scheme? Is not the house built by the labour of the carpenter and the bricklayer? Is it not built for the profit only of the architect and for the use of the inhabitant, who could not easily have placed one brick upon another? Is not the cloth or the silk, wrought in its form, and variegated with all the beauty of colours, by those who are forced to content themselves with the coarsest and vilest part of their work, while the profit and enjoyment of their labours fall to the share of others?'[3]

It is this generalised moral concern which gives force to the particular touches of satirical description in the book, touches which would otherwise seem often crude and heavy-handed. When, for instance, in the highway robbery mentioned above, the Count La Ruse has been robbed (through the agency of Wild) of the money he has just won by dishonesty at the gambling table, Fielding's comment is

The Count was obliged to surrender to savage force what he had in so genteel and civil a manner taken at play. . . .

The irony that comes into play here extends far beyond the particular situation. It is not merely that the Count was in fact scared stiff so that Bagshot had to use no force, nor that he had in fact cheated at play: what Fielding is bringing to our attention here is the utter inadequacy of the normal eighteenth-century polite, literary use of such concepts as 'force' and 'civility'. It is not the Count but the whole genteel tradition that is being held up to criticism.

Almost every aspect of bourgeois society is satirised in *Jonathan Wild*. Whigs and Tories, the party system itself, the corruption of office, all are transported to Newgate jail where, in the fantastic world of conscious criminals and unfortunate debtors, everything is seen with a new and piercing clarity. An election is fought in the jail between two parties of rogues. Both use the same catch-phrase, 'the liberties of Newgate', which, remarks Fielding, 'in cant language signifies plunder'.

The force of *Jonathan Wild* comes from Fielding's social vision which is what puts life into the great passages of the book. The conversations between Wild and his cronies, the Newgate scenes, the final grotesque, appalling journey to the gallows, these are what capture the imagination. Many of the descriptions (such as that of Miss Tishy Snap)[4] have a ruthless realism which even Swift does not surpass. Here there is more than a precise sordidness, more than a determination to leave no horror unspoken. And when Fielding speaks of Tishy as 'dishonouring the human species' one realises how much of humanity as well as of bitterness lies in this strange book. Fielding is not without positive values. You cannot dishonour the human species unless there is honour there. The picture of women in *Jonathan Wild*, either, like Mrs Heartfree, so constantly at the mercy of men that life becomes one long battle for the retention of virtue, or else, like the Snap sisters, almost totally degraded by the world they live in, this picture throws a not irrelevant light on all the Pamelas and Molls of eighteenth-century fiction.

But for all its power and its extraordinary insight *Jonathan Wild* is not quite a great novel and its weaknesses as well as its strength derive from Fielding's social vision. There are, I think, three major weaknesses in the book: Heartfree; a too-insistent reiteration of the ironical antithesis of 'great' and 'good'; and certain compromises—embedded in the plot—which betray inadequacies in Fielding's own moral attitude.

The weakness of Heartfree is important because, as the chief representative of 'goodness' in the novel, he is essential to its pattern. Only once in the book does Heartfree truly come to life, in the interesting, satirical and yet moving soliloquy (Book III, ch. II) which is a kind of eighteenth-century 'to be or not to be'. And even here his weakness as a symbolic figure is revealed in the feebleness of his final positive affirmation: 'I will do my utmost to lay the foundations of my children's happiness; I will carefully avoid educating them in a station superior to their fortune, and for the event trust to that Being in whom whoever rightly confides must be superior to all worldly sorrows.' Because in a fable like *Jonathan Wild* the vitality of the characters is wholly dependent on their part in the moral pattern one cannot separate what Wild or Heartfree 'stands for' from what he is. Wild and the rogues are vital characters (not, in Mr Forster's sense 'round' characters, but nevertheless alive in the way they must be) because all that they stand for is fully realised.

Heartfree is not vital because Fielding castrates him as a moral agent and yet at the same time makes him bear the positive values of the fable on his shoulders. Therefore it is precisely Heartfree's passive acceptance, in the sentence I have just quoted, of the inevitability of class society (which Fielding has, through Wild, with such ruthless honesty dissected) and the commonplaces of conventional religion that makes him unfit to be the hero of the book, morally and therefore aesthetically. When Heartfree tells us that 'what we seek in this world is vanity' our hearts sink and the vital tension of the book is weakened, not because the philosophy he is expressing is in the abstract true or untrue, but because we know perfectly well that what Heartfree is seeking is not vanity, but a happy marriage and a decent living.

And if in the conception of Heartfree there is a core of defeatism which makes him an inadequate hero, this same defeatism emerges also in Fielding's prose. The irony, after the first pages, becomes a little too insistent. The reiteration of the good-great antithesis comes after a time somewhat to pall. Is not Fielding protesting, perhaps, too much? And is not his insistence, like the player queen's, a mark for suspicion? Repetition of this kind reveals not full confidence but an underlying doubt, a problem not fully realised, something hollow somewhere.

If we probe the weaknesses of *Jonathan Wild* our examination always leads us towards the same diagnosis. In the last chapter of Book I there is one of the fullest and richest of Fielding's analyses of the great ('Mankind are first properly to be considered under two grand divisions—those that use their own hands, and those who employ the hands of others . . . etc.'), but out of the vigorous clarity emerges one unresolved ambiguity, his attitude to the 'middle' and particularly the professional class. Again, one notices a tendency (the only hint of sentimentality in Fielding's attitude towards Wild) to treat the villain of the piece as his own worst enemy. This tends to blur the central pattern; if Wild is the victim of a delusion his force as a typical symbol is weakened. Finally, there is in this novel a critical weakness in the resolution of the plot which involves more than once the production of a *deus ex machina* —the 'good magistrate'—who ultimately ensures that right prevails (and, incidentally, runs the 'rational' Utopian city that Mrs Heartfree finds in Africa).

It is the good magistrate (it is perhaps not irrelevant to recall that Fielding was one himself) who saves Heartfree and brings down Wild. He is above party, above class and therefore does not fit into the world of the novel, the world of 'the two grand divisions'. And for this reason he weakens the book and blurs the full power and horror of it. For the real horror of the *Jonathan Wild* world, as Fielding has already convinced us, is that the Wilds do not inevitably end on the gallows and that the Heartfrees, in-adequately armed as they are seen to be, may well be themselves corrupted. And from this final horror Fielding averts his eyes, consoling us with the spectacle of the good magistrate administer-ing an impartial justice. And it is precisely owing to the presence of the magistrate that the 'good' characters in the novel remain passive and unalive, are neither corrupted nor transformed by their participation in the *Wild* world. For if they were corrupted the magistrate could not save them, and if they were transformed, made rebels, he would not need to.

The basic weakness of *Jonathan Wild*, to which the various details I have mentioned all contribute, is that no one on the 'good' side actually fights for human values (as Tom Jones, for instance, does). This is why as far as the success and vitality of the book go, the rogues have all the life. And the weakness is not an abstractable 'aesthetic' weakness. It is a weakness which springs direct from the limitations of Fielding's social vision.

I have dwelt in some detail on an analysis of *Jonathan Wild* because it is a typical example of the moral fable and there is no other way of indicating the kind of approach relevant to this kind of book. If we encounter *Jonathan Wild*, or any novel with a serious moral structure, with the preconception that what is most important in a novel is 'character' (in the Dickensian sense) or 'story' (of the kind Stevenson does well) or 'atmosphere' (as in Hardy) or 'plot-construction' (as in Wilkie Collins), then we shall make little of Fielding's wonderful book. That is not to say that 'character' etc., are not important. But it is to say that such terms can only be discussed in relation to the central core and purpose of each particular book.

The eighteenth-century moral fable does not end with *Jonathan Wild*. Thomas Day, in his popular *Sandford and Merton*, Godwin (and other, lesser, radicals of the last two decades of the eighteenth century), Mrs Inchbald (her *Nature and Art* is an intriguing example of the genre), Maria Edgeworth, Hannah More, all worked in the tradition. And the form has persisted, not only through the nine-teenth century,[5] but into the twentieth: the novels of Mr Rex Warner are an obvious example, those of Mr Graham Greene perhaps less obvious.

And here we cannot avoid the question, 'At what point does the moral fable become something else?' Every novel which has within it some basic moral pattern (that is to say, every good novel) has something of the fable in it. And yet for the novels of, say, Richardson or Jane Austen or George Eliot, the term 'moral fable' is inadequate. The point at which it becomes inadequate is not easy to define. Perhaps it may be put in this way: once a novel ceases to be an illustration, once it becomes an expression of something of life in its own right, once the discoveries we make in it are no longer adequately expressible in the terms alongside which we set out, then we cease to feel that 'moral fable' is a fair description.

Mr Henry Reed has said of a novel of Mr Graham Greene: 'The strength of his initial beliefs seems to leave him nothing to discover while writing the book; in consequence the reader discovers nothing either.'[6] I am not here concerned to argue whether this is a just estimate of Mr Greene, and I would, in any case, prefer the word 'nature' to 'strength' (it is not the strength but the nature of a man's philosophy that makes him narrow); but I think Mr Reed is saying something valuable here, something relevant to the moral fable as such.

An interesting example of an eighteenth-century novel which is basically a moral fable, although in the end it becomes something rather different, is Godwin's *Caleb Williams*, published in 1794 and for two decades regarded as the finest novel of the time. The nature of Godwin's moral concern is evident throughout the book (he looked upon it as a sweetened pill containing the ideas of *Political Justice*) and is enshrined in the motto on the title page:

> Amidst the woods the leopard knows his kind;
> The tyger prays not on the tyger brood;
> Man only is the common foe of man.

Godwin has left us a fascinating account of the conception of *Caleb Williams*:

I formed a conception of a book of fictitious adventure, that should in some way be distinguished by a very powerful interest. Pursuing this idea I invented first the third volume of my tale, then the second, and last of all the first. I bent myself to a series of adventures of flight and pursuit, the fugitive in perpetual apprehension of being overwhelmed with the worst calamities, and the pursuer, by his ingenuity and resources, keeping his victim in a state of the most fearful alarm. This was the project of my third volume.

I was next called upon to conceive a dramatic and impressive situation adequate to account for the impulse that the pursuer should feel, incessantly to alarm and harass the victim. . . . This I apprehended could best be affected by a secret murder, to the investigation of which the innocent victim should be impelled by an unconquerable spirit of curiosity. The murderer would thus have a sufficient motive to persecute the unhappy discoverer . . . and have him for ever in his power. This constituted the outline of my second volume.

The subject of the first volume was still to be invented. To account for the fearful events of the third, it was necessary that the pursuer should be invested with every advantage of fortune, with a resolution that nothing could defeat or baffle, and with extraordinary resources of intellect. Nor could my purpose . . . be answered, without his appearing to have been originally endowed with a mighty store of amiable dispositions and virtues, so that his being driven to the first act of murder should be judged worthy of the deepest regret, and should be seen in some measure to have arisen out of his virtues themselves. . . .[7]

After this description (which, incidentally, throws interesting light on the social origins of the novel of pursuit of which Mr Greene has been an exponent) it is scarcely surprising to find, particularly in the early part of *Caleb Williams*, a peculiarly arid quality. It is all far too glib and our interest in it today is almost entirely an historical one. And the trouble is that Godwin so clearly knows all the answers before he begins; he has left himself, in Mr Reed's words, 'nothing to discover'. But then, towards the end of the book, something happens. Falkland—the villain of the piece, the murderer, the landed aristocrat formed (in true Godwinian fashion) by the prejudices of his class, who has used all his social power and almost the entire state apparatus to hound the innocent Caleb Williams who knows his secret—Falkland gradually, almost imperceptibly, ceases to be the villain of the book and becomes its hero. So that when finally Caleb triumphs and Falkland dies, the wretched Williams is haunted by the sensation that a better man than he has perished.

Now this theme of the fatal fascination of the villain Falkland (a fascination rich in implication to any student of the Romantic movement) is clearly the element in the story which had escaped even the meticulous Godwin's calculations. It is the element which gives the book what vitality it has and it is also—if we compare Godwin's description of the novel in composition with the finished work—the element of 'discovery' in it. It is not as it stands, for all its interest, a very valuable discovery. On the contrary, the vitality it brings the book is a sort of hysteria, something uncontrolled, unrealised, neurotic.

The fascination which Falkland exercises upon Caleb (and Godwin) is indeed a fatal one, the fascination exercised by a decadent order on those who would like intellectually to free themselves from it but emotionally are unable to do so. And because Godwin does not understand the nature of this problem he is not able to turn it into art. He *feels* the problem but does not have it under control. Because he feels it something striking happens to his book which quickens our pulses. But because he does not have it under control his presentation of the problem is merely hysterical, without artistic significance. But from the moment that the new 'discovery' emerges in the novel, the discovery that the Falkland-Williams relationship is something vital, complex, many-sided, passionate, *Caleb Williams* ceases to be a moral fable.

3

DEFOE AND THE PICARESQUE TRADITION

The form—and the formlessness—of the early picaresque stories corresponded, as we have seen, to the consciousness of the people whose lives those stories portrayed. They are the literature of the feudal outcasts, of men and women who have no satisfactory place in feudal society, and their characteristics—variety, adventurousness, colour, irreverence, a lack of guiding principle—are the characteristics of the rebels and adventurers who had not yet become a self-conscious class.

Defoe's novels are in the picaresque tradition, but it is not adequate to describe them as picaresque. For by the time of Defoe the consciousness, and therefore the art, of the feudal outcasts had undergone the profoundest changes. By the beginning of the eighteenth century the *picaro* was no longer an outcast and therefore no longer a *picaro*; he might not be a fully fledged bourgeois, but he participated in a society in which the bourgeoisie had become a powerful section of the ruling class, a society whose standards and values he shared and accepted. By 1748, when *Roderick Random* was published, Smollett's hero, though he experiences all the adventures of the *picaro*, is a thoroughly eighteenth-century character and 'values himself on his taste in the *Belle Lettre*'.

What places Defoe in the picaresque tradition is his anti-romantic, anti-feudal realism, his concern with the feel and texture of the life he conveys and his lack of pattern. It is not true to say that there is no pattern in any of Defoe's novels, but certainly there is not the kind of concern which infuses and shapes the moral fable. Defoe's novels are not illustrations. He is careful to point out the moral, insistent in his claim to be instructing the reader, but in fact the insistence is quite bogus. There is no 'moral discovery' to be made in *Moll Flanders* for all the moral talk.*

Interestingly Defoe expresses the hope in the Preface that the discriminating reader 'will be more pleased with the moral than the fable'. But Defoe's moral attitudes are almost as ambiguous as those of Moll herself who repents of her sins every few pages with perfect sincerity and precious little consequence. This is, indeed, the very delight of *Moll Flanders*. Moll is magnificently real, magnificently alive because her moral limitations are caught and paralleled so precisely by the sensibility of the writer. Were Defoe to have seen her from any other point of view the same kind of vitality could not have been achieved. One of the limiting factors of the autobiographical technique in a novel (Defoe's chief characters always write as 'I') is that the total effect of the novel depends inevitably on the quality of the consciousness of the narrator. What 'I' does not perceive can be perceived by the reader only by implication. Defoe turns this limitation into a strength. *Moll Flanders* is completely convincing because Moll and 'I' are triumphantly identical.

The supreme quality in Defoe's novels is their sense of solidity, their painstaking but vital verisimilitude. Fiction was never nearer truth—the surface truth of the 'average' reader's view of life—nor did any novelist ever take greater pains to convince the reader of this truth. This concern of Defoe's is due to a large extent to the prejudices of his Puritan audience, who started often with the assumption that fiction, since it dealt in illusion, must be wrong. As Mrs Leavis, in her admirable pages on Defoe, has put it: 'If fiction could be disguised so that it could be acceptable to the virtuous (for whom "invention" meant lying, and more particularly the immoral literature and drama of the Restoration court), fiction could be made to pay.'[8] Not the least of Defoe's triumphs was his ability to overcome the Puritan suspicion of the imagination.

This suspicion was the by-product of success. Puritanism (the growth of which was inseparably linked with the rise of the commercial classes)[9] had little need of fantasy because real life was, not merely literally, paying such high dividends. Only to people who feel a fundamental confidence in the possibility of prosperity can 'self-help' be a satisfactory moral attitude, and it is the predominant

* For a fuller and later discussion of *Moll Flanders* see my essay 'In Defence of *Moll Flanders*' in *Of Books and Humankind*, Essays and Poems Presented to Bonamy Dobrée (ed. J. Butt), (Routledge, 1964).

attitude both of Defoe and his audience. Crusoe's father points out
in his eulogy of the middle class

> '. . . that the calamities of life were shared among the upper and lower
> part of mankind; but that the middle station had the fewest disasters, and
> was not expos'd to so many vicissitudes as the higher or lower part of
> mankind; nay, they were not subjected to so many distempers and un-
> easinesses, either of body or mind, as those were who, by vicious living,
> luxury, and extravagancies on one hand, or by hard labour, want of
> necessaries, and mean or insufficient diet on the other hand, bring dis-
> tempers upon themselves by the natural consequences of their way of
> living; that the middle station of life was calculated for all kinds of
> vertues and all kinds of enjoyments; that peace and plenty were the hand-
> maids of a middle fortune; that temperance, moderation, quietness,
> health, society, all agreeable diversions, and all desirable pleasures, were
> the blessings attending the middle station of life; that this way men went
> silently and smoothly thro' the world, and comfortably out of it, not
> embarass'd with the labours of the hands or of the head, not sold to the
> life of slavery for daily bread, or harrast with perplex'd circumstances,
> which rob the soul of peace, and the body of rest; not enrag'd with the
> passion of envy, or secret burning lust of ambition for great things; but
> in easy circumstances sliding gently thro' the world, and sensibly tasting
> the sweets of living without the bitter, feeling that they are happy, and
> learning by every day's experience to know it more sensibly.'[10]

For such people real life was obviously good enough, hence
Defoe's concern to persuade them that what he is writing is indeed
'real life'. Hence also his concern to add a moral 'when he remembers'.[11]

Defoe, then, seems more interested in 'life' than in 'pattern'. The
excellent things in his books are the descriptions of actions, of
people doing things. Moll comparing three estimates—ranging
from £13. 13s. 0d. to £53. 14s. 0d.—for a confinement, Colonel
Jack deciding what clothes he shall buy with the money he has
stolen, Robinson Crusoe making his pot and his oven, these are
the moments one remembers and returns to. Here is a description
from *Colonel Jack* of the 'Colonel's' youthful activities in London:

> I was now rich, so rich that I knew not what to do with my money or
> with myself. I had lived so near and so close, that although, as I said, I
> did now and then lay out twopence or threepence for mere hunger, yet
> I had so many people who, as I said, employed me, and who gave me
> victuals and sometimes clothes, that in a whole year I had not quite spent
> the fifteen shillings which I had saved of the custom-house gentleman's

money, and I had the four guineas, which was of the first booty before that, still in my pocket—I mean the money that I let fall into the tree.

But now I began to look higher, and though Will and I went abroad several times together, yet when small things offered, as handkerchiefs and such trifles, we would not meddle with them, not caring to run the risk for small matters. It fell out one day that as we were strolling about in West Smithfield, on a Friday, there happened to be an ancient country-gentleman in the market selling some very large bullocks. It seems they came out of Sussex, for we heard him say there were no such bullocks in the whole county of Sussex. His Worship, for so they called him, had received the money for these bullocks at a tavern, whose sign I forget now, and having some of it in a bag, and the bag in his hand, he was taken with a sudden fit of coughing, and stands to cough, resting his hand, with the bag of money in it, upon a bulkhead of a shop just by the Cloister gate in Smithfield—that is to say, within three or four doors of it. We were both just behind him. Says Will to me, 'Stand ready.' Upon this he makes an artificial stumble, and falls with his head just against the old gentleman, in the very moment when he was coughing ready to be strangled and quite spent for want of breath.

The violence of the blow beat the old gentleman quite down; the bag of money did not immediately fly out of his hand, but I ran to get hold of it, and gave it a quick snatch, pulled it clean away, and ran like the wind down the Cloister with it, turned on the left hand as soon as I was through and cut into Little Britain, so into Bartholomew Close, then across Aldersgate Street, through Paul's Alley into Red Cross Street, and so across all the streets, through innumerable alleys, and never stopped till I got into the second quarter of Moorfields, our old agreed rendezvous.

Will in the meantime fell down with the old gentleman but soon got up. The old knight (for such it seems he was) was frighted with the fall, and his breath so stopped with his cough that he could not recover himself to speak till some time, during which nimble Will was got up again and walked off; nor could he call out 'Stop thief!' or tell anybody he had lost anything for a good while; but coughing vehemently, and looking red till he was almost black in the face, he cried, 'The ro——hegh-hegh-hegh, the rogues, hegh, have got, hegh-hegh-hegh-hegh-hegh-hegh'; then he would get a little breath, and at it again—'the rogue——hegh-hegh'—and after a great many 'heghs' and 'rogues', he brought it out—'have got away my bag of money.'[12]

This is an admirable example of Defoe's method. Utter verisimilitude is achieved by the insistence on detail: the precise financial calculations, the naming of the day of the week and the actual streets. The rhythm of the prose is the ordinary rhythm of speech: we get the flavour of colloquial talk in the passing reference to 'no such bullocks in the whole county of Sussex', and the whole is remarkably simple and vivid. And the informing moral interest is equally simple. No insights are offered beyond the surface statements and when Colonel Jack's conscience makes its appearance, as it does from time to time, it is treated in much the same matter-of-fact way as the other elements in the book.

And yet it would not be quite true to say that there is no pattern in Defoe's novels. There is a tentative sort of pattern, the pattern of a man's or woman's life. The shape of these books is the shape of their heroes' existence. We follow them from birth to old age and even the most immense section, like Crusoe's time on the island, has the status of an episode. This is something rather different from the early 'rogue' novels in which there is no attempt thus to see a man's life whole, and this biographical element in Defoe has its importance. It corresponds to the bourgeois—as opposed to the feudal—way of looking at the world, this sense of life's being what a man makes it, this essentially individualist attitude to existence.

During the eighteenth century the middle-class writers, secure in the outcome of the successful bourgeois revolution, take stock of the new world which the members of their class, now comfortably allied with the old landed aristocracy, already control politically and which they are confident they will—with the aid of Locke's philosophy and Newton's science—totally subjugate. The medieval world-picture gradually becomes mere superstition and prejudice; hope and confidence replace the doubt and uncertainty, the lack of coherence of the earlier seventeenth century. The proper study of mankind, it is widely felt, is man.

Defoe's novels are among the first and most excellent of such proper studies. Behind these novels is the same impulse that brought about the scientific advances and the new prose associated with the Royal Society—'a close, naked, natural way of speaking; positive expressions, clean senses; a native easiness; bringing all things as near the Mathematical plainness, as they can; and preferring the language of Artisans, Countrymen and Merchants, before that of Wits, or Scholars'. It was this impulse that was to lead such a man as Boswell in his *Journal* to examine and record with scrupulous honesty, and little thought of their 'propriety', the motives and reactions of his day-to-day experience. This spirit of curiosity, this eager and uninhibited desire to see things and men as they really are, is the driving force behind the best literature of the eighteenth century, and when we see it as a by-product of the bourgeois revolution we must beware of an over-simplification.

For it is not adequate to describe Defoe, for instance, simply as a
bourgeois. He is that, but he is more than that. We must not forget
that when Robinson Crusoe sets off on his life of adventure and
uncertainty he goes *against* the advice of his middle-class father. And
the vitality and interest of *Robinson Crusoe* which come, as we have
noticed, from the continuous sense of action and achievement, of
actual physical effort, do not arise from specifically bourgeois virtues.

On the contrary it is a characteristic of the bourgeois, as Jonathan
Wild well knew, that he makes his money from the toil not of his
own hands but of other people's. When we say, then, that *Robinson
Crusoe* is a product of, and can be fully understood only in relation
to, the bourgeois revolution, we must by no means think of it as a
mere 'reflection' of that revolution and the society which arose as
its consequence. Such a view takes the guts out of literature. If
Robinson Crusoe were merely a reflection of bourgeois society no
one except members of the capitalist class needing a little consola-
tion would trouble to read it. The truth is a good deal more complicated and much more rich. The bourgeois revolution, because
it *was* a revolution and *did* destroy (though not utterly) the social
relationships and therefore the outlook and philosophy of feudalism, set in motion actions and ideas which were of the greatest use
not merely to the bourgeoisie. Just as, in order to win their own
freedom, the English merchant-capitalists of the seventeenth century needed to create the new Model Army which quickly turned
out to be far more democratic and revolutionary than its creators,
so in breaking the ideological chains of feudalism men like Bacon
and Hobbes and Hume released ideas which scared not only the
new ruling class but themselves as well.

Robinson Crusoe is in one sense a story in praise of the bourgeois
virtues of individualism and private enterprise.* But in another, and
more important sense, it celebrates the necessity of social living and
the struggle of mankind through work to master nature, a struggle
in which the bourgeois virtues are as sands upon the Red Sea shore.
For where would Crusoe have been without the products of social
living which he could salvage from the wreck? And what seeker
after 'the blessings attending the middle station of life . . . not
embarrassed with the labours of the hands or of the head . . .' could
cry out to Crusoe: 'No joy at a thing of so mean a nature was ever
equal to mine, when I found that I had made an earthen pot that
would bear the fire'?

* For a relevant and interesting discussion of this whole question see 'Robinson
Crusoe as a Myth' by Ian Watt (*Essays in Criticism*, Vol. I, no. 2).

The fact is that while Defoe's novels could only have arisen out of the social situation of the early eighteenth century and are a direct and undeniable product of the seventeenth-century revolution, his strength as a writer comes from his inability to *feel* the strength of the code of his class as glibly as he accepted it intellectually. It is because he cannot in his heart and therefore in his writing quite take the orthodox Puritan attitude towards Moll that the fable goes (in spite of his protests) so much deeper than the moral. It is because when he describes Colonel Jack robbing the Sussex gentleman he forgets his conscience that the passage lives so joyously. This is Defoe's strength, that he is able to extricate himself as an artist from conventional morality (even in the very act of paying lip-service to it) and to concentrate on the surface-texture of life. And his limitation is that he has no other morality to put in its place. This is why his books, except perhaps *Robinson Crusoe* and *Roxana*, are ultimately without pattern. For the mere presentation of a man's life is not pattern enough, and the assumption that surface-texture is in the end an alternative to, or indeed separable from, point of view is an illusion.

But we should not underestimate the contribution of the picaresque tradition to the English novel. Even though it made for a neglect of pattern it did demonstrate that the novel must draw its vitality from a concern with the actual life of the people. It made impossible any serious attempt to move back to the pastoral and courtly traditions of the early romances. *The Unfortunate Traveller*, *Moll Flanders*, *Roderick Random*, *Kim*, Joyce Cary's *The Horse's Mouth*: it is not a line that anyone who delights in the novel will despise.

We have come (and rightly) in the last fifty years, to look in a novel for a controlling intelligence, a total significance which these books can scarcely claim to possess. Criticism of the novel has come (and rightly) to distrust an undifferentiated 'vitality' as criterion enough of a novel's worth and to see the amorphous, sprawling tendencies of the earlier English novels as an unfortunate influence on later novelists. Yet we should beware of too narrow an approach. The reader who sees in Smollett, for instance, nothing but a failure to impose a significant form is not merely missing something delightful but is casting some doubt on the adequacy of his idea of 'significance'. A vitality that captures our imagination is in itself significant. Energy is Eternal Delight.

4

RICHARDSON, FIELDING, STERNE

Sophia was in her chamber, reading, when her aunt came in. The moment she saw Mrs Western, she shut the book with so much eagerness, that the good lady could not forbear asking her, What book that was which she seemed so much afraid of showing? 'Upon my word, madam,' answered Sophia, 'it is a book which I am neither ashamed nor afraid to own I have read. It is the production of a young lady of fashion, whose good understanding, I think, doth honour to her sex, and whose good heart is an honour to human nature.' Mrs Western then took up the book, and immediately after threw it down, saying—'Yes, the author is of a very good family; but she is not much among people one knows. I have never read it; for the best judges say, there is not much in it.'—'I dare not, madam, set up my own opinion,' says Sophia, 'against the best judges, but there appears to me a great deal of human nature in it; and in many parts so much true tenderness and delicacy, that it hath cost me many a tear.'—'Ay, and do you love to cry then?' says the aunt. 'I love a tender sensation,' answered the niece, 'and would pay the price of a tear for it at any time.'   TOM JONES

SAMUEL RICHARDSON

No considerable writer in our language is so easily made fun of as Richardson. The very length of his books has become a joke; his concern to extract from his reader on every occasion the price of a tear of sensibility is not likely to recommend him to an age which regards tears as either superficial or shameful; and his moral attitudes have been vulnerable targets from the moment that someone (who was almost certainly Fielding) countered *Pamela* with the uproarious and only too apt burlesque called *Shamela*. And yet, having made all the jokes and agreed with all the strictures, we are left with the fact that Richardson is not just an 'important' writer, interesting only to literary historians, but a very remarkable one who brings something not merely new but vital to the English novel.

Pamela is by no conceivable standard a great novel. Technically it is crude: the letter-form leads not merely to gross improbability but to tedious repetition. The improbability does not, in itself, matter. It is no more improbable that Pamela should pause at a moment of crisis to pen a letter to her parents than that an 'impersonal' novelist should know exactly what is going on simultaneously in the minds of half a dozen characters or that the principal boy in the pantomime should be a girl. All art has its conventions which we must accept if we are to accept the art, and what arouses our mistrust in *Pamela* is not the fundamental improbability of the novel of letters, but Richardson's self-consciousness in the use of his technique. When *Pamela* stops to explain how it comes that she—a simple servant-girl—can spend so much time and money in correspondence it is as though Hamlet were to apologise before a soliloquy for speaking his thoughts aloud.

But the technical crudity, forgivable anyway in a pioneer, is the least of the faults of *Pamela*. The fundamental trouble is that we are asked to admire actions and characters whose moral basis is quite unadmirable. 'Virtue Rewarded' is the sub-title of the novel, and by the end of four volumes the well-guarded chastity of the heroine is indeed rewarded by a considerable income, not to mention social position. Had it been the purpose of Richardson to reveal ironically that Pamela's chastity (or that of any maiden of the day) was indeed her only material asset, a commodity which she could ill afford to prize cheaply, here would have been legitimate moral criticism, as both Defoe and Fielding show. But this is by no means the theme of *Pamela*. On the contrary the hard-headed scheming of the girl and her parents for a decent social position is presented in terms of a high-falutin religiosity, Pamela's decision to marry a man whom she could only heartily despise is accepted without criticism and the subsequent 'reformation' of Mr B—— produced for our additional edification. The result is that every thrust of *Shamela* (not to mention *Joseph Andrews*) is a palpable hit, and *Pamela* remains only as a record of a peculiarly loathsome aspect of bourgeois puritan morality.

The extraordinary thing is that *Pamela* was followed by *Clarissa*, a novel of quite astonishing subtlety and fascination.

What is remarkable about *Clarissa* is its power. There is an intensity here, an intimate involvement of the reader which is quite outside anything previously achieved in the English novel or, for that matter, achieved again before Jane Austen.

In Defoe's novels or Fielding's or in any of the moral fables the reader remains at a certain distance from all that happens. We care about Moll or Tom Jones or Parson Adams, and we become involved in their problems and experiences. They have their odd and subtle flavour, as other people do, and we are tempted, as we so often are with actual acquaintances, to look at them rather simply, to encompass with a phrase or mental gesture what cannot really be encompassed. And this simplification of feeling does no violence to their author's intention. With *Clarissa* it is different. We are involved in a way in which we are seldom involved in the lives of others in actual life. As Clarissa's position is revealed and the intolerable situation closes in on her there is recorded on our own consciousness with a quite horrible intensity the sense of being trapped, of being unable to break through the web of misunderstanding and hatred and jealousy and sheer insensibility that are going to destroy her.

I do not think that this experience should be described as 'self-identification'. We know perfectly well that we are not Clarissa, and one of the elements in our experience is that we do indeed know more than she, do in fact see the situation with an objectivity she cannot attain. Nor do I think the experience is different in *kind* from the experience of a Defoe or Fielding novel. In each case we give ourselves up (yet consciously and not utterly) to a fantastic world in which our intelligence and sympathies and interests become involved. The distinction is in the *intensity* of the experience, not necessarily in its value. (There is not more of life in the total experience of *Clarissa* than in that of *Tom Jones*.) And perhaps the best description of this peculiar intensity is that it is tragic. We are involved in a situation to which there is no obvious solution, no solution that does not imply changes that are unlikely to occur.

This, then, we can say of Richardson: not that he is the first English novelist but that he is the first tragic novelist, and this is where the power of *Clarissa* lies. For *Clarissa*, unlike *Pamela*, expresses and encompasses a truly tragic situation. There are strands and tints in this second and greater novel which weaken it, sometimes quite disastrously. The religiosity is still there; the moral distribution of reward and punishment is offensive; the dwelling almost *ad nauseam* on the affecting moments (particularly in the last volumes) is distasteful, so is the prurient playing

on the reader's anticipation of the rape. But the power remains
because the situation is indeed tragic.

'If you were to read Richardson for the story, your impatience
would be so much fretted that you would hang yourself,' wrote
Johnson; 'but you must read him for the sentiment, and consider
the story only as giving occasion to the sentiment.' Johnson's
remark is true and helpful so long as we remember that he was not
using the word sentiment in its modern pejorative sense of 'sentimental' and so long as we do not draw an antithesis (as Johnson
did not) between sentiment and realism. For the tragedy of Clarissa
is a very real tragedy and the reason we sympathise with her is
because, unlike Pamela, she faces (rather passively but nevertheless
bravely) the lewd machinations of her conventional bourgeois
family and will not give in. She, the middle-class girl, timid and
virtuous, will not subscribe to one of the first and essential dicta of
eighteenth-century morality, that a daughter is the property of her
parents to be married as they think fit—and profitable.

The conflict of Clarissa—the individual heart versus the conventional standards of the property-owning class—is one of the
essential, recurring conflicts of the modern novel, as of all literature
of class society. It is the conflict of love (i.e. human dignity, sympathy, independence) versus money (i.e. property, position, 'respectability', prejudice), which lies at the heart of almost all the
novels of Fielding, Jane Austen, the Brontës, Thackeray, unalike
as they are in almost every other respect. And it is no chance or
subsidiary theme. When we are moved by a novel it is because our
human sympathies are aroused. Such sympathies are not awoken
by nothing or by imaginary issues and conflicts which have no
relevance to actual facts. We are moved by problems and situations
which we know through our experience of life to be the real and vital
problems. What engages our interest and holds it in Clarissa is not
some abstract quality of sentiment or analysis, but the presentation
and examination of a real and concrete human problem.

The presentation is extremely realistic—sharp, nervous sentences, colloquial speech-rhythms, sudden swooping detail. The
good Clarissa cannot resist—at a moment when she is trying hard
to be fair—describing her sister:

'The poor Bella has, you know, a plump high-fed face, if I may be
allowed the expression.'

When Clarissa is shut up in disgrace because she will not marry rich Solmes she is visited by her aunt and sister. The aunt is all but won over by Clarissa's innocence but the sister is merciless:

'My sister left my aunt musing at the window, with her back towards us; and took that opportunity to insult me still more barbarously: for, stepping to my closet, she took up the patterns which my mother had sent me up, and bringing them to me, she spread them upon the chair by me; and, offering one, and then another, upon her sleeve and shoulder, thus she ran on, with great seeming tranquillity, but whisperingly, that my aunt might not hear her. *This*, Clary, is a pretty pattern enough; but *this* is quite *charming*! I would advise you to make your appearance in it. And *this*, were I you, should be my wedding night-gown, and *this* my second dressed suit! Won't you give orders, love, to have your grand-mother's jewels new set? Or will you think to show away in the new ones Mr Solmes intends to present to you? He talks of laying out two or three thousand pounds in presents, child! Dear heart! how gorgeously you will be arrayed! What! silent, my dear! Mamma Norton's *sweet dear*! What! silent still? But, Clary, won't you have a velvet suit? It would cut a great figure in a country church, you know: and the weather may bear it for a month yet to come. Crimson velvet, suppose! Such a fine com-plexion as yours, how would it be set off by it! What an agreeable blush would it give you! High-ho? (mocking me; for I sighed to be thus fooled with): and do you sigh, love? Well then, as it will be a solemn wedding, what think you of *black* velvet, child? Silent still, Clary! Black velvet, so fair as you are, with those charming eyes, gleaming through a wintry cloud, like an April sun! Does not Lovelace tell you they are charming eyes! How lovely will you appear to every one! What! silent still, love! But about your laces, Clary!

She would have gone on still further had not my aunt advanced towards us, wiping her eyes. What! whispering, ladies! You seem so easy and so pleased, Miss Harlowe, with your private conference that I hope I shall carry down good news.

I am only giving her my opinion of her patterns, *here*. Unasked indeed; but she seems, by her silence, to approve of my judgment.'[13]

Richardson catches the tone and movement of speech with immense skill. The taunts, which might so easily be crude, have the keenness of a refined and subtle torture. The force of the 'but whisperingly' is a poetic force, dependent on the whole structure of the sentence.

Richardson's psychological insight and subtlety have been re-marked often enough; the solidity of his scene seems to have been less generously recognised. Both the Harlowe household in the earlier part of the book and the world of brotheldom in the later have a firm and solid reality which gives a necessary depth of back-ground to the scene after scene of intense emotion. This is why the accusation of sentimentality carries less force than it might. There is no doubt that Richardson's approach is, in the modern sense, sentimental, that he deliberately plays on the emotions of his reader because a play on the emotions is regarded as being *for its own sake* desirable; and this is undoubtedly the danger point both in his novels and in his influence. But although he squeezes every atom of emotion (and sometimes more) out of every incident, yet because the central conflict is so strong and true and because the scene he has built is so real and solid, the book can in fact, to an astonishing measure, bear such treatment.

Hence the paradox that though Richardson is sentimental *Clarissa*, by and large, is not. This success, one is tempted to feel, is almost fortuitous: what Richardson is out to find are situations that will wring the tender heart because the tender hearts of his audience were waiting, with delicious expectation, to be wrung; that he should have achieved in *Clarissa* a situation so truly impressive that his sentimental approach is not ridiculous was due either to his luck or his genius, and perhaps it is unreasonable to expect luck to last for seven volumes. But that his success was less than fully conscious is shown by his insistence in Preface and Postscript that his novel is illustrating the 'doctrine of future rewards'.

In fact, as Mr Brian Downs has excellently pointed out,

the real effectiveness . . . of the novel and its true ethical significance lie in the precise opposite of this notion, in that sublime cry of Clarissa's in which the story culminates, '*The man who has been the villain to me that you have been shall never make me his wife.*'[14]

It is from this assertion of a woman's dignity within the moral jungle of the world of arranged marriages and hypocritical prostitution, an assertion that is the very antithesis of *Pamela*'s 'message', that the power of *Clarissa* to move us really springs.

It is the irrevocability of human action that *Clarissa* inculcates, the stern truth that no reparation is possible to cancel out selfish cruelty, wantonly devised to give the maximum of anguish.[15]

This 'stern truth' would not, of course, move us were it not presented in the terms of art, and it is here that Richardson's realism of presentation and psychological acuteness must get their just emphasis. Not the least of his achievements is his ability to convey, with a subtlety that eludes quotation, the quality of

Lovelace's *attraction* for Clarissa as well as the repugnance she feels
for him. And Lovelace himself is a most impressive creature. I
cannot feel that Mr Downs does justice (emotionally, I mean, not
ethically) to 'this consummate cad' when he refers to him as an
'overgrown schoolboy'. What is effective and even terrifying about
Lovelace in the pattern of the book is that he *is* so much the
eighteenth-century gentleman, that he is indeed what passed for
a civilised man, with a great deal—in contrast to the Harlowes—
of what Jane Austen called elegance of manner. That Lovelace
should be all this and *at the same time* unspeakable is what Richardson so powerfully (and again, one suspects, not quite consciously)
reveals, and the revelation illumines, as no abstract moral thesis
could ever do, the full horror of the position of Clarissa and of
women in general in a society which it is still not uncommon to
hear described as polite.

How, then, to summarise Richardson's contribution? He produced—as Defoe had not quite succeeded in doing but as *The
Spectator* had begun to do—a form of fiction ethically and emotionally fully agreeable to the new reading-public. Despite his hope
'to turn young people into a course of reading different from the
pomp and parade of romance writing', his novels performed on one
(and the most obvious) level the exact functions of romance, the
titillation of emotion for its own sake and the explicit recommenda-
tion of a bogus philosophy of life. Technically he did almost all
that was to be done with the epistolary form: in *Pamela* he uses it
realistically and crudely, in *Clarissa* and *Grandison* it becomes
merely a convention—probability is no longer a serious concern.
And as a convention it had its uses for it permitted, through the
intimacies involved, that closer examination of 'the human heart'
for which Richardson is famous—justly.

Here we reach the point at which he ceases to be merely of
historical interest. For in his delving into the private feelings and
secret motives of his characters he achieved something quite
different from the mere evocation of the sentimental moment which
he seems to have intended. He got deeper into the subtle, wayward
and contradictory feelings of human beings than any previous
novelist had managed, and he did so because, in his search for the
easily pathetic, he stumbled on a situation fully tragic, a situation
so wrought with real contradictions that in its revelation strings and
chords are touched which reverberate deep into human experience,
and tensions are experienced which are the actual tensions of life
in motion.

Tragedy occurs when a situation arises which men, at the particular point in development that they have reached, are unable to solve. Such a situation in the eighteenth and nineteenth centuries—and the problem is not yet answered—was the growing consciousness of women of the necessity of their emancipation (by which is not meant mere formal emancipation, parliamentary votes, etc.), and the inability of class society to admit such freedom without destroying something essential to itself. Clarissa *has* to fight her family and Lovelace; they for their part *cannot* let her win without undermining all that is to them necessary and even sacred. It is from the examination of such situations that the artist makes contact with the stuff and movement of life. The actual material of tragedy changes. Clarissa today could solve her problem, at any rate after a fashion. But we still respond to Richardson's novel because in the world of the novel the problem is not soluble and yet the direction of its solution is indicated in the quality of the sympathy which Clarissa herself (silly as she often is) evokes. *Pamela*, in which there is no such insight, we throw aside. But by *Clarissa* our human sympathy and understanding is quickened. It is in this sense that works of art are timeless; they capture the tensions and movement of life which, though for ever altering in form, are nevertheless perpetually going on.

Life develops through struggle and change. The particular struggle is solved, another emerges. The particular tragedy is solved, but we are faced with our own tragic dilemma. This will be solved in its turn, though not perhaps by us, and the experience of the past will help to solve it, just as life, though it involves tragedy, is not tragic (or it would not have gone on for thousands of years), so art, though it springs from its own time and situation, is not merely transient and relative in value. We shall not enjoy *Clarissa* unless we approach it sympathetically, through history. But if we approach it *only* through history we shall not enjoy it either. The past and the present are at once different and inseparable. It is precisely because he stumbled on one of the real, contemporary dilemmas of his own time that Richardson achieved an art which has relevance to ours.

HENRY FIELDING

Fielding, unlike Richardson, is not a tragic novelist, and he does not work on anything like the same level of intensity. His own description of his first novel, *Joseph Andrews*, as a comic romance or a 'comic epic poem in prose', is important. Much more seriously than Richardson, Fielding is concerned to write anti-romances, and *Joseph Andrews* is, indeed, an anti-*Pamela*, attacking all that seems to Fielding to be unrealistic and false in Richardson's novel. Fielding, in fact, tries quite consciously (his debt to Cervantes is explicit) to create an art-form that will be to eighteenth-century society what the epic had been in a more primitive world: it is to be at once a realistic mirror and a critical consideration of the life of the time. Human nature, nothing more or less, is, he announces in the first chapter of *Tom Jones*, his subject.

This claim is a large one and tactically unwise. It advertises that side of Fielding, a cheerful imprecision degenerating too often into mere heartiness, which today seems one of his less sympathetic qualities. But the claim is also symptomatic of that large confidence, that serene facing of the unpleasant as well as the amiable, which gives the novels their warmth and spaciousness. Fielding (despite the impression one gets from Dr Leavis's patronising strictures)[16] is neither smug nor insensitive nor unsubtle. True, he does not explore the darker recesses of the soul, nor does he aim at the concrete intensity of Jane Austen's concern with living; but what he does achieve is a panoramic vision and critical commentary of society both invigorating and satisfying.

Apart from *Jonathan Wild*, Fielding's novels owe more to the picaresque tradition than to that of the moral fable. But, like his master Cervantes, Fielding transcends the random formlessness of the picaresque and imposes a pattern upon that loose and liberal chunk of 'life' which is his raw material. Nor is the pattern merely one of a contrived plot, though it sometimes degenerates into that.

No one could maintain that *Joseph Andrews* has too much plot. Indeed, in so far as plot has the function of holding together the subject-matter in an organised way, it has too little. It is held together, not by a story but by certain themes and also, in a subtle way, by its basic form, that of a journey. The journey of Joseph and Adams from London to Lady Booby's country seat has a certain symbolic quality about it: it is a journey not simply of adventure but of discovery. Now this use of a journey as some kind of a symbol of man's life and striving is, of course, common in literature. It is not always easy to say precisely why some of the journeys of literature—those, for instance, of Ulysses, of Don Quixote, of Robinson Crusoe, of Joseph Andrews—achieve a symbolic significance, while others—those of Roderick Random, of Gil Blas, of David Balfour in *Kidnapped*, of Tom Jones—do not. Clearly the question is one involving the total organisation of the books concerned. In so far as in the journey certain moral discoveries are involved the journey does itself symbolise a striving for clarity; the rhythms of the journey become identified with (as in the *Odyssey*) or in some obscure way hint at (as in *Crusoe* or *Joseph Andrews*) the rhythms of life itself.

The central theme of *Joseph Andrews*, as of *Don Quixote*, is anti-romance, the showing-up of the dangers and inadequacies of romantic attitudes and the assertion of a humane realism. And *Joseph Andrews*, like *Don Quixote*, contains elements of burlesque which it is wrong to exaggerate. Richardson's *Pamela* is burlesqued throughout: Joseph protecting his virginity from the onslaughts of Lady Booby is a situation which only the reader of romance will fully appreciate; but Fielding's intention goes far beyond burlesque. In an interesting passage in his Preface he associates himself with Hogarth and remarks, 'He who should call the ingenious Hogarth a burlesque painter would, in my opinion, do him very little honour.' To recognise the inadequacy of seeing *Joseph Andrews* merely as a burlesque of *Pamela* one has only to compare it with *Shamela*, which has, uproariously, no further intention.

Shamela has, of course, no Parson Adams, and Adams's importance in *Joseph Andrews* is central, not because he is a well-done 'character' (though he is that), but because he raises Fielding's anti-romantic criticism far above a mere common-sense repudiation of Richardson's moral pornography. Just as Quixote is wildly impractical—his head filled with romantic ideas of honour and chivalry—and yet humane, so is Adams—his mind stuffed with the classics and Platonic philosophy—always coming into the sharpest conflict with hard facts. He loses his way, forgets he has no money, sleeps when he should be awake, fights his imaginary windmills (who turn out to be lads of the village engaged in the sport of bird-batting); and, like Quixote, he is a better man than those who do him down.

In the conflicts of the novel—which are always those of humanity versus hypocrisy and bogus morality—Adams, for all his idealistic impracticability, is always on the right side. A consideration of charity is one of the recurring themes of the book. Adams's discussion with Peter Pounce, the steward, is typical.

'I thank God I have a little,' replied the other, 'with which I am content and envy no man: I have a little, Mr Adams, with which I do as much good as I can.' Adams answered, That riches without charity were

nothing worth; for that they were a blessing only to him who made them
a blessing to others.—'You and I,' said Peter, 'have different notions of
charity. I own, as it is generally used, I do not like the word, nor do I
think it becomes one of us gentlemen; it is a mean parson-like quality;
though I would not infer many parsons have it neither.' 'Sir,' said Adams,
'my definition of charity is, a generous disposition to relieve the distressed.'—'There is something in that definition,' answered Peter, 'which
I like well enough; it is, as you say, a disposition, and does not so much
consist in the act as in the disposition to do it; but, alas! Mr Adams, who
are meant by the distressed? Believe me, the distresses of mankind are
mostly imaginary, and it would be rather folly than goodness to relieve
them.' 'Sure, sir,' replied Adams, 'hunger and thirst, cold and nakedness,
and other distresses which attend the poor, can never be said to be
imaginary evils.'[17]

There is nothing casual about this dialogue. The theme has
already been introduced early on by the appalling Mrs Towwouse,
whose views are vigorous:

'Common charity a f—t!' says she; 'common charity teaches us to
provide for ourselves, and our families; and I and mine won't be ruin'd
by your charity, I assure you.'[18]

and it is taken up again by Joseph, who soliloquises (sending
Adams to sleep), contrasting charity with honour.

The conversation with Peter Pounce is an admirable example
not only of the vigour of Fielding's dialogue, but of the subtlety
of his dialectic. Pounce begins with a typical, apparently common-
sense, materialist definition of charity. But by the end of the
dialogue his materialism is revealed as an empty idealism ('the
distresses of mankind are mostly imaginary'), while the impractical
idealist Adams is left asserting the reality of hunger and thirst, cold
and nakedness.

It is this kind of insight, which goes beyond a mere hearty
sympathy for what is decent and dislike of what is hypocritical,
that gives *Joseph Andrews* its quality. But neither should we undervalue the sheer common-sense decency and strong (albeit unsubtle)
moral concern which is at the basis of Fielding's vision. In the
continual conflicts in *Joseph Andrews* around the theme of charity,
conflicts in which Adams and Joseph are always in trouble, generally because they have no money, it is interesting that the unkind
are invariably the great and fashionable and lustful, the mercenary
and servile and hypocritical—the Mrs Slipslops and Parson Trul-

libers—while the kind are the humble people—the postillion who
gives Joseph his cloak, the common soldier who pays the bill at
the inn, the farmer who has seen through the ways of the world.
If we stop to analyse the pervading sense, in Fielding's novels, of
generous humanity (and it is, when all is said, the dominant quality
of his books), we shall find that it springs not from a vague, undifferentiated bonhomie but from a very explicit social awareness
and understanding of the people. Nor is it a sentimental view. The
common people in Fielding's novels are often cruel, stupid, ignorant, bestial. But they are human beings and he doesn't despise them.

How far Fielding has come from the picaresque school is well
illustrated in *Joseph Andrews* in his use of the interpolated tale.
Twice the narrative is held up while an unimportant character
relates a long tale which has no obvious connection with the novel
—a device frequently used by the picaresque writers. But in fact
both *Leonora* (the first of these tales) and Mr Wilson's story do
contribute to the plan of *Joseph Andrews*; neither is a mere casual
interlude. Not only do the two tales contrast with and balance each
other, both provide variations on the main themes of the book:
romance, charity, and love. The *Leonora* story is not just a crude
homily on the evil consequences of Leonora's conduct; its important
purpose is that it allows Fielding to comment on the inadequacy of
conception of such a story. *Leonora* has all the crudities, moral and
technical (including the idiotic letters got by heart) of a *Pamela*.
Fielding is not presenting it to us for our approval. (Such a phrase
as 'the refinement of your mind . . .' with which Leonora's reply to
Horatio's entirely artificial love-letter opens, bears an immense
weight of irony.) *Leonora* underlines the incipient immorality of
Pamela's attitude to love. Mr Wilson's story fills in more of the
picture, telling us something of the world of the Boobys that needs,
for the pattern of the novel, to be told.

If *Joseph Andrews* is very different from *Jonathan Wild*, *Tom
Jones* is almost as different again. What strikes one most, perhaps,
returning to this novel, is how very tentative and experimental a
book it is. In spite of all the apparent self-confidence, the easy
handling of his puppet-master role and the great expertness in
plot-construction, Fielding is for ever feeling his way, moving
from one plane of narrative to another, tentatively exploring the
possibilities of his *milieu*.

The immediate impression is the opposite of tentative. Fielding
appears to be very much in control of the situation. The plot, as
numerous critics have pointed out, is worked out with the greatest

skill; it is the job, indeed, of the successful professional dramatist Fielding had been. Even more basic to the impression of assuredness is the nature of Fielding's philosophy, sceptical but optimistic. He takes the world in his stride, always curious, frequently indignant, but never incurably hurt. It is not, in the academic sense, a philosophy at all, certainly not a conscious metaphysical system. Rather is it an attitude of mind, an acceptance of certain standards and approaches. Fielding, like most of the writers of the eighteenth century, is very sure of his world. He is not complacent but he is fundamentally confident—confident that the problems of human society, that is to say *his* society, can and will be solved by humane feeling and right reason. It is this broad and tolerant confidence which gives *Tom Jones* its particular tone and which also (one suspects) alienates those critics who feel less confidence in social man than Fielding, whose optimism they mistake for insensitiveness.

The tentative note can be isolated as emerging from Fielding's constant preoccupation with method. How best to gain the reader's interest? How to project a character on to the page? How to achieve any kind of suspense without either playing a trick on the reader or forfeiting his own position as omniscient puppet master? He is constantly finding that the contrivance of his plot does violence to the characters he has created. The truth is that in *Tom Jones* there is too much plot. Scenes take place which do not arise inevitably from character and motive. And the characters themselves are not, in the fullest sense, people. They are almost all 'flat' characters in the tradition of the comedy of humours, that useful though unsubtle theory based on the crude physiological psychology of the Middle Ages. The very language of the 'humours' tradition lingers on. Tom Jones's 'complexion' is referred to when his amorous exploits are under discussion. Mr Allworthy's name betrays the manner of his conception.

The point, here, is not that the 'humours' tradition is invalid but that it does not quite square with the larger claims of Fielding to present a true and realistic picture of 'human nature'. There is any amount of 'life' in *Tom Jones*, but it is not presented with any kind of consistency of convention. Some episodes are fully dramatic, developing through and out of their own internal potentialities, like the scene in which Sophia finds Tom in Lady Bellaston's room; others, like the muddles in the inn, are simply contrivances with no point beyond the exploitation of the farcical moment; others again, like Molly Seagrim's fracas in the churchyard, are realistic narrative which make up the larger panorama, but in which the reader is not at all closely involved. The characters, too, are conceived on various planes. Allworthy is almost an allegorical figure, scarcely individualised at all; Square and Thwackum are like ninepins, put up in order to be knocked down; Mrs Blifil is a realistic character, essentially a type, not presented in the round, but subtly observed; Tom himself and Squire Western are unsubtle but fully rounded figures; Partridge is a great deal larger than life, a creation conceived and introduced almost in terms of the later music-hall.

And yet for all this the novel has a unity and a pattern, which is something beyond the artificial unity of its carefully contrived but entirely non-symbolic plot.

Tom Jones is a panoramic commentary on England in 1745, and it is also the story of Tom Jones and Sophia Western. And what engages our sympathy in that story is (oddly enough, one might suppose, for the two books are otherwise quite dissimilar), just what engaged our sympathy on behalf of Clarissa. Tom and Sophia, like Clarissa, are rebels, revolting against the respectably accepted domestic standards of eighteenth-century society. By such standards Sophia should obey her father and Tom should be, what Blifil thinks him, an illegitimate upstart who ought to be put firmly in his place.

Now it is true that, for the purposes of the plot (and to placate conventional taste), Fielding makes Tom a gentleman after all; but that is not really important. What does matter, because the whole movement and texture of the book depend on it, is that Tom and Sophia fight conventional society, embodied in the character of Blifil. They fight with every stratagem, including, when necessary, fists and swords and pistols. Unlike Clarissa, they are not passive in their struggle, and that is why *Tom Jones* is not a tragedy but comedy. It is not the conventionally contrived happy ending but the confidence we feel throughout the book that Tom and Sophia can and will grapple with their situation and change it that gains our acceptance of Fielding's comic view of life. It is, of course, no real contradiction that the same reader who is convinced by the tragedy of Clarissa should also be convinced by the comedy of *Tom Jones*. Tragedy and comedy, even in the same situation, are not mutually exclusive.

The struggle of Tom and Sophia against Blifil and all that he stands for is at the very centre of the novel. It is neither Allworthy, whose standards are shown to be wanting but who is genuinely deceived, nor the superbly presented old idiot, Squire Western, who is the villain of *Tom Jones*, but Blifil. Indeed, it is the particular weakness of both Allworthy and Western that they are taken in by Blifil, whom they accept at his face value. Blifil, 'sober, discreet and pious', is in fact treacherous, lecherous, hypocritical and entirely self-seeking. From the moment he betrays Black George, whom Tom has protected with an admirable lie, we know what Blifil is like. He is for ever on the side of conventional respectability, the friend (significantly) of both Square and Thwackum, despite their mutual (and logical) incompatibility. And when his fell schemes—centring as they do upon the orthodox ruling-class concern with property and a 'good' marriage—are defeated, Fielding's description of him is significant:

He cast himself on his bed, where he lay abandoning himself to despair, and drowned in tears; not in such tears as flow from contrition, and wash away guilt from minds which have been seduced or surprised into it unawares, against the bent of their dispositions, as will sometimes happen from human frailty, even to the good; no, these tears were such as the frighted thief sheds in his cast, and are indeed the effect of that concern which the most savage natures are seldom deficient in feeling for themselves.

Inevitably our minds are carried back to *Jonathan Wild*, and it is not by a casual stroke. It is relevant to recall that the weakness of *Jonathan Wild* lies in Heartfree; the strength of *Tom Jones* lies to a high degree in Tom. For Tom, unlike Heartfree, *is* able to carry the positive values of Fielding's world. Unlike Heartfree, he is not afraid to fight, if necessary to tell lies. He has all the vigour and spirit that Heartfree lacks. In him Fielding's positives—the values of the open heart—become more concrete and more fully realised. In Tom the prevailing positive is spontaneity: he acts 'naturally' and therefore the excesses into which his animal spirits lead him are forgiven. There is an interesting link here with that recurring eighteenth-century figure, the noble savage (glimpsed by Mrs Heartfree in Africa), a personage who becomes in time (Mrs Inchbald's *Nature and Art* is a link here) the 'natural man' of Rousseau and the Romantics.

The 'natural man' (descending from a 'golden age') and the 'noble savage' are of course sentimental idealisations, but they play nevertheless an important part in the struggle of eighteenth-century man to free himself from the limitations of mechanical materialism and the consequences of class society. They are vigorous concepts because they oppose the static world-view of the eighteenth-century ruling class. Their strength lies in their revolutionary assertion of the capacity of human nature to change itself and the world; their weakness lies in the idealist nature of that assertion.

Now the strengths and weaknesses of Fielding's conception of Tom Jones have precisely these same qualities. The strength lies in the vigour and spontaneity of Tom's reactions; the weakness in the element of idealism implicit in Fielding's simple confidence in the values of the heart. After all, is not Tom just a little too ready to wash his hands of Molly Seagrim and does not the inadequacy here spring from an unwillingness to evaluate the morality of spontaneity within the bounds of a particular social situation? More important, can one happy marriage really justify a world in which the Blifils rule the roost? Are the weapons of Tom and Sophia weapons enough?

It is, nevertheless, the central story of Tom and Sophia that best expresses in concrete form the view of life which Fielding is concerned to encompass in his novel (or, perhaps one should say that it is from the effect on us of the story of Tom and Sophia that we are best able to judge the nature and validity of Fielding's view of life). Yet we do not get very close to Tom and Sophia. Fielding deliberately keeps them at a distance. The ironical opening description of Sophia[19] is really a way of *not* describing her. And later in the novel Fielding writes of his heroine:

> As to the present situation of her mind, I shall adhere to a rule of Horace, by not attempting to describe it, from despair of success. Most of my readers will suggest it easily to themselves; and the few who cannot, would not understand the picture, or at least would deny it to be natural, if ever so well drawn.'[20]

Now this deliberate refusal to bring us really close to his characters, so that all the time he tends to describe rather than convey a situation, cannot just be dismissed as a failure in Fielding's art. On the contrary it is essential to his comic method. He asks that the reader should survey life rather than experience it. And so he tends always to approach the particular situation through the general comment. Hence the quality of his style,* brimming with abstract nouns which generalise the narrative, remove the particular emotion to a distance and yet—because Fielding's own social attitudes (and therefore his language) are so secure and confident—evoke a

---

* e.g. 'Matrimony, therefore, having removed all such motives, he grew weary of this condescension, and began to treat the opinions of his wife with that haughtiness and insolence which none but those who deserve some contempt can bestow, and those only who deserve no contempt can bear.' (Book II, ch. VII)

response remarkably precise and controlled though not, of course, intimate. It is with English society at large, not with the precise quality of feeling of individual characters, that he is primarily concerned. And between this large panorama, this general interest, and ourselves Fielding himself stands (larger, more insistent than any of his creations) directing our attention, controlling our reactions, imposing the pattern. Henry James, of all novelists perhaps the furthest removed from Fielding in method and outlook, has admirably made the essential point:

It is very true that Fielding's hero in *Tom Jones* is but as 'finely', that is as intimately, bewildered as a young man of great health and spirits may be when he hasn't a grain of imagination: the point to be made is, at all events, that his sense of bewilderment obtains altogether on the comic, never on the tragic plane. He has so much 'life' that it amounts, for the effect of comedy and application of satire, almost to his having a mind, that is to his having reactions and a full consciousness; besides which his author—*he* handsomely possessed of a mind—has such an amplitude of reflection for him and round him that we see him through the mellow air of Fielding's fine old moralism, fine old humour and fine old style, which somehow really enlarge, make everyone and everything important.[21]

LAURENCE STERNE

Tristram Shandy (published between 1759 and 1767) is so individual and, in many respects, so eccentric a work, that one might suppose it to have no integral place in the development of the art of the novel. It is true that in few other novels does the hero take three volumes to be born or is finally abandoned before the age of adolescence; but, then, few other novels have as one of their chief subjects the pre- and post-natal influences which are to determine the character of the central personage (though it is as reasonable a theme for a novel as any). It is true also that in few other novels— at any rate until the twentieth century—do digressions form the major part of the narrative; but, then, to refer to Sterne's method as digressive is—as he himself insists[22]—to miss much of the point of the book. *Tristram Shandy* is not without plan. The digressions cannot indeed be separated from the progression. And if the progression is wayward, perverse, frustrating, so—Sterne is insisting— is life itself, or at least the particular side of life he is concerned with.

Nor is *Tristram Shandy* so far outside the eighteenth-century tradition (if the word can yet be applied to a body of work so experimental and tentative) of fiction as may at first appear. Sterne's

debt to Rabelais is as clear as Fielding's to Cervantes, though it will
immediately be admitted that his tone is very different and (with
its tendency to the snigger) a good deal less virile. This aspect of
Sterne—the garrulous social-climber trying his best to come to
terms with aristocratic society—I do not propose to discuss: it is
there and a great deal has been made of it; but it should not distract
us from the real charm and value of his work. The principal theme
of *Tristram Shandy*, as Mr Jefferson has put it, 'may be seen in
terms of a comic clash between the world of learning and that of
human affairs'.* The relation (a conscious debt is not implied) to
Joseph Andrews and thence *Don Quixote* does not need to be
stressed. Mr Shandy's obsession with abstract learning—metaphysical, legal, physiological, philological—and Uncle Toby's
hobby-horse—military science—are in the line of Quixote's
chivalry and Parson Adams' absorption in the classics. And they
take a similar significance in the pattern of Sterne's book: they are
for ever at odds with reality.

Mr Jefferson has pointed out how, at every point in *Tristram
Shandy*, the misfortunes which are to determine Tristram's future
are either the actual consequences of the hobby-horses or else
derive from hard facts which fly direct in the face of Mr Shandy's
darling theories. At the very moment of begetting, Mr Shandy's
physical and metaphysical assurance is scattered by his wife's
practical question about the winding of the clock. It is a pedantic
legalism which leads to Tristram's being born in the country, hence
to Dr Slop, hence to the tragedy of his nose. Through the cussed-
ness of life Mr Shandy's elaborate theory of names comes to naught
—Tristram is the worst of all possible names. And the fall of the
sash-window, due to Uncle Toby's need (satisfied all too diligently
by the faithful Trim) for lead for his miniature field-pieces, is not
merely another ghastly blow at the hopes of the young hero but
adds a special piquancy to the *Tristapaedia* and to Mr Shandy's
researches (involving a full investigation into the wardrobe of the
ancients) on the question of breeches.

Now the pedantic learning which is thus the butt and indeed the
perverse driving-force of *Tristram Shandy* is not just *any* learning,
any concern with theory. It is true that part of the effect of the book
could be got by any contrast at all between theory and practice, that
one of the levels of its appeal is in its sense of the waywardness of

* I should like to express my particular debt, in this section, to conversations with
Mr D. W. Jefferson as well as to his essay on 'Tristram Shandy and the Tradition of
Learned Wit' (*Essays in Criticism*, Vol. I, no. 3).

life, the difficulty of theorising adequately about anything so complex as the countless facts of actual existence; but Sterne's book depends in the end very little on generalisations; it is only with some difficulty that we abstract the principles behind it. Thus to describe it as a satire on the theme of the conflict between theory and practice, though true enough in a way, does not adequately convey its basic quality which is very concrete and particular.

For Sterne's 'world of learning' is not simply, as has sometimes been assumed, the philosophical works of Locke and the eighteenth-century Enlightenment. No doubt Sterne, soaked as he was in Locke, did exploit, and most effectively, the Lockean theory of association. It is possible to see this theory as the principle underlying not only the digressions of *Tristram Shandy* but a great deal of modern 'stream of consciousness' literature. But to over-simplify Sterne's debt to Locke is to risk missing much of the point of his book, for there is in *Tristram Shandy* a continuous and subtle tension between what might be described as eighteenth-century common-sense enlightenment and the old scholastic tradition of the medieval world.

The jokes in *Tristram Shandy* are only thinkable, or indeed comprehensible, in relation to the scholastic tradition. The reason for this lies in the intellectual habits of the pre-scientific epoch. Whitehead has described the later phase of scholastic thought as one of 'unbridled rationalism', referring to its freedom in abstract speculation uncurbed by the discipline later imposed by the scientific method. Scholastic wit, as exemplified in some parts of Rabelais and in the more strictly metaphysical poems of Donne, exploits this freedom, learned ideas being ingeniously applied to unwonted ends. Sterne is essentially in this tradition (and so is the Swift of *A Tale of a Tub*) in so far as the flexible handling of ideas in the interests of wit is one of its main characteristics—a point that should not be obscured by the fact that the ideas are not all scholastic, but include those of the new scientists and philosophers. He differs in spirit from most of the other writers of the eighteenth century who were influenced by Locke—and from Locke himself—in that he sees in his ideas an opportunity for a play of fancy.

Under the old régime of learning, as illustrated by the work of Sir Thomas Browne, there was no problem in the universe which the erudite amateur might not tackle, reasoning from abstract principles and citing hosts of traditional authorities which are usually impressively listed. It would be a mistake to suppose that this mentality vanished with the first generation or two of the new

science. Mr Shandy, who is its very incarnation, represents what
was certainly old-fashioned but not quite dead in the middle of the
eighteenth century. Sterne was writing of mental habits which,
with all their extravagance, were humanly familiar to him. That is
why there is nothing arid about *Tristram Shandy*. We feel the force
of the hobby-horses at the same time as we feel their absurdity.
Like all good satirists Sterne has, on a certain level, the deepest
sympathy for and indeed participates in the attitudes he is satirising.

This then is one aspect of *Tristram Shandy*—this satirical
examination of an outworn mode of thinking—that reveals Sterne's
novel not as a mere idiosyncratic curiosity but as anti-romance, a
contribution towards a more realistic and satisfying literature. And
closely bound up with this is Sterne's success in catching certain
subtleties of human experience which had eluded previous novelists.
This success will best be illustrated by a quotation—the arrival
belowstairs of the news of the death of Master Bobby:

——My young master in *London* is dead! said *Obadiah*. ——A green
sattin night-gown of my mother's which had been twice scoured, was
the first idea which *Obadiah's* exclamation brought into *Susannah's* head.
—Well might *Locke* write a chapter upon the imperfection of words.—
Then, quoth *Susannah*, we must all go into mourning.—But note a
second time: the word *mourning*, notwithstanding *Susannah* made use of
it herself—failed also of doing its office; it excited not one single idea,
tinged either with grey or black,—all was green.——The green sattin
night-gown hung there still.

——O! 'twill be the death of my poor mistress, cried *Susannah*.—My
mother's whole wardrobe followed.—What a procession! her red
damask,—her orange tawney,—her white and yellow lutestrings,—her
brown taffata,—her bone-laced caps, her bedgowns, and comfortable
under-petticoats.—Not a rag was left behind.—*No,—she will never look
up again*, said *Susannah*.

We had a fat, foolish scullion—my father, I think, kept her for her
simplicity;—she had been all autumn struggling with a dropsy.—He is
dead, said *Obadiah*,—he is certainly dead!—So am not I, said the foolish
scullion.

——Here is sad news, *Trim*, cried *Susannah*, wiping her eyes as *Trim*
stepp'd into the kitchen,—master *Bobby* is dead and *buried*—the funeral
was an interpolation of *Susannah's*—we shall have all to go into
mourning, said *Susannah*.

I hope not, said *Trim*.—You hope not! cried *Susannah* earnestly.—
The mourning ran not in *Trim's* head, whatever it did in *Susannah's*.—I
hope—said *Trim*, explaining himself, I hope in God the news is not true.
—I heard the letter read with my own ears, answered *Obadiah*; and we

shall have a terrible piece of work of it in stubbing the Ox-moor.—Oh!
he's dead, said *Susannah*.—As sure, said the scullion, as I'm alive.
   I lament for him from my heart and my soul, said *Trim*, fetching a
sigh.—Poor creature!—poor boy!—poor gentleman.
   ——He was alive last *Whitsontide*! said the coachman.—*Whitsontide*!
alas! cried *Trim*, extending his right arm, and falling instantly into the
same attitude in which he read the sermon,—what is *Whitsontide*,
Jonathan (for that was the coachman's name), or *Shrovetide*, or any tide
or time past, to this? Are we not here now, continued the corporal
(striking the end of his stick perpendicularly upon the floor, so as to give
an idea of health and stability)—and are we not—(dropping his hat upon
the ground) gone in a moment!—'Twas infinitely striking! *Susannah*
burst into a flood of tears.—We are not stocks and stones.—*Jonathan*,
Obadiah, the cook-maid, all melted.—The foolish fat scullion herself,
who was scouring a fish-kettle upon her knees, was rous'd with it.—The
whole kitchen crowded about the corporal.[23]

This is not merely brilliant comic drama, very much of a *scene* with
the simultaneous actions and reactions of several characters contrasted, grouped, individualised and, at the same time, brought
together interpenetrating; it does things which the stage cannot
ever do. That green satin night-gown is beyond the reach of the
theatre or of Defoe or Fielding. With it (and it is only one trivial
example of the kind of thing Sterne is for ever achieving) new
potentialities in the art of the novel appear. The assumption, implicit in Fielding, that it is possible to describe a character in two-
dimensional terms, in *Tristram Shandy* is questioned. Sterne, in his
sense of the unpredictable quality in life, sees the texture of experience as something more subtle, more complex, less easily to be
captured than his predecessors—Richardson included—had revealed. The resources of language are explored with a new precision and a new adventurousness (the ghost of Rabelais presiding):
the ambiguity of words, the daring invention, the sentence that dies
away as you raise your voice, 'What prodigious armies you had in
Flanders!'
   Too high a claim must not be made. Many of the felicities of
Tristram Shandy are mere gestures, hints as to future insights.
There is too much in the book that is perverse and too much that
is trivial. But it is a great book nevertheless, a book whose detail
one can continually relish even though the total effect is less than
satisfying. And it is a book which vastly and intricately extended
the scope and possibilities of the English novel.

PART III

The Nineteenth Century

(to George Eliot)

I

INTRODUCTION

To say that Jane Austen is the last of the eighteenth-century novelists is to indicate something beyond the 'classicism' of her style. Jane Austen belongs to the eighteenth century in that her world is still the world established by the English revolution of the seventeenth century. Professor George Lukács in his *Studies in European Realism* has remarked:

> The great English novelists of the eighteenth century lived in a *post-revolutionary* period, and this gives their works an atmosphere of stability and security and also a certain complacent shortsightedness.[1]

This atmosphere of stability and security Jane Austen emphatically shares. The impulse of realism which permeates her novels is an extension, a refinement of that impulse of controlled and objective curiosity which we have noticed as a by-product of the bourgeois revolution and the underlying characteristic of the eighteenth-century novel.

But by the time of Jane Austen the eighteenth-century world—that apparently secure society ruled by a self-consciously enlightened alliance of landed aristocrat and commercial gentleman—that world is almost gone. The industrial revolution is under way and a new and immensely powerful class—that of the industrial capitalists—is in the ascendancy. And the world of the nineteenth century is a world infinitely less amicable to art of any kind than the eighteenth-century world.

It is important, if we are to understand the nature of the literature of the era, to emphasise how bitterly the Mr Bounderbys, who played so vital a part in shaping the Victorian world, were opposed to art and how conscientiously they strove to degrade it. From the utilitarians who preferred pushpin to poetry to the hard-faced men whom Keynes watched negotiating the Treaty of Versailles, the industrial bourgeoisie as a class (one does not forget of course enlightened individuals struggling against the current) hated and feared the implications of any artistic effort of realism and integrity. And throughout the century, from the days of Shelley's Castlereagh through those of Dickens's Gradgrind to the triumph of Matthew Arnold's Philistines, honest writers were bound to feel a deep revulsion against the underlying principles and the warped relationships of the society they lived in.

It is for this reason that, after Jane Austen, the great novels of the nineteenth century are all, in their differing ways, novels of revolt. The task of the novelists was the same as it had always been—to achieve realism, to express (with whatever innovations of form and structure they needs must discover) the truth about life as it faced them. But to do this, to cut through the whole complex structure of inhumanity and false feeling that ate into the consciousness of the capitalist world, it was necessary to become a rebel.

Much of the literary rebellion of the nineteenth century was of a purely individualistic and practically ineffective kind. Those in authority encouraged indirectly and by implication the view of the artist as crank, knowing well enough that garret deaths, Bohemian dissipation and art for art's sake, while charged with a certain seductive glamour, would leave the fundamental structure of their society untouched save for a few rude pictures on the wall. Hence the degrading of art by the 'arbiters of taste' into a nice mixture of neurosis and prettiness, the poetry of Swinburne, the novels of Mrs Henry Wood. Inferior art was elevated; great work treated in a way that shrouded its greatness. Dickens became a creator of juicy 'characters', *Wuthering Heights* a romantic love idyll.

The great novelists were rebels, and the measure of their greatness is found in the last analysis to correspond with the degree and consistency of their rebellion. It was not of course always a conscious, intellectualised rebellion; very seldom was it based on anything like a sociological analysis. It was, rather, a rebellion of the spirit, of the total consciousness, and it was often only indirectly reflected in the lives the writers led. Emily Brontë, Henry James and Joseph Conrad, outwardly appearing to conform to the accepted standards of their day, sensed no less profoundly than the more radical Dickens and George Eliot and Samuel Butler the degradation of human existence in Victorian society. In a moving letter written on the day after the outbreak of the First World War (the day the nineteenth century as a social era ended) the tired and elderly Henry James, very much the upper-middle-class gentleman in his habits of life and thought, wrote (in his most deeply tortured manner):

How can what is going on not be to one as a huge horror of blackness? . . . The plunge of civilisation into this abyss of blood and darkness by the wanton feat of those two infamous autocrats is a thing that so gives away the whole long age during which we have supposed to world to be, with whatever abatement, gradually bettering, that to have to take it all now for what the treacherous years were all the while really making for and *meaning* is too tragic for any words.[2]

The section that follows does not claim, of course, to deal fully or adequately with the nineteenth-century English novel. Historically interesting figures like Bulwer Lytton and Meredith are left out altogether. And one would have liked the space to demonstrate for instance, why Trollope is an inferior writer to, say, George Eliot. In the essays that follow the attempt is made to evaluate the particular qualities of a number of separate novels and to suggest the direction of some of the contributions of their authors to the art of fiction. Against the background I have indicated the novels will not, I hope, seem so separate and isolated as might at first appear. They are linked, not easily or crudely, by history and by the struggles of the individual novelists, themselves characters in history, to mould out of the accumulated consciousness and tensions of their age an honest and vital art.

2

JANE AUSTEN: *EMMA*

(1816)

My strong point is those little things which are more important than big ones, because they make up life. It seems that big ones do not do that, and I daresay it is fortunate. . . . I. COMPTON-BURNETT: *A Family and a Fortune*

The subject of *Emma* is marriage. Put that way the statement seems ludicrously inadequate, for *Emma*—we instinctively feel—is not about anything that can be put into one word. And yet it is as well to begin by insisting that this novel does have a subject. There is no longer, especially after Mrs Leavis's articles,[1] any excuse for thinking of Jane Austen as an untutored genius or even as a kind aunt with a flair for telling stories that have somehow or other continued to charm. She was a serious and conscious writer, absorbed in her art, wrestling with its problems. Casting and recasting her material, transferring whole novels from letter to narrative form, storing her subject-matter with meticulous economy, she had the great artist's concern with form and presentation. There is nothing soft about her.*

Emma* is about marriage. It begins with one marriage, that of Miss Taylor, ends with three more and considers two others by the way. The subject is marriage; but not marriage in the abstract. There is nothing of the moral fable here; indeed it is impossible to conceive of the subject except in its concrete expression, which is the plot. If, then, one insists that the subject of *Emma* is important it is not in order to suggest that the novel can be read in the terms of *Jonathan Wild*, but rather to counteract the tendency to treat

---

* Mrs Leavis has emphasised, too, how strong a part in Jane Austen's novels is played by her conscious war on the romance. She did to the romance of her day (whether the domestic romance of Fanny Burney or the Gothic brand of Mrs Radcliffe) what Cervantes had done in his. *Pride and Prejudice* is as much an anti-*Cecilia* as *Northanger Abbey* is an anti-*Udolpho*.

plot or story as self-sufficient. If it is not quite adequate to say that *Emma* is about marriage it is also not adequate to say it is about Emma.

The concrete quality of the book, that is what has to be emphasised. We have no basic doubts about *Emma*. It is there, a living organism, and it survives in the vibrations of its own being. In *Clarissa* time and again our attention is shifted in a particular direction not because it *must* be so directed but because Richardson wishes to give his reader an 'exquisite sensation'; in *Tom Jones* the happenings are too often contrived, so that we sense Fielding's presence behind the scenes, pulling a string. But *Emma* lives with the inevitable, interlocking logic of life itself; no part of it is separable from any other part. Even those episodes of the plot which seem at first mere contrivances to arouse a little suspense and keep the story going (such as the mystery of the pianoforte, Jane's letters at the post office, the confusion as to whether Harriet referred to Mr Knightley or to Frank Churchill), such passages all have a more important purpose. They reveal character, or they fail to reveal it. This latter function is subtle and important.

Jane Austen, like Henry James, is fascinated by the complexities of personal relationships. What is a character *really* like? Is Frank Churchill *really* a bounder? She conveys the doubt, not in order to trick, but in order to deepen. The more complex characters in *Emma*, like people in life, reveal themselves gradually and not without surprises. Putting aside for the moment certain minor faults which we will return to, it is not an exaggeration to say that *Emma* is as convincing as our own lives and has the same kind of concreteness.

It is for this reason that the subject of *Emma*, its generalised significance, is not easily or even usefully abstracted from the story. Just as in real life 'marriage' (except when we are considering it in a very theoretical and probably not very helpful way) is not a problem we abstract from the marriages we know, so marriage in *Emma* is thought of entirely in terms of actual and particular personal relationships. If we learn more about marriage in general from Jane Austen's novel it is because we have learned more—that is to say experienced more—about particular marriages. We do, in fact, in reading *Emma* thus enrich our experience. We become extremely closely involved in the world of Hartfield so that we experience the precise quality of, say, Mr Woodhouse's affection for his daughters, or Harriet's embarrassment at meeting the Martins in the draper's. When Emma is rude to Miss Bates on Box Hill we *feel* the flush rise to Miss Bates's cheek.

The intensity of Jane Austen's novels is inseparable from their concreteness and this intensity must be stressed because it is so different from the charming and cosy qualities with which these novels are often associated. Reading *Emma* is a delightful experience but it is not a soothing one. On the contrary our faculties are aroused, we are called upon to participate in life with an awareness, a fineness of feeling and a moral concern more intense than most of us normally bring to our everyday experiences. Everything matters in *Emma*. When Frank Churchill postpones his first visit to Randalls it matters less finely to Mr Weston than to his wife, but the reader gauges precisely the difference in the two reactions and not only appreciates them both but makes a judgment about them. We do not 'lose ourselves' in *Emma* unless we are the kind of people who lose ourselves in life. For all the closeness of our participation we remain independent.

Jane Austen does not demand (as Richardson tends to) that our subjective involvement should prejudice our objective judgment. On the contrary a valid objective judgment is made possible just because we have been so intimately involved in the actual experience. This seems to me a very valuable state of mind. How can we presume to pass judgment on the Emma Woodhouses of the world unless we have known them, and how can we valuably know them without bringing to bear our critical intelligence?

Because the critical intelligence is everywhere involved, because we are asked continuously, though not crudely, to judge what we are seeing, the prevailing interest in *Emma* is not one of mere 'aesthetic' delight but a moral interest. And because Jane Austen is the least theoretical of novelists, the least interested in Life as opposed to living, her ability to involve us intensely in her scene and people is absolutely inseparable from her moral concern. The moral is never spread on top; it is bound up always in the quality of feeling evoked.

Even when a moral conclusion is stated explicitly, as Mr Knightley states it after the Box Hill incident or while he reads Frank Churchill's letter of explanation, its force will depend not on its abstract 'correctness' but on the emotional conviction it carries, involving of course our already acquired confidence in Mr Knightley's judgment and character. Some of Mr Knightley's remarks, out of their context, might seem quite intolerably sententious.

'My Emma, does not everything serve to prove more and more the beauty of truth and sincerity in all our dealings with one another?'[2]

The sentiment, abstracted, might serve for the conclusion of one of Hannah More's moral tales. In fact, in the novel, it is a moment of great beauty, backed as it is (even out of context the 'my Emma' may reveal something of the quality) by a depth of feeling totally convincing.

How does Jane Austen succeed in thus combining intensity with precision, emotional involvement with objective judgment? Part of the answer lies, I think, in her almost complete lack of idealism, the delicate and unpretentious materialism of her outlook. Her judgment is based never on some high-falutin irrelevancy but always on the actual facts and aspirations of her scene and people. The clarity of her social observation (the Highbury world is scrupulously seen and analysed down to the exact incomes of its inmates) is matched by the precision of her social judgments and all her judgments are, in the broadest sense, social. Human happiness not abstract principle is her concern. Such precision—it is both her incomparable strength and her ultimate limitation—is unimaginable except in an extraordinarily stable corner of society. The precision of her standards emerges in her style. Each word—'elegance', 'humour', 'temper', 'ease'—has a precise unambiguous meaning based on a social usage at once subtle and stable. Emma is considering her first view of Mrs Elton:

> She did not really like her. She would not be in a hurry to find fault, but she suspected that there was no elegance;—ease, but no elegance— she was almost sure that for a young woman, a stranger, a bride, there was too much ease. Her person was rather good; her face not unpretty; but neither feature, nor air, nor voice, nor manner, were elegant. Emma thought at least it would turn out so.[3]

The exquisite clarity, the sureness of touch, of Jane Austen's prose cannot be recaptured because in a different and quickly changing society the same sureness of values cannot exist.

But to emphasise the stability and, inevitably too, the narrowness of Jane Austen's society may lead us to a rather narrow and mechanical view of the novels. *Emma* is *not* a period-piece. It is *not* what is sometimes called a 'comedy of manners'. We read it not just to illuminate the past, but also the present. And we must here face in both its crudity and its importance the question: exactly what relevance and helpfulness does *Emma* have for us today? In what sense does a novel dealing (admittedly with great skill and realism) with a society and its standards dead and gone for ever

have value in our very different world today? The question itself—
stated in such terms—is not satisfactory. If *Emma* today captures
our imagination and engages our sympathies (as in fact it does)
then either it has some genuine value for us or else there is something wrong with the way we give our sympathy and our values
are pretty useless.

Put this way, it is clear that anyone who enjoys *Emma* and then
remarks 'but of course it has no relevance today' is in fact debasing
the novel, looking at it not as the living work of art which he has
just enjoyed, but as something he does not even think it is—a mere
dead picture of a past society. Such an attitude is fatal both to art
and to life. The more helpful approach is to enquire why it is that
this novel does in fact still have the power to move us today.

One has the space only to suggest one or two lines of consideration. The question has, I hope, been partly answered already.
An extension of human sympathy and understanding is never
irrelevant and the world of *Emma* is not presented to us (at any
rate in its detail) with complacency. Emma faced (Vol. I, ch. xvi)
with what she has done to Harriet, the whole humiliating horror of
it, or Emma finding—the words are not minced—that, save for her
feeling for Mr Knightley 'every other part of her mind was disgusting':[4] these are not insights calculated to decrease one's moral
awareness. And in none of the issues of conduct arising in the novel
is Jane Austen morally neutral. The intensity with which everything matters to us in *Emma* is the product of this lack of complacency, this passionate concern of Jane Austen for human values.
Emma is the heroine of this novel only in the sense that she is its
principal character and that it is through her consciousness that
the situations are revealed; she is no heroine in the conventional
sense. She is not merely spoilt and selfish, she is snobbish and
proud, and her snobbery leads her to inflict suffering that might
ruin happiness. She has, until her experience and her feeling for
Mr Knightley brings her to a fuller, more humane understanding,
an attitude to marriage typical of the ruling class. She sees human
relationships in terms of class snobbery and property qualifications:
Harriet, for the sake of social position, she would cheerfully hand
over to the wretched Elton and does in fact reduce to a humiliating
misery; her chief concern about Mr Knightley is that his estate
should be preserved for little Henry. It is only through her own
intimate experiences (which we share) that she comes to a more
critical and more fully human view.

The question of Jane Fairfax is relevant here. Many readers find her and her relationship with Frank Churchill less than fully convincing. Does she quite bear the full weight of admiration which clearly we are supposed to feel for her? If she is indeed the person she is intended to be, would she love Frank Churchill? Has not Jane Austen here failed, perhaps, completely to reconcile the character she has created and the plot and pattern to which she is committed?

I think it is worth pausing for a moment on these criticisms, in order to consider not only their justice (which can be fairly objectively tested by careful reading) but their relevance. May we not here be slipping into the undisciplined habit of judging a novel according to rather vague criteria of 'probability' or 'character'? We all know the old lady who doesn't like *Wuthering Heights* because it's so improbable and the old gentleman who reads Trollope for the characters (not to mention the 'Janeites' whose chief interest in *Emma* is to determine how many nursemaids Isabella Knightley brought with her to Hartfield); and we all know how unsatisfactory such criteria are when it comes to the point.

It is worth emphasising, therefore, that a just criticism of Jane Fairfax has nothing to do with the question of whether we should like to meet her at dinner or even whether we think she acted rightly or wrongly. Jane Fairfax is a character in a novel. We know nothing of her except what we gather in the course of the novel. What we learn while we read (and we learn, of course, more than mere 'facts'), is that, although unduly reserved (for reasons which when revealed make the fault pardonable), she is a young woman of singular refinement, and 'true elegance', a phrase carrying great significance ('elegance of mind' involves a genuine sensibility to human values as well as the more superficial refinements of polished manner). She is, moreover, especially singled out for commendation by Mr Knightley (whose judgment is recommended as invariably sound) and warmly liked (e.g. the very, very earnest shake of the hand) by Emma herself.

Now the critical question is whether the reader can be convinced that this Jane Fairfax would in fact play her essential part in the novel and marry Frank Churchill, a young man whose total quality is a good deal less than admirable. Many readers are not convinced. Are they right?

I think they are not right. It is true that Jane Fairfax is—we have been convinced—as good as she is clever and as clever as she is beautiful. But it is also true that Jane Fairfax is an unprovided woman with no prospects in life beyond those of earning her living

as governess at Mrs Smallridge's (and how well the nature of that
establishment has been revealed to us through Mrs Elton!) and
passing her hard-earned holidays with Miss Bates. The quality of
Jane's reaction to such a future has been clearly indicated:

'I am not at all afraid [she says to Mrs Elton] of being long unem-
ployed. There are places in town, offices, where enquiry would soon
produce something—Offices for the sale—not quite of human flesh—but
of human intellect.'
'Oh! my dear, human flesh! You quite shock me; if you mean a fling
at the slave-trade I assure you Mr Suckling was always rather a friend to
the abolition.'
'I did not mean, I was not thinking of the slave-trade,' replied Jane,
'governess-trade, I assure you, was all that I had in view; widely different
certainly as to the guilt of those who carry it on; but as to the greater
misery of the victims, I do not know where it lies. . . .'[5]

It is her horror of this alternative (notice the extraordinary force of
the word 'offices'; the sentence is broken in the sense of degradation) that those who are unconvinced by Jane's decision to marry
Frank Churchill have, I think, overlooked. Perhaps all this makes
Jane Fairfax less 'good' than Emma thought her; but it does not
make her less convincing to us. On the contrary a good deal of the
moral passion of the book, as of her other novels, does undoubtedly
arise from Jane Austen's understanding of and feeling about the
problems of women in her society. It is this realistic, unromantic
and indeed, by orthodox standards, subversive concern with the
position of women that gives the tang and force to her consideration of marriage. Jane Fairfax's marriage has not, indeed, been made
in heaven, and it is unlikely that Frank Churchill will turn out to be
an ideal husband; but is that not precisely Jane Austen's point?
    More vulnerable is the marrying-off of Harriet Smith and Robert
Martin. Here it is not the probability that is to be questioned but
the manner. The treatment is altogether too glib and the result is
to weaken the pattern of the novel. Since the experiences of Emma
—her blunders and romanticisms—are the core of the book, and
what most intimately illuminate the theme of marriage, it is essential to Jane Austen's plan that these experiences should be in no
way muffled or sentimentalised. We must feel the whole force of
them. The marriage of Harriet is presented in a way which does,
to some extent, sentimentalise. Emma is allowed too easy a way out
of her problem and the emotional force of the situation is thereby
weakened. The objection to too conventional a sense of happy

ending is not that it is happy (we do not question that) but that it is conventional and so lulls our feelings into accepting it too easily.

Sufficient has perhaps been said to suggest that what gives *Emma* its power to move us is the realism and depth of feeling behind Jane Austen's attitudes. She examines with a scrupulous yet passionate and critical precision the actual problems of her world. That this world is narrow cannot be denied. How far its narrowness matters is an important question.

Its *smallness* does not matter at all. There is no means of measuring importance by size. What is valuable in a work of art are the depth and truth of the experience it communicates, and such qualities cannot be identified with the breadth of the panorama. We may find out more about life in a railway carriage between Crewe and Manchester than in making a tour round the world. A conversation between two women in the butcher's queue may tell us more about a world war than a volume of despatches from the front. And when Emma says to Mr Knightley: 'Nobody, who has not been in the interior of a family, can say what the difficulties of any individual of that family may be,' she is dropping a valuable hint about Jane Austen's method. The silliest of all criticisms of Jane Austen is the one which blames her for not writing about the battle of Waterloo and the French Revolution. She wrote about what she understood and no artist can do more.

But did she understand enough? The question is not a silly one, for it must be recognised that her world was not merely small but narrow. Her novels are sometimes referred to as miniatures, but the analogy is not apt. We do not get from *Emma* a condensed and refined sense of a larger entity. Neither is it a symbolic work suggesting references far beyond its surface meaning. The limitations of the Hartfield world which are indeed those of Surrey in about 1814 are likely therefore to be reflected in the total impact of the novel.

Thel imitation and the narrowness of the Hartfield world are the limitations of class society. And the one important criticism of Jane Austen (we will suspend judgment for the moment on its truth) is that her vision is limited by her unquestioning acceptance of class society. That she did not write about the French Revolution or the Industrial Revolution is as irrelevant as that she did not write about the Holy Roman Empire; they were not her subjects. But Hartfield is her subject and no sensitive contemporary reader can fail to sense here an inadequacy (again, we will suspend judgment on its validity). It is necessary to insist, at this point, that the question at issue is not Jane Austen's failure to suggest a *solution* to the problem of class divisions but her apparent failure to notice the *existence* of the problem.

The values and standards of the Hartfield world are based on the assumption that it is right and proper for a minority of the community to live at the expense of the majority. No amount of sophistry can get away from this fact and to discuss the moral concern of Jane Austen without facing it would be hypocrisy. It is perfectly true that, within the assumptions of aristocratic society, the values recommended in *Emma* are sensitive enough. Snobbery, smugness, condescension, lack of consideration, unkindness of any description, are held up to our disdain. But the fundamental condescension, the basic unkindness which permits the sensitive values of *Emma* to be applicable only to one person in ten or twenty, is this not left unscathed? Is there not here a complacency which renders the hundred little incomplacencies almost irrelevant?

Now this charge, that the value of *Emma* is seriously limited by the class basis of Jane Austen's standards, cannot be ignored or written off as a non-literary issue. If the basic interest of the novel is indeed a moral interest, and if in the course of it we are called upon to re-examine and pass judgment on various aspects of human behaviour, then it can scarcely be considered irrelevant to face the question that the standards we are called upon to admire may be inseparably linked with a particular form of social organisation.

That the question is altogether irrelevant will be held, of course, by the steadily decreasing army of aesthetes. Those who try to divorce the values of art from those of life and consequently morality will not admit that the delight we find in reading *Emma* has in fact a moral basis. It is a position, I think, peculiarly hard to defend in the case of a Jane Austen novel, because of the obvious preoccupation of the novelist with social morality. If *Emma* is *not* concerned with the social values involved in and involving personal relationships (and especially marriage) it is difficult to imagine what it *is* about.

That the question though relevant is trivial will be held by those readers who consider class society either good or inevitable. Clearly to those who think aristocracy today a morally defensible form of society, and are prepared to accept (with whatever modifications and protestations of innocence) the inevitability of a cultural *élite* whose superior standards depend on a privileged social position based on the exploitation of their inferiors, clearly such readers will not feel that Jane Austen's acceptance of class society weakens or

limits her moral perspicacity. The suspicion that the true elegance
which Emma so values could not exist in Hartfield without the
condemnation to servility and poverty of hundreds of unnamed
(though not necessarily unpitied) human beings will not trouble
their minds as they admire the civilised sensibility of Jane Austen's
social standards. The position of such readers cannot of course be
objected to on logical grounds so long as all its implications are
accepted.

At the other extreme of critical attitudes will be found those
readers whose sense of the limitations of Jane Austen's social
consciousness makes it impossible for them to value the book at
all. How can I feel sympathy, such a reader will say, for characters
whom I see to be, for all their charm and politeness, parasites and
exploiters? How can I feel that the problems of such a society have
a relevance to me? Now if art were a matter of abstract morality it
would be impossible to argue against this puritan attitude; but in
truth it misses the most essential thing of all about *Emma*, that it
is a warm and living work of art. To reject *Emma* outright is to
reject the humanity in *Emma*, either to dismiss the delight and
involvement that we feel as we read it as an unfortunate aberration,
or else to render ourselves immune to its humanity by imposing
upon it an attitude narrower than itself.

More sophisticated than this philistine attitude to the problem is
that which will hold that *Emma* does indeed reflect the class basis
and limitations of Jane Austen's attitudes, but that this really does
not matter very much or seriously affect its value. This is a view,
plausible at first sight, held by a surprisingly large number of
readers who want to have their novel and yet eat it. Yes indeed,
such a reader will say, the moral basis of Jane Austen's novels is,
for us, warped by her acceptance of class society; her standards
obviously can't apply in a democratic society where the Emmas
and Knightleys would have to work for their living like anyone
else. But, after all, we must remember when Jane Austen was
writing; we must approach the novels with sympathy in their
historical context. Jane Austen, a genteel bourgeoise of the turn of
the eighteenth century, could scarcely be expected to analyse class
society in modern terms. We must make a certain allowance,
reading the book with a willing suspension of our own ideas and
prejudices.

This represents a view of literature which, behind an apparently
historical approach, debases and nullifies the effects of art. It invites us to read *Emma* not as a living, vital novel, relevant to our

own lives and problems, but as a dead historical 'document'. A work of art which has to be read in such a way is not a work of art. The very concept of 'making allowances' of this sort for an artist is both insulting and mechanical. It has something of the puritan's contempt for those who have not seen the light, but it lacks the puritan's moral courage, for it is accompanied by a determination not to be done out of what cannot be approved. The final result is generally to come to terms with the aesthetes. For if *Emma* is morally undesirable and yet Art, then Art can have little to do with morality and some new, necessarily idealist, criteria must be found.

It is important, I believe, to realise the weakness of this pseudo-historical view of *Emma*. If, in whatever century she happened to live, Jane Austen were indeed nothing but a genteel bourgeoise 'reflecting' the views of her day, she would not be a great artist and she could not have written *Emma*. The truth is that in so far as *Emma* does reveal her as a conventional member of her class, blindly accepting its position and ideology, the value of *Emma* is indeed limited, not just relatively, but objectively and always. But the truth is also that this is not the principal or most important revelation of *Emma*.

The limitation must not be ignored or glossed over. There can be no doubt that there *is* an inadequacy here, an element of complacency that does to some extent limit the value of *Emma*. The nature of the inadequacy is fairly illustrated by this description of Emma's visit, with Harriet, to a sick cottager.

They were now approaching the cottage, and all idle topics were superseded. Emma was very compassionate; and the distresses of the poor were as sure of relief from her personal attention and kindness, her counsel and her patience, as from her purse. She understood their ways, could allow for their ignorance and their temptations, had no romantic expectations of extraordinary virtue from those, for whom education had done so little, entered into their troubles with ready sympathy, and always gave her assistance with as much intelligence as good-will. In the present instance, it was sickness and poverty together which she came to visit; and after remaining there as long as she could give comfort or advice, she quitted the cottage with such an impression of the scene as made her say to Harriet, as they walked away——

'These are the sights, Harriet, to do one good. How trifling they make every thing else appear!—I feel now as if I could think of nothing but these poor creatures all the rest of the day; and yet who can say how soon it may all vanish from my mind?'

'Very true,' said Harriet. 'Poor creatures! one can think of nothing else.'

'And really, I do not think the impression will soon be over,' said Emma, as she crossed the low hedge and tottering doorstep which ended the narrow, slippery path through the cottage garden, and brought them into the lane again. 'I do not think it will,' stopping to look once more at all the outward wretchedness of the place, and recall the still greater within.

'Oh! dear no,' said her companion. They walked on. The lane made a slight bend; and when that bend was passed, Mr Elton was immediately in sight; and so near as to give Emma time only to say farther,

'Ah! Harriet, here comes a very sudden trial of our stability in good thoughts. Well (smiling), I hope it may be allowed that if compassion has produced exertion and relief to the sufferers, it has done all that is truly important. If we feel for the wretched, enough to do all we can for them, the rest is empty sympathy, only distressing to ourselves.'

Harriet could just answer. 'Oh! dear, yes,' before the gentleman joined them.[6]

Now there can be no doubt about the quality of the feeling here. Harriet's silly responses underline most potently the doubt that Emma herself feels as to the adequacy of her own actions. There can be no point in this passage (for it has no inevitable bearing on the plot) save to give a sense of the darker side of the moon, the aspect of Hartfield that will not be dealt with. And it does indeed to a great extent answer the doubt in the reader's mind that an essential side of the Hartfield world is being conveniently ignored. But the doubt is not entirely answered. After all, the important question is not whether Emma recognises the existence of the poor at Hartfield, but whether she recognises that her own position depends on their existence. 'Comfort or advice' moreover remain the positives in Emma's attitudes and one's doubts as to their sufficiency are in fact, like Emma's, swept away by the arrival of Mr Elton and the plot. The essential moral issue is shelved; and it is, in general, the supreme merit of Jane Austen, that essential moral issues are *not* shelved.

But that the inadequacy is not crippling the passage just quoted will also suggest. That final remark of Emma's is very significant. The parenthesised 'smiling' and the idiocy of Harriet's comment have the effect of throwing into doubt the whole aristocratic philosophy that Emma is expounding and that doubt, though it does not balance the shelving of the problem, does at least extenuate it. We are not wholly lulled.

Against the element of complacency other forces, too, are at work. We should not look merely to the few specific references to the poor to confirm our sense that the inadequacies of Jane Austen's social philosophy are overtopped by other, more positive vibrations. Among these positive forces are, as we have seen, her highly critical concern over the fate of women in her society, a concern which involves a reconsideration of its basic values. Positive also are her materialism and her unpretentiousness. If aristocracy is implicitly defended it is at least on rational grounds; no bogus philosophical sanctions are called in to preserve the *status quo* from reasonable examination. And no claim is made, explicit or implicit, that we are being presented with a revelation of a fundamental truth. Hartfield is offered to us as Hartfield, not as Life.

And this is ultimately, I think, the strength of *Emma*; this rejection of Life in favour of living, the actual, concrete problems of behaviour and sensibility in an actual, concrete society. It is Jane Austen's sensitive vitality, her genuine concern (based on so large an honesty) for human feelings in a concrete situation, that captures our imagination. It is this concern that gives her such delicate and precise insight into the problems of personal relationships (how will a group of individuals living together best get on, best find happiness?). And the concern does not stop at what, among the ruling class at Hartfield, is pleasant and easily solved.

It gives us glimpses of something Mr Woodhouse never dreamed of—the world outside the Hartfield world and yet inseparably bound up with it: the world Jane Fairfax saw in her vision of offices and into which Harriet in spite of (no, *because of*) Emma's patronage, was so nearly plunged: the world for which Jane Austen had no answer. It is this vital and unsentimental concern which defeats, to such a very large extent, the limitations. So that when we think back on *Emma* we do not think principally of the narrow inadequacies of Hartfield society but of the delight we have known in growing more intimately and wisely sensitive to the way men and women in a particular, given situation, work out their problems of living.

3

SCOTT: THE HEART OF MIDLOTHIAN

(1818)

Jane Austen, the literary histories tell us, is a 'Classical' writer; Scott a 'Romantic'. And certainly there are some very obvious differences between *Emma* and *The Heart of Midlothian*, though whether the conventional antithesis is very helpful is a matter for question.

It is worth glancing more than once at a passage (not in itself of very vital importance in the novel) towards the end of Scott's book:

> . . . she listened in placid silence; and whenever the point referred to common life, and was such as came under the grasp of a strong natural understanding, her views were more forcible, and her observations more acute, than his own. In acquired politeness of manners, when it happened that she mingled a little in society, Mrs Butler was, of course, judged deficient. But then she had that obvious wish to oblige, and that real and natural good-breeding depending on good sense and good-humour, which, joined to a considerable degree of archness and liveliness of manner, rendered her behaviour acceptable to all with whom she was called upon to associate. Notwithstanding her strict attention to all domestic affairs, she always appeared the clean well-dressed mistress of the house, never the sordid household drudge. . . .[1]

It would be hard to say, if one came upon these sentences out of their context, whether they had been written by Scott or by Jane Austen. The secure and confident rhythms, binding together words used with a precise social significance, belong to any humane yet aristocratic writer of the day. The ease and clarity of writing depend entirely on the precision with which each word is invested, a precision involving not only the thing looked at but the way of looking at it. 'Common life', 'a strong natural understanding', 'acquired politeness of manners', 'real and natural good-breeding', 'good sense and good humour', 'a considerable degree of archness and liveliness of manners', etc.: each phrase reflects an accepted and savoured way of life which forms a firm, confident basis to the writer's firm and confident point of view.

Let us now add to our quotation the sentences which flank it at either end and read the entire paragraph they form:

If he talked to Jeanie of what she did not understand,—and (for the man was mortal, and had been a schoolmaster) he sometimes did harangue more scholarly and wisely than was necessary,—she listened in placid silence: and whenever the point referred to common life, and was such as came under the grasp of a strong natural understanding, her views were more forcible, and her observations more acute, than his own. In acquired politeness of manners, when it happened that she mingled a little in society, Mrs Butler was, of course, judged deficient. But then she had that obvious wish to oblige, and that real and natural good-breeding depending on good sense and good-humour, which, joined to a considerable degree of archness and liveliness of manner, rendered her behaviour acceptable to all with whom she was called upon to associate. Notwithstanding her strict attention to all domestic affairs, she always appeared the clean well-dressed mistress of the house, never the sordid household drudge. When complimented on this occasion by Duncan Knock, who swore, 'that he thought the fairies must help her, since her house was always clean, and nobody ever saw anybody sweeping it,' she modestly replied, 'That much might be dune by timing ane's turns.'[2]

The paragraph (it will be generally agreed) could not be Jane Austen's. And the difference is not merely a matter of Jeanie's brogue in the last phrase. In the first sentence there are two moments at which we catch an accent that we have not found in *Emma*. The phrase in parenthesis ('for the man was mortal, etc.') is indicative. Implied in it is a breadth of reference to which Jane Austen does not aspire. 'Appraising the exact shade of mere mortal man with his many passions and his miserable ingenuity in error' (the expression is Conrad's) is not the kind of language one could use in writing of Jane Austen (she deals, as we have seen, with men not Man, with Hartfield not with mortality) even though the depth of her penetration is not necessarily any the less for that. But with Scott such terms of reference are at once appropriate, even though his performance may not necessarily satisfy all the claims they call up.

In the sentence under consideration there is implied, both in the words in parenthesis and the use of the adverb 'wisely', a broader worldliness, a loose (the irony is vague, not at all sharp and explicit) and hearty tolerance which takes us back to Fielding rather than to Jane Austen. While in the closing sentence of the paragraph, with its fairies and its dialect we are within a range of subject-matter which Jane Austen does not touch.

It is dangerous to judge a novel from a paragraph or even to use a short passage to demonstrate the peculiar quality of a particular writer; but the kind of examination which we have just been making has, nevertheless, its value. For it cannot be insisted too often that the basis for all literary judgments must be the actual words an author writes; and it is in the choice and arrangement of those words, carrying as they do the weight and illumination of his view of life, that the qualities of a novelist are revealed. And we shall find that the revelations of that single paragraph of *The Heart of Midlothian* give us a very fair start to our enquiry: in what ways does this novel differ from *Emma*, what is this element in Scott that it is usual to call Romantic?

Partly it is a question of subject-matter. The span of social life which Scott depicts is far broader than that of Jane Austen. Jeanie Deans is a peasant and speaks the language of the Lowland peasantry. The characters of *The Heart of Midlothian* range socially from the dregs of the criminal world to Queen Caroline herself and this range, wider than that of any eighteenth-century novel (even Fielding's), is important for it involves a series of relationships more complex (though not necessarily more intense) than any Jane Austen has to deal with. For Jane Austen's people, though their social positions may vary, all move within the same periphery, all share (though not with equal sensitiveness) the standards, social and spiritual, of the same class. And it is from this common acceptance, the common partaking from the same point of view of an identical cultural tradition, that both the discipline and the limitation of Jane Austen's art spring.

To have followed Jane Fairfax, for instance, to the offices where governesses are bought and sold, to have looked closely at the gypsies who frightened Harriet or even to have gone into the lives of the Martin family at the same level as she examines the Woodhouses, would have involved Jane Austen in technical and artistic problems of formidable dimensions, for it would necessarily have meant a shifting of her own point of vantage and view.

It is the range of his subject-matter which, more than anything

else, gives Scott's novels an epic quality. It is to do him less than
justice to call him a historical novelist, for he was not interested in
history for its own sake, or even primarily, as is sometimes asserted,
as an escape. But he had a remarkable sense of history, of the forces
which go to make a situation and lead individuals to act as they do.
Jeanie and Effie Deans are, in the profoundest, least artificial sense,
characters in history. As Mr V. S. Pritchett, in his very suggestive
essay on Scott, has said:

. . . Scott's strength in the handling of the situation between the two
women comes from his knowledge of the effect of history upon them.
They are children of history. And the one part of history Scott knew
inside out was its effect upon the conscience. Jeanie's refusal to tell a lie
had generations of Calvinistic quarrelling behind it, the vituperations of
the sectaries who had changed the sword of the clan wars and the civil
wars for the logic-chopping of theology. Instead of splitting skulls, they
had taken to splitting hairs. The comedies, the tragedies, the fantastic
eloquence and tedious reiteration of these scruples of conscience are
always brilliantly described by Scott, who has them in his blood. And so
Jeanie's refusal to lie and her journey to London on foot to seek her
sister's pardon were not the result of conceit, heartlessness or even
literalness of mind: they are the fruit of history. . . .[3]

We shall come back later to this point. My immediate concern
is to emphasise that the breadth of Scott's panorama and the depth
of it, the extra dimension achieved by his sense of history, make
inevitable certain fundamental differences from Jane Austen's
manner of writing. When he is describing (as in the first sentences
I quoted) a domestic scene within a prescribed social *milieu*, Scott
can write like Jane Austen. But when he has to portray vast clashes
of classes and ideas, when the Covenanting fanaticism of David
Deans comes into conflict with the commercial morality of Barto-
line Saddletree or the down-to-earth peasant realism of Jeanie meets
the romantic clan-born fantasy of Duncan Knock, there Jane
Austen's secure values cannot serve. Comment cannot be made
from within; the novelist must straddle history and Scotland. It is
a high ambition.

The Romantic movement in English literature coincides with
the transformation of Britain from the agricultural and commercial
country of Dr Johnson's day into 'the workshop of the world'. It
coincides with the Industrial Revolution at home and the French
Revolution abroad. It was (to simplify a very complicated question) the expression of the need of the British writers to come to

grips with the new world that the Industrial Revolution created. In this task the old secure standards of the eighteenth-century ruling class were inevitably insufficient. The old horizons were inadequate; a thousand new problems, new relationships, new ideas, came crowding in.

The writers whom we have come to see as belonging to the Romantic movement were men and women of widely differing attitudes to life and ways of writing. Wordsworth and Byron, Coleridge and Keats, Shelley and Scott have, when we come to look at their work, remarkably little in common in the way of positive achievement or philosophy. But they have this that links them together: each is responding in his particular way to the new situation brought about by the Industrial Revolution. They have differing philosophies, but they are all in revolt against the mechanical and undialectical materialism of the eighteenth-century philosophers and its later development, the utilitarianism of the theorists of industrial capitalism.

The Romantic movement was not a literary movement away from realism. On the contrary it was the aim of the Romantic writers to achieve a more significant, more inclusive realism than the conventions of aristocratic literature had permitted. They did not always succeed, for it was one thing to recognise the inadequacies of the class-bound standards of the 'classical' writers and quite another to achieve a satisfactory democratic art. For reasons which, from our point of vantage a hundred and fifty years on, it is not hard to understand, it was easier for the Romantic writers to sense that it was impossible for them to attach themselves any longer to the eighteenth-century tradition, than to discover a positive force upon which to base their work and aspirations. Hence the tendency of a good deal of Romantic literature to lose itself in vagueness and individualist frustration and to become in the end romantic in the pejorative sense.

Scott's Romanticism lies in his rejection of the eighteenth-century polite tradition and his attempt to write a literature of and for far broader sections of the people. In contrast to the 'Gothic' novelists like Mrs Radcliffe from whom technically he learned a good deal, Scott does not write exclusively from the point of view of the ruling class. There is an escapist, romantic element in all his books (particularly those dealing with the Middle Ages), but in his best novels—*Old Mortality*, *The Antiquary*, *The Heart of Midlothian*, the novels about eighteenth-century Scotland—he makes a serious attempt to capture realistically the strains and tensions of the experiences of the Scottish people. And what ultimately gives these books their strength is Scott's feeling for the plight and problems of the Lowland peasantry. It would not be true to say that they are written consistently from the point of view of the peasantry; in so far as Scott had a consistent conscious standpoint it was that of the paternalist landowner.

Like all the Romantic writers, he loathed the new capitalism, seeing the Industrial Revolution as destroying the old social ties which made in the old society if not for equality (he was no democrat) at least for a certain kindliness in human relationships. 'To Scott, as to Carlyle,' Professor Grierson has said in his admirable biography, 'the main source of the evil was the divorce of any tie between the employer and the labourer but the cash-nexus.'[4]

The reaction of Scott to the Industrial Revolution expressed itself often in an escape into a dream-world of medieval romance. Just how conscious in his mind was this contrast between an ugly present and an idealised past is shown by an interesting passage in the Introduction to *Chronicles of the Canongate*. He is describing Edinburgh and its surroundings as a background to the stories he is about to narrate:

> I think even the local situation of Little Croftangry may be considered as favourable to my undertaking. A nobler contrast there can hardly exist than that of the huge city, dark with the smoke of ages, and groaning with the various sounds of active industry or idle revel, and the lofty and craggy hill, silent and solitary as the grave, one exhibiting the full tide of existence, pressing and precipitating itself forward with the force of an inundation; the other resembling some time-worn anchorite, whose life passes as silent and unobserved as the slender rill which escapes unheard, and scarce seen, from the fountain of his patron saint. The city resembles the busy temple, where the modern Comus and Mammon hold their court, and thousands sacrifice ease, independence and virtue itself at their shrine; the misty and lonely mountain seems as a throne to the majestic but terrible genius of feudal times, when the same divinities dispensed coronets and domains to those who had heads to devise and arms to execute bold enterprises.[5]

The contrast could scarcely be clearer—the industrial city on the one hand, 'Nature' on the other, and 'Nature' identified with 'the majestic but terrible genius of feudal times'. The passage throws fascinating light on the whole of the 'Gothic' revolt against industrialism.

The Heart of Midlothian is concerned, in its first half, at any rate, with the very scene described in the *Chronicles of the Canongate*, but the story is set back eighty years—in 1736. And the atmosphere of the novel is realistic as opposed to romantic, although, as we shall see, it contains a number of romantic elements. It is one of Scott's most successful novels precisely because in it he manages to express his Romantic vision in realistic form, to encompass aspects of life which Jane Austen ignores and yet avoid for the most part the seductive escape into an idealised dream-world. How is it that Scott succeeds in this novel (despite weaknesses that we must examine) in responding to the liberating influences of Romanticism without losing himself (as he does, for instance, in *Ivanhoe*) in the world of romance?

The answer does not lie in his technical skill, the ability (that Mr E. M. Forster has emphasised) to tell a story. *Rob Roy* is as good a story as *The Heart of Midlothian*, but not as good a novel. Nor is it his interest in history or folk-lore, in the academic sense, that saves him. What gives *The Heart of Midlothian* its 'body', its solid sense of real life and real issues, is Scott's ability to see his subject from the point of view of the peasantry, a point of view with its own limitations but one that is nevertheless neither idealistic nor dishonest. The trouble with many of his novels (*Waverley*, for instance, and even *Old Mortality*), is that he limits their sense of integrity from the start by taking as his heroes and heroines ladies and gentlemen whose existence rests on activities and attitudes so trivial that they can produce no vital and gripping prose. In these novels one skips the stilted conversations of the main characters and is reconciled only by the liveliness of the incidentals. But in *The Heart of Midlothian* the Deanses are at the very centre of the book; Scott has something solid to work on.

It is a well-constructed novel, grouped effectively around its central situation, the trial of Effie Deans, with the black gallows as a central symbol throwing its shadow across the whole book. Is it merely a 'story', i.e. a consecutive narrative of interesting events held together by suspense? I do not think so. True, the plot is important, a bit too important, perhaps, for the use of so much coincidence gives a certain sense of artificiality. The ends are a little too neatly gathered; everyone is at the right place just a little too often. But these are not important faults; we should regard them rather as part of the convention in which the novel is written, a convention which has become rather old-fashioned but is by no means indefensible. The main point about the plot, however, is that it successfully serves and subordinates itself to the essential pattern of the book. That pattern is the consideration of the trial of Effie, the causes which bring it about and the consequences that follow from it. And the trial is seen not merely in sensational terms, not merely as a melodramatic incident well suited for an 'ado' which will wring our hearts, but as a significant event involving clashes of opposing cultures and differing values. In a word, it is seen in history.

On one level the clash is between country and town; it is when she goes to live in Edinburgh that temptation assails Effie. More deeply it is a conflict between the old peasant world of David Deans with its strict, fanatical, Covenanting morality and the world of the city 'where the modern Comus and Mammon hold their court', the world of successful rich and criminal poor, of slick lawyers and desperate smugglers, of well-to-do merchants and the City Guard. It is this world that seduces Effie, almost destroys her and then turns her into a great lady. And against it, in total contrast, is set the world of Jeanie and her father.

The sense of the personal story as a part of history which permeates the book is evoked at the very beginning, of course, in the chapters on the Porteous riots. The picture here of a sullen, determined, angry people is excellently done. It is done, one might say, on Scott's part with the maximum of research but the minimum of conscious understanding. We do not know, save in the vaguest terms, *why* the people are angry. We do not know *why* they behave with such disciplined fanaticism in the storming of the Tolbooth and the hanging of Porteous. Indeed, by reducing the whole riot to terms of the personal story of Robertson and Effie, Scott makes it almost impossible for himself to explain these things. And yet despite this he manages to convey a sense of the real conflict between people and City Guard and of the bitter hostility of the Scottish burghers to the alien English state, and it is this success that sets the whole tone and tenor of the novel. We know we are confronted here with something deeper, more interesting than the melodramatic story of a young blood's attempt (disguised as a woman) to rescue the girl he has ruined from jail. Indeed, if we did not know this we should be intolerably irritated by Effie's refusal to be rescued (she has no such compunction a few weeks later) and by her bold seducer's acceptance of that refusal (why on earth, on that level, didn't Robertson drag the silly girl away?).

The opening chapters of the novel underline, too, what is to be one of its fundamental themes, one of the principal strands of the pattern: the consideration of the values and validity of law. It is not by accident that the strangers whom Peter Patterson meets when the stage-coach overturns are lawyers, nor that the first conversation in the story proper turns on a point of law. The townsfolk who have been done out of Porteous's execution are indignant.

'An unco thing this, Mrs Howden,' said old Peter Plumdamas to his neighbour the rouping-wife, or saleswoman, as he offered her his arm to assist her in the toilsome ascent, 'to see the grit folk at Lunnon set their face against law and gospel, and let loose sic a reprobate as Porteous upon a peaceable town!'

'And to think o' the weary walk they hae gien us,' answered Mrs Howden, with a groan; 'and sic a comfortable window as I had gotten, too, just within a penny-stane-cast of the scaffold—I could hae heard every word the minister said—and to pay twalpennies for my stand, and a' for naething!'

'I am judging,' said Mr Plumdamas, 'that this reprieve wadna stand gude in the auld Scots law, when the kingdom *was* a kingdom.'

'I dinna ken muckle about the law,' answered Mrs Howden; 'but I ken, when we had a king, and a chancellor, and parliament-men o' our ain, we could aye peeble them wi' stanes when they werena gude bairns—But naebody's nails can reach the length o' Lunnon.'

'Weary on Lunnon, and a' that e'er came out o't!' said Miss Grizel Damahoy, an ancient seamstress; 'they hae taen awa our parliament, and they hae oppressed our trade. Our gentles will hardly allow that a Scots needle can sew ruffles on a sark, or lace on an owerlay.'

'Ye may say that, Miss Damahoy, and I ken o' them that hae gotten raisins frae Lunnon by forpits at ance,' responded Plumdamas; 'and then sic an host of idle English gaugers and excisemen as hae come down to vex and torment us, that an honest man canna fetch sae muckle as a bit anker o' brandy frae Leith to the Lawnmarket, but he's like to be rubbit o' the very gudes he's bought and paid for.—Weel, I winna justify Andrew Wilson for pitting hands on what wasna his; but if he took nae mair than his ain, there's an awfu' difference between that and the fact this man stands for.'

'If ye speak about the law,' said Mrs Howden, 'here comes Mr Saddletree, that can settle it as weel as ony on the bench.'[6]

It is far more than quaint, amusing talk; central themes are being stated. Law is being bandied against law—the law of London against that of Scotland, an alien law against gospel law. What has this law dispensed by Queen Caroline got to do with the people, with the facts? It is to be Effie's problem, too, and the problem which goads Jeanie into action. But without this general discussion, without Porteous, without the pedantries of Saddletree and the

Latin tags of the young men in the opening chapter, the story of
Jeanie and Effie would only be the tale of a novelette.

It is because the problem of Effie is linked to that of Porteous
by more than coincidence that she becomes a typical, a symbolic
figure. David Deans's pangs of conscience as to whether or not he
can take an oath in the court of a government which has not
ratified the Covenant are not mere personal idiosyncrasies, rich in
'character', they embody the deepest issues of the day. And Jeanie's
refusal to tell a white lie to save her sister's life, a refusal which, in
the abstract, should make her immediately forfeit all our sympathy,
is convincing and dramatically moving because we know what is
behind her refusal. History is behind it, the history of generations
of Lowland peasants fighting for the right; the secret, fanatical
gatherings in the valleys of the Border country; the martyrdoms
which we may cull from David Deans's conversation.

How well Scott catches the complex relationship between the
personal and impersonal forces in a man's life! David Deans is a
character in history, but he is not *merely* that. And in his own
conduct the intertwining of personal relationships and theoretical
obsessions is admirably conveyed (the hint of absurdity, even of
humbug, in the scene is beautifully done) when Reuben Butler
comes to visit him after his wife's death.

'Young man,' said the sufferer, 'lay it not to heart, though the righteous
perish and the merciful are removed, seeing it may well be said, that they
are taken away from the evils to come. Woe to me, were I to shed a tear
for the wife of my bosom, when I might weep rivers of water for this
afflicted Church, cursed as it is with carnal seekers, and with the dead of
heart.'

'I am happy,' said Butler, 'that you can forget your private affliction
in your regard for public duty.'

'Forget, Reuben?' said poor Deans, putting his handkerchief to his
eyes,—'She's not to be forgotten on this side of time; but He that gives
the wound can send the ointment. I declare there have been times during
this night when my meditation has been so wrapt, that I knew not of my
heavy loss. It has been with me as with the worthy John Semple, called
Carspharn John, upon a like trial,—I have seen this night on the banks
of Ulai, plucking an apple here and there.'[7]

Scott is not, by and large, a subtle writer but at such moments,
deeply sunk in the history of his people, his insights are profound.

It is not always easy in *The Heart of Midlothian* to disentangle
the false and the true, the conventional and the original, the

romantic and the real. The figure of Madge Wildfire is an interesting example. Superficially she appears to be essentially a 'literary' figure, owing a good deal to Shakespeare's mad characters and a convenient foil in working out the plot and lending it a certain romantic colouring. But this is not the whole truth about Madge Wildfire. She is a conventional figure—the crazy jilted girl turned harlot—but not merely in a literary sense. These mad, semi-prophetic women who are constantly appearing in Scott's novels (Meg Merrilies is perhaps the best example) have a significance which is not simply that of the exploited theatrical figure.* Sometimes these half-crazy women reach strange heights of eloquence—colloquial eloquence springing out of the language of the people—as when Meg Merrilies curses the Laird of Ellangowan:

'Ride your ways, ride your ways, Laird of Ellangowan, ride your ways, Godfrey Bertram!—This day have ye quenched seven smoking hearths—see if the fire in your ain parlour burn the blyther for that. Ye have riven the thack off seven cottar houses—look if your ain roof-tree stand the faster. Ye may stable your stirks in the shoalings at Derncleugh—see that the hare does not couch on the hearth-stane at Ellangowan.—Ride your ways, Godfrey Bertram; what do ye glower after our folk for?—There's thirty hearts there, that hae wanted bread ere ye had wanted sunkets, and spent their life-blood ere ye had scratched your finger. Yes—there's thirty yonder, from the old wife of an hunder to the babe that was born last week, that ye have turned out o' their bits o' bields, to sleep with the tod and the black-cock in the muirs!—Ride your ways, Ellangowan.—Our bairns are hinging at our weary backs—look that your braw cradle at home be the fairer spread up—not that I am wishing ill to little Harry, or to the babe that's yet to be born—God forbid—and make them kind to the poor and better folk than their father!—And now, ride e'en your ways; for these are the last words ye'll ever hear Meg Merrilies speak, and this is the last reise that I'll ever cut in the bonny woods of Ellangowan.'⁸

What gives such a passage its remarkable power is the force of real suffering behind it. Meg Merrilies is not simply a proud, defiant gypsy woman; she is the symbol of a class suffering and dispossessed by the enclosure movement and the power of the great landowners. Scott's knowledge of poverty is not, for all his Toryism, academic, though it is often tinged with unrealism.

The odd figure of the Whistler at the end of *The Heart of Midlothian* is a case in point. This wild boy, the unfortunate child

* The same character turns up, interestingly enough, in John Galt's *Annals of the Parish*, a down-to-earth, realistic contemporary Scottish novel which is not at all Romantic in texture.

of Effie and her lover (he is interesting as a forerunner of Heath-cliff, also called a gypsy, whose physical characteristics are very similar), is presented with the oddest mixture of real compassion and romantic nonsense. 'The eyes of the lad were keen and spark-ling; his gesture free and noble, like that of all savages.'[9] We have already noticed the part that the myth of the noble savage played in the emancipation of the eighteenth-century writers from the limiting attitudes of their society. It is appropriate that the Roman-tic Scott should take up the theme. And it is a measure of Scott's honesty that he should be able to see even this stock figure with a certain realism. When Jeanie goes to release the Whistler from his bonds she asks him

'O ye unhappy boy . . . do ye ken what will come o' ye when ye die?'
'I shall neither feel cauld nor hunger more,' said the youth doggedly.[10]

It is not quite the answer the conventional noble savage should make.

Neither is Madge Wildfire quite what she threatens to be—an amalgam of literary mad-women. There is a kind of dreadful pity behind the presentation of her and her wretched mother which, for all the unconvincing detail, does grip the imagination. They are figures out of that ghastly underworld which Fielding and Hogarth looked into with such honesty and which we associate above all with Dickens. The writer's problem of presenting poverty in the eighteenth and nineteenth centuries sometimes seems an almost insoluble one because the poverty is of a kind which degraded men and women to a sub-human level. It is perhaps only when the products of the underworld can be presented as successful rogues and therefore seen with humour as well as accuracy that the prob-lems of their presentation can be satisfactorily solved. We need not pity Jonathan Wild for he can take care of himself, and the same goes for Ratcliffe in *The Heart of Midlothian*. He is a magnificent creation, this highwayman-turned-jailer, and the bargaining scene between him and Sharpitlaw is one of the novel's most complete successes. Scott is generally underestimated as a comic writer. He is without wit but his sense of the comic clash between characters working within different sets of assumptions is sharp and delightful.

The Heart of Midlothian has three sections to it: the opening (and most important) one set in Edinburgh, the second in England, the third in the Duke of Argyle's estate in the West of Scotland. The Edinburgh section as well as being the longest is by far the best. Real issues, real people, real conflicts form it, the central conflict being, as I have already suggested, between the peasant world of the Deanses and the more sophisticated but more uncertain world of the city, while cutting across this theme is always another—the relation of Scotland to the English state. This relationship permeates the novel, giving to the city of Edinburgh a curious consciousness, a wholeness, such as the towns of England in the eighteenth-century novels never have. Fielding's London (perhaps the difference in size has something to do with it) is quite without this organic unity. It is a place where people live, but as a place, a community, a centre of conflicting and co-operating men and women which achieves a consciousness of its own, it is never encompassed; whereas Scott's Edinburgh is not just a casual dwelling-centre but a Scottish city, unified by its Scottish consciousness, set in history so that the very title of the book, *The Heart of Midlothian*, comes to have a rich ambiguity which refers not merely to the place of execution, but to Edinburgh itself, the heart of Scotland.

We shall be mistaken if we look on Scott's national consciousness as something merely quaint, the kind of regional loyalty which is exploited from affectation or narrowness, a provincialism. On the contrary, this feeling for the culture and aspirations of the people of the Lowlands, this intense awareness of a Scottish national tradition, is an aspect of Scott's genius which contributes most deeply to the positive qualities of his novels. It is when Scott is least Scottish, most cosmopolitan, most urbane that his weaknesses emerge. It is then that his plots become most tiresome, his characters most wooden, his style most cumbersome. It is then that Mr E. M. Forster's complaint that Scott lacks passion has the greatest force.[11]

The first section of *The Heart of Midlothian* has certain weaknesses, but they are relatively unimportant. The most disastrous perhaps is the character of Reuben Butler, as dim a hero as any novelist ever conceived and in the worst tradition of Scott's leading figures. Why is Butler such a failure? Fundamentally, I believe, because Scott's genteel conservatism, his vision of himself as the benevolent aristocrat (Hazlitt's picture in *The Spirit of the Age* though not altogether fair, is significant) could never allow him to make his heroes rebels even when their situation cries out for rebellion. Reuben Butler, like Waverley himself, is a congenital fence-sitter. He has most of David Deans's ideas without the passion (which is history) that should attend them. His reaction to the Porteous riot is that of Blake's lily-livered anti-Jacobin who would smile on the wintry seas and pity the stormy roar. He is horrified by the mob not from conviction but from pusillanimity and he finds his level at the end of the book as a successful ecclesiastical politician at the General Assembly of the Scottish Church, a thoroughly safe man who will undoubtedly go far.

But while Butler reflects the least satisfactory side of Scott, there is more than enough in this first section of the novel to compensate for this weakness. Besides the Deanses there are the two lairds of Dumbiedikes, there is Saddletree and Ratcliffe and Sharpitlaw and Porteous himself and there is the magnificent evocation of the Covenanting past through David Deans's own conversation; and these varying elements and characters are welded into a fully significant pattern so that when in chapter XXII the climax (Effie's trial) is reached the accumulated tensions—sister against sister, humanity against legalism, puritanism against worldliness, extreme presbyterianism against the episcopalian tradition, peasantry against town, Scotland against England—are all in play with no puny Butlerisms to weaken and blur the force and truth of the central contradictions.

If the second half of *The Heart of Midlothian* were as good as the first it would be—despite the minor irritations of Scott's writing, his ponderousness and 'literary' affectations—a great novel. But the second half is spoiled, in the first place by the scenes in Lincolnshire (those tedious and unconvincing conversations with the Stauntons) and in the second by the emergence of the Duke of Argyle as *deus ex machina*. It is not the presentation of the Duke himself that is at fault; this is done by and large with a good deal of tact and the scene between Jeanie and Queen Caroline is surprisingly successful. The trouble with Argyle is not in himself as a character in the novel but rather in his star as a part of the novel's pattern. For it is his part in the book to resolve all the conflicts, to reconcile all the contradictory forces and to turn the drama of the destiny of the Deanses into something like a cheerful domestic comedy.

There are felicities in this latter half of the novel but they are of a different kind from the merits of the first half. The treatment of Effie, who is allowed to show that the wages of sin are not wholly unpalatable, has a great deal of truth and insight to it. Scott's ability to achieve a sense of community makes itself clear again in his building up of the solid world of Roseneath; but the picture is this time tinted with unrealism. The Duke's estate is altogether too

idyllic and the softening of all the characters which occurs in the
final chapters of the book is not a mellowing. They soften because
all the opposing forces which have, in their clashes, generated
vitality are removed beneath the paternal eye of the enlightened
Duke. The city, symbol of the stresses and strains of the new
world, disappears altogether. True, there are the Highlanders and
smugglers in the offing, but they too (as opposed to Ratcliffe and
Meg Murdockson) are romanticised (we have noticed already the
'noble savage' theme). Even David Deans loses his edge and is
prepared to make some ruinous compromises. And the reason for
the change in tone is, at bottom, that Scott has stopped looking at
the world from the peasant's angle and sees it now from the idealised
standpoint of the paternalist landowner.

The point is not, of course, that peasants are *better* than landowners but that in the paternalist attitude there is inevitably an
element of wishful thinking which precludes realism, whereas in
the earlier reaches of the novel Scott is able to penetrate to the real
and vital clashes of forces within Scottish society through his
imaginative comprehension of the true situation of the Lowland
peasantry. It is from this penetration that the artistic vitality of *The
Heart of Midlothian* derives. The artistic success of Jeanie Deans
comes from the depth of Scott's understanding of her as a historically typical figure, and she alone totally survives the novel,
renewing even in the final pages her artistic vitality through her
treatment of the captured Whistler.

Ralph Fox, one of the few modern critics to attempt a defence
of Scott, has said:

. . . He knew that man had a past as well as a present, and his astonishing
and fertile genius attempted to make the synthesis which the eighteenth
century had failed to produce, in which the novel should unite the poetry
as well as the prose of life, in which the nature love of Rousseau should
be combined with the sensibility of Sterne and the vigour and amplitude
of Fielding.

He failed, but it was a glorious failure, and the reasons are worth
examination. It is popular today to deprecate Scott as a mere teller of
skilfully contrived and intolerably sentimental stories. Mr E. M. Forster
sees him as that, but Balzac had a different view. Scott is the only novelist
to whom Balzac acknowledges a real and deep debt, and with all respect
to Mr Forster, himself our only considerable contemporary novelist, I
prefer the view taken by Balzac.

Why did Scott fail in his immense task? Because impenetrable blinkers
obscured his vision.[12]

It is true that Scott wore blinkers, the blinkers of the humane aristocrat; but they were not impenetrable blinkers. They limited his range of vision but they did not blind him. I do not think any of his novels, even *The Heart of Midlothian*, is a great novel or that he is ever again likely to be compared (as he regularly was during the last century) to Shakespeare. But he is not a writer we can afford to despise, and the very qualities that have made him unfashionable —a certain lack of sophistication, his national consciousness, the absence of a narrowly 'aesthetic' concern in his books—may well contribute one day to a more securely based esteem than he has enjoyed in the past.

4

DICKENS: OLIVER TWIST

(1837–8)

In the twelfth chapter of *Oliver Twist*, Oliver, carried insensible by Mr Brownlow from the magistrate's court, wakes up to find himself in a comfortable bed:

> Weak, and thin, and pallid, he awoke at last from what seemed to have been a long and troubled dream. Feebly raising himself in the bed, with his head resting on his trembling arm, he looked anxiously round.
> 'What room is this? Where have I been brought to?' said Oliver. 'This is not the place I went to sleep in.'
> He uttered these words in a feeble voice, being very faint and weak, but they were overheard at once; for the curtain at the bed's head was hastily drawn back, and a motherly old lady, very neatly and precisely dressed, rose as she withdrew it from an armchair close by, in which she had been sitting at needlework.
> 'Hush, my dear,' said the old lady softly. 'You must be very quiet, or you will be ill again; and you have been very bad—as bad as bad could be, pretty nigh. Lie down again; there's a dear!' With these words, the old lady very gently placed Oliver's head upon the pillow, and, smoothing back his hair from his forehead, looked so kindly and lovingly in his face, that he could not help placing his little withered hand in hers, and drawing it round his neck.
> 'Save us!' said the old lady, with tears in her eyes, 'what a grateful little dear it is! Pretty creature! What would his mother feel if she had sat by him as I have, and could see him now?'[1]

It is a central situation in the book—this emergence out of squalor into comfort and kindliness—and it is repeated later in the story when once again Oliver, after the robbery in which he has been wounded, wakes to find himself cared for and defended by the Maylies. There is more than mere chance in the repetition and we meet here, indeed, a pattern recurring throughout Dickens's novels. It is worth while examining it more closely.

The first eleven chapters of *Oliver Twist* are an evocation of misery and horror. We have been drawn straight with the first sentence (of which workhouse is the key word) into a world of the most appalling poverty and ugliness, a world of brutality and violence in which life is cheap, suffering general and death welcome. That the evocation is crude, that it is marred by moments of false feeling and by a heavy-handed irony which weakens all it comments on, is not for the moment the consideration. By and large, the effect is of extraordinary power. No such effect (for good or ill) has emerged from any novel we have previously discussed. It is an effect which is, in the precise sense of a hackneyed word, unforgettable. The workhouse, the parochial baby-farm, Mr Sowerberry's shop, the funeral, the Artful Dodger, Fagin's lair: they have the haunting quality, but nothing of the unreality, of a nightmare. It is a curious comment on Victorian civilisation that this was considered suitable reading for children.

What is the secret of the power? Is it merely the objective existence of the horror, the fact that such things were, that strikes at our minds? Fairly obviously not or we should be moved in just the same way by a social history. There is a particularity about this world which is not the effect of even a well-documented history. It is not just any evocation of the life of the poor after the Industrial Revolution; when we read the Hammonds' *Town Labourer* or Engels's *Condition of the Working Class in England in 1844* our reaction may not be less profound than our reaction to *Oliver Twist*, but it is different, more generalised, less vivid, less intense.

The most obvious difference between *Oliver Twist* and a social history is, of course, that it deals with actual characters whose personalities we envisage, whose careers we follow, and whose feelings we share. But this difference is not, I think, quite so important as we might assume. For in fact we do not become involved in the world of *Oliver Twist* in the way we become involved in the world of *Emma*. We do not really know very much about any of these characters, even Oliver himself, or participate very closely in their motives and reactions. We are sorry for Oliver; we are on his side; but our feeling for him is not very different from our feeling for any child we see ill-treated in the street. We are outraged and our sense of outrage no doubt comes, ultimately, from a feeling of common humanity, a kind of identification of ourselves with the child in his misery and struggles; but our entanglement in his situation is not really very deep.

In the famous scene when Oliver asks for more it is not the precise sense of Oliver's feelings and reactions that grips us; we do not feel what he is feeling in the way we share Miss Bates's emotion on Box Hill, and in this sense Oliver is less close to us and matters to us less than Miss Bates and Emma. But in another way Oliver matters to us a great deal more. For when he walks up to the master of the workhouse and asks for more gruel, issues are at stake which make the whole world of Jane Austen tremble. We care, we are involved, not because it is Oliver and we are close to Oliver (though that of course enters into it), but because every starved orphan in the world, and indeed everyone who is poor and op-pressed and hungry is involved, and the master of the workhouse (his name has not been revealed) is not anyone in particular but every agent of an oppressive system everywhere. And that, inci-dentally, is why millions of people all over the world (including many who have never read a page of Dickens) can tell you what happened in Oliver Twist's workhouse, while comparatively few can tell you what happened on Box Hill.

That this episode from *Oliver Twist* should have become a myth, a part of the cultural consciousness of the people, is due not merely to its subject-matter but to the kind of novel Dickens wrote. He is dealing not, like Jane Austen, with personal relationships, not with the quality of feelings involved in detailed living, but with something which can without fatuity be called Life. What we get from *Oliver Twist* is not a greater precision of sensitiveness about the day-to-day problems of human behaviour but a sharpened sense of the large movement of life within which particular problems arise. It is pointless to argue whether the way Dickens tackles life is better or worse than the way Jane Austen tackles it. One might just as well argue whether it is better to earn one's living or to get married. Not merely are the two issues not exclusive, they are indissolubly bound up. In a sense they are the same problem—how best to live in society—but, for all their interdependence, one does not tackle them in precisely the same way.

What distinguishes the opening chapters of *Oliver Twist* from, on the one side, a social history and, on the other side, *Emma*, is that they are symbolic. It is not a sense of participation in the personal emotions of any of the characters that engages our imagination but a sense of participation in a world that is strikingly, appallingly relevant to our world.

The *Oliver Twist* world is a world of poverty, oppression and death. The poverty is complete, utterly degrading and utterly realistic.

The houses on either side were high and large, but very old and tenanted by people of the poorest class: as their neglected appearance would have sufficiently denoted, without the concurrent testimony afforded by the squalid looks of the few men and women who, with folded arms and bodies half-doubled, occasionally skulked along. A great many of the tenements had shop fronts; but these were fast closed, and mouldering away, only the upper rooms being inhabited. Some houses which had become insecure from age and decay were prevented from falling into the street, by huge beams of wood reared against the walls, and firmly planted in the road; but even these crazy dens seemed to have been selected as the nightly haunts of some houseless wretches, for many of the rough boards, which supplied the place of door and window, were wrenched from their positions, to afford an aperture wide enough for the passage of a human body. The kennel was stagnant and filthy. The very rats, which here and there lay putrefying in its rottenness, were hideous with famine.[2]

The oppression stems from the 'board'—eight or ten fat gentlemen sitting round a table—and particularly (the image is repeated) from a fat gentleman in a white waistcoat; but its agents are the (under) paid officers of the state: beadle, matron, etc., corrupt, pompous, cruel. The methods of oppression are simple: violence and starvation. The workhouse is a symbol of the oppression but by no means its limit. Outside, the world is a vast workhouse with the 'parish' run by the same gentleman in a white waistcoat, assisted by magistrates fatuous or inhuman, by clergymen who can scarcely be bothered to bury the dead, by Mr Bumble. London is no different from the parish, only bigger.

The oppressed are degraded and corrupted by their life (plus a little gin) and either become themselves oppressors or else criminals or corpses. Of all the recurring themes and images of these opening chapters that of death is the most insistent. Oliver's mother dies. ' "It's all over, Mrs Thingummy," said the surgeon. . . .'[3] The note of impersonal and irresponsible horror is immediately struck. It is not fortuitous that Mr Sowerberry should be an undertaker, presiding over an unending funeral. Oliver and Dick long for death. Fagin gives a twist of new and dreadful cynicism to the theme: ' "What a fine thing capital punishment is! Dead men never repent;

dead men never bring awkward stories to light." '⁴ The ultimate sanction of the oppressive state becomes the ultimate weapon of its degraded creatures in their struggles against one another.

The strength of these opening chapters lies in the power and justice of the symbols, through which is achieved an objective picture arousing our compassion not through any extraneous comment but through its own validity. The weakness lies in Dickens's conscious attitudes, his attempts to comment on the situation. These attempts are at best (the ironical) inadequate, at worst (the sentimental) nauseating.

Although I am not disposed to maintain that the being born in a workhouse is in itself the most fortunate and enviable circumstance that can possibly befall a human being . . .⁵

The heaviness of the prose reflects the stodginess and unsubtlety of the thought. So does the reiteration of the 'kind old gentleman' as a description of Fagin. (The less satisfactory side of Dickens's treatment of the thieves obviously comes direct from *Jonathan Wild*; the same irony—even to the very words—is used, but because it is not based on Fielding's secure moral preoccupation it becomes tedious far more quickly.) The incursions of 'sentiment' (i.e. every reference to motherhood, the little scene between Oliver and Dick) are even more unsatisfactory. After Dickens has tried to wring an easy tear by playing on responses which he has done nothing to satisfy, we begin to be suspicious of the moments when we really *are* moved, fearing a facile trick.

But the weaknesses—which may be summed up as the inadequacy of Dickens's conscious view of life—are in the first eleven chapters of *Oliver Twist* almost obliterated by the strength. The subjective inadequacy is obscured by the objective profundity. Again and again Dickens leaves behind his heavy humour, forgets that he ought to be trying to copy Fielding or vindicating our faith in the beauty of motherhood, and achieves a moment of drama or insight which burns into the imagination by its truth and vividness. We have already noticed the surgeon's comment on Oliver's mother's death. Most of the Mr Bumble-Mrs Mann conversations, the whole of the undertaker section, the meeting with the Artful Dodger, the first description of the thieves' kitchen are on the same level of achievement. So is the moment when Oliver asks for more and the passage when Oliver and Sowerberry go to visit the corpse of a dead woman.

The terrified children cried bitterly; but the old woman, who had hitherto remained as quiet as if she had been wholly deaf to all that passed, menaced them into silence. Having unloosed the cravat of the man, who still remained extended on the ground, she tottered towards the undertaker.

'She was my daughter,' said the old woman, nodding her head in the direction of the corpse; and speaking with an idiotic leer, more ghastly than even the presence of death in such a place. 'Lord, Lord! Well, it *is* strange that I who gave birth to her, and was a woman then, should be alive and merry now, and she lying there, so cold and stiff! Lord, Lord!— to think of it; it's as good as a play—as good as a play!'

As the wretched creature mumbled and chuckled in her hideous merriment, the undertaker turned to go away.

'Stop, stop!' said the old woman in a loud whisper. 'Will she be buried tomorrow, or next day, or tonight? I laid her out and I must walk, you know. Send me a large cloak—a good warm one, for it is bitter cold. We should have cake and wine, too, before we go! Never mind; send some bread—only a loaf of bread and a cup of water. Shall we have some bread, dear?' she said eagerly, catching at the undertaker's coat, as he once more moved towards the door.

'Yes, yes,' said the undertaker, 'of course. Anything, everything.' He disengaged himself from the old woman's grasp, and, drawing Oliver after him, hurried away.[6]

There is no sentimentality here, only horror, and with something of the quality which one associates particularly with Dostoievsky, the strengthening of realism by the moment of fantasy, the blurring of the line between reality and nightmare, a stretching to the ultimate of the capacity of the mind to deal with the world it has inherited.

And then from the desperate horror of the nightmare world Oliver awakes, lying in a comfortable bed, surrounded by kindly middle-class people. He has become all of a sudden a pretty creature, a grateful little dear. And from that moment the plot of the novel becomes important.

It is generally agreed that the plots of Dickens's novels are their weakest feature but it is not always understood why this should be so. The plot of *Oliver Twist* is very complicated and very unsatisfactory. It is a conventional plot about a wronged woman, an illegitimate baby, a destroyed will, a death-bed secret, a locket thrown into the river, a wicked elder brother and the restoration to the hero of name and property. That it should depend on a number of extraordinary coincidences (the only two robberies in which Oliver is called upon to participate are perpetrated, fortuitously, on his father's best friend and his mother's sister's guardian!) is the least of its shortcomings. Literal probability is not an essential quality of an adequate plot. Nor is it a damning criticism that Dickens should have used his plot for the purposes of serial-publication, i.e. to provide a climax at the end of each instalment and the necessary twists and manœuvres which popular serialisation invited. (It is not a fault in a dramatist that he should provide a climax to each act of his play, and the serial instalment is no more or less artificial a convention than the act of a play.) What we may legitimately object to in the plot of *Oliver Twist* is the very substance of that plot in its relation to the essential pattern of the novel.

The conflict in the plot is the struggle between the innocent Oliver, aided by his friends at Pentonville and Chertsey, against the machinations of those who are conspiring from self-interest to do him out of his fortune. These latter stem from and centre in his half-brother Monks. It is not, even by its own standards, a good plot. Oliver is too passive a hero to win our very lively sympathy and Monks is a rather unconvincing villain who is, anyway, out-shone in interest by his agents. The good characters are, by and large, too good and the bad too bad. If the centre of interest of the novel were indeed the plot then the conventional assessment of a Dickens novel—a poor story enlivened by magnificent though irrelevant 'characters'—would be fair enough. But in fact the centre of interest, the essential pattern of the novel, is not its plot, and it is the major fault of the plot that it does not correspond with this central interest.

The core of the novel, and what gives it value, is its consideration of the plight of the poor. Its pattern is the contrasted relation of two worlds—the underworld of the workhouse, the funeral, the thieves' kitchen, and the comfortable world of the Brownlows and Maylies. It is this pattern that stamps the novel on our minds. We do not remember, when we think back on it, the intricacies of the plot; we are not interested in the affairs of Rose and Harry Maylie; we do not care who Oliver's father was and, though we sympathise with Oliver's struggles, we do not mind whether or not he gets his fortune. What we do remember is that vision of the underworld of the first eleven chapters, the horror of Fagin, the fate of Mr Bumble, the trial of the Artful Dodger, the murder of Nancy, the end of Sikes. What engages our sympathy is not Oliver's feeling for the mother he never saw, but his struggle against his oppressors of which the famous gruel scene is indeed a central and adequate symbol.

The contrast of the two worlds is at the very heart of the book, so that we see a total picture of contrasted darkness and light. Often the two are explicitly contrasted in divided chapters. The two worlds are so utterly separate that Oliver's two metamorphoses from one to the other must inevitably take the form of an awakening to a new existence and the root of the weakness as 'characters' of both Oliver and Monks is that they are not fully absorbed in either world. Oliver is rather a thin hero because, though he is called upon to play a hero's part, he never becomes identified with the heroic forces of the book; while Monks's stature as the fountainhead of evil is wrecked by his parentage; how can he compete with Sikes and Fagin when he is to be allowed, because he is a gentleman, to escape his just deserts?

The power of the book, then, proceeds from the wonderful evocation of the underworld and the engagement of our sympathy on behalf of the inhabitants of that world. Its weakness lies in Dickens's failure to develop and carry through the pattern so powerfully presented in the first quarter of the novel. It is by no means a complete failure; on the contrary, there are passages in the latter part of the book quite as successful as the early scenes: and in the final impression of the novel the sense of the two worlds is, as has been suggested, the dominant factor. But the failure is, nevertheless, sufficiently striking to be worth consideration.

It is not by chance that the plot and Mr Brownlow emerge in the novel at the same moment, for their purpose is identical. It is they who are to rescue Oliver from the underworld and establish him as a respectable member of society. It is not through his own efforts that the metamorphosis takes place and indeed it cannot be. For if the whole first section of the novel has convinced us of anything at all it is that against the whole apparatus set in motion by the gentleman in the white waistcoat the Oliver Twists of that world could stand no possible chance.

The introduction of the plot, then, savours from the very first of a trick. It is only by reducing the whole of Oliver's experiences up till now to the status of 'a long and troubled dream' that he can be saved for the plot. But we know perfectly well that these experiences are not a dream; they have a reality for us which the nice houses in Pentonville and Chertsey never achieve. Indeed, as far as the imaginative impact of the novel is concerned, it is the Brownlow–Maylie world that is the dream, a dream-world into which Oliver is lucky enough to be transported by the plot but which all the real and vital people of the book never even glimpse. The

Brownlow–Maylie world is indeed no world at all; it is merely the romantic escape-world of the lost wills and dispossessed foundlings and idiotic coincidences which make up the paraphernalia of the conventional romantic plot.

The plot makes impossible the realisation of the living pattern and conflict of the book. This conflict—symbolised, as we have seen, by the gruel scene—is the struggle of the poor against the bourgeois state, the whole army of greater and lesser Bumbles whom the gentleman in the white waistcoat employs to maintain morality (all the members of the board are 'philosophers') and the *status quo*. The appalling difficulties of this struggle are impressed on our minds and it is because Oliver, however unwillingly, becomes an actor in it that he takes on a certain symbolic significance and wins more than our casual pity.

It is notable that Dickens makes no serious effort to present Oliver with any psychological realism: his reactions are not, for the most part, the reactions of any child of nine or ten years old; he is not surprised by what would surprise a child and his moral attitudes are those of an adult. And yet something of the quality of precocious suffering, of childish terror, is somehow achieved, partly by the means by which other characters are presented, with a kind of exaggerated, almost grotesque simplicity, and partly through the very fact that Oliver is—we are persuaded—a figure of symbolic significance. Because he is *all* workhouse orphans the lack of a convincing individual psychology does not matter; it is Oliver's situation rather than himself that moves us and the situation is presented with all of Dickens's dramatic symbolic power.

Once he becomes involved in the plot the entire symbolic significance of Oliver changes. Until he wakes up in Mr Brownlow's house he is a poor boy struggling against the inhumanity of the state. After he has slept himself into the Brownlow world he is a young bourgeois who has been done out of his property. A complete transformation has taken place in the organisation of the novel. The state, which in the pattern of the book is the organ of oppression of the poor and therefore of Oliver, now becomes the servant of Oliver. The oppressed are now divided (through the working of the plot) into the good and deserving poor who help Oliver win his rights and the bad and criminal poor who help Monks and must be eliminated. It is a conception which makes a mockery of the opening chapters of the book, where poverty has been revealed to us in a light which makes the facile terms of good and bad irrelevant.

By the end of the book Nancy can be pigeon-holed as good, Sikes as bad. But who can say whether the starving creatures of the opening chapters are good or bad? It is for this kind of reason that the plot of *Oliver Twist* has so disastrous an effect on the novel. Not merely is it silly and mechanical and troublesome, but it expresses an interpretation of life infinitely less profound and honest than the novel itself reveals.

The disaster, happily, is not complete. For one thing, the plot does not immediately, with the entrance of Mr Brownlow, gain entire ascendancy. The kidnapping of Oliver by Nancy and Sikes and his return to the thieves gives the novel a reprieve. The robbery episode is excellently done. But in this section (chs. XII to XXIX) the plot is beginning to seep into the underworld. Monks appears. And the reintroduction of the workhouse (the death of old Sally, the marriage of Mr Bumble), despite some delicious moments ('It's all U.P. here, Mrs Corney'; Noah and Charlotte eating oysters; 'Won't you tell your own B?'), too obviously serves the contrivances of the plot.

Once, however, the robbery is done with and Oliver awakes for a second time in the respectable world, the plot completely reasserts itself. The third quarter of the book (chs. XXIX to XXXIX) is its weakest section. Oliver is here entirely at the mercy of the Maylies and the plot. Monks bobs up all over the place. And our interest is held (if at all) only by the Bumble passages, now completely involved in the plot, and the incidental 'characters', Giles and Brittles, Blathers and Duff. And because these characters have no part in the underlying pattern of the book and are therefore, unlike Bumble and Fagin and the Artful Dodger and Noah Claypole, without symbolic significance, they are merely eccentrics, comic relief, with all the limitations the phrase implies.

The basic conflict of the novel is brought, in this quarter, almost to a standstill; the people who have captured our imagination scarcely appear at all. The world of the opening chapters has been replaced by another world in which kindly old doctors like Losberne and crusty but amiable eccentrics like Grimwig are in control of the situation. But after what we have already experienced, we simply cannot believe in this world in the way we believed in the other.

In the final quarter of the book (ch. XXXIX onwards) plot and pattern, artifice and truth, struggle in a last, violent encounter. The plot wins the first round by extracting Nancy from the clutches of the pattern. The girl's genuine humanity, revealed earlier in the novel by the simple moving language of her moment of compassion for the suffering wretches within the walls of the jail, is debased by the plot into the conventional clichés of cheap melodrama. But Nancy's abduction is countered almost at once by one of the great episodes of the novel, the trial of the Artful Dodger. This scene is irrelevant to the plot except in so far as the Dodger has to be got out of the way before the final dispensing of reward and punishment. It is an interesting instance of the power of Dickens's genius that he should have realised that in the Dodger he had created a figure which the plot was quite incapable either of absorbing or obliterating. And so he is obliged to give the irrepressible boy his final fling, a fling which again raises the book into serious art and plays an essential part in its (by this time) almost forgotten pattern.

The trial of the Artful Dodger (it is a greater because emotionally and morally a profounder scene than Jonathan Wild's dance without music) re-states in an astonishing form the central theme of *Oliver Twist*: what are the poor to do against the oppressive state? The Dodger throughout the book is magnificently done: his precosity, the laboured irony of his conversation (which becomes involuntarily a comment on the quality of Dickens's own irony), his shrewdness, his grotesque urbanity, his resourcefulness (gloriously at variance with his appearance), his tremendous vitality, all are revealed without false pathos but with an effect of great profundity.

For what is so important about the Artful Dodger is not his oddity but his normality, not his inability to cope with the world but his very ability to cope with it on its own terms. Oliver is afraid of the world, the Dodger defies it; it has made him what he is and he will give back as good as he got. His trial contrasts in the novel with all the other trials. He turns up with all his guns loaded and fires broadside after broadside which for all their fantastic unexpectedness and apparent inappropriateness have an irony beyond any other statements in the novel.

It was indeed Mr Dawkins, who, shuffling into the office with the big coat-sleeves tucked up as usual, his left hand in his pocket, and his hat in his right hand, preceded the jailer, with a rolling gait altogether indescribable, and, taking his place in the dock, requested in an audible voice to know what he was placed in that 'ere disgraceful sitivation for.

'Hold your tongue, will you?' said the jailer.

'I'm an Englishman, ain't I?' rejoined the Dodger; 'where are my priwileges?'

'You'll get your privileges soon enough,' retorted the jailer, 'and pepper with 'em.'

'We'll see wot the Secretary of State for the Home Affairs has got to say to the beaks, if I don't,' replied Mr Dawkins. 'Now then! Wot is this here business? I shall thank the madg'strates to dispose of this here little affair, and not to keep me while they read the paper for I've got an appointment with a genelman in the city, and as I'm a man of my word and wery punctual in business matters, he'll go away if I ain't there to my time, and then pr'aps there won't be an action for damage against them as kept me away. Oh, no, certainly not!'

At this point the Dodger, with a show of being very particular with a view to proceedings to be had thereafter, desired the jailer to communicate 'the names of them two files as was on the bench', which so tickled the spectators, that they laughed almost as heartily as Master Bates could have done if he had heard the request.

'Silence there!' cried the jailer.

'What is this?' inquired one of the magistrates.

'A pick-pocketing case, your worship.'

'Has the boy ever been here before?'

'He ought to have been, a many times,' replied the jailer. 'He has been pretty well everywhere else. I know him well, your worship.'

'Oh! you know me, do you?' cried the Artful, making a note of the statement. 'Wery good. That's a case of deformation of character anyway.'

Here there was another laugh, and another cry of silence.

'Now then, where are the witnesses?' said the clerk.

'Ah! that's right,' added the Dodger. 'Where are they? I should like to see 'em.'

This wish was immediately gratified, for a policeman stepped forward who had seen the prisoner attempt the pocket of an unknown gentleman in a crowd, and indeed take a handkerchief therefrom, which, being a very old one, he deliberately put back again, after trying it on his own countenance. For this reason, he took the Dodger into custody as soon as he could get near him, and the said Dodger being searched, had upon his person a silver snuff-box, with the owner's name engraved upon the lid. This gentleman had been discovered on reference to the Court Guide, and being then and there present, swore that the snuff-box was his, and that he had missed it on the previous day, the moment he had disengaged himself from the crowd before referred to. He had also remarked a young gentleman in the throng particularly active in making his way about, and that young gentleman was the prisoner before him.

'Have you anything to ask this witness, boy?' said the magistrate.

'I wouldn't abase myself by descending to hold no conversation with him,' replied the Dodger.

'Have you anything to say at all?'

'Do you hear his worship ask if you have anything to say?' inquired the jailer, nudging the silent Dodger with his elbow.

'I beg your pardon,' said the Dodger, looking up with an air of abstraction. 'Did you redress yourself to me, my man?'

'I never see such an out-and-out young wagabond, your worship,' observed the officer with a grin. 'Do you mean to say anything, you young shaver?'

'No,' replied the Dodger, 'not here, for this ain't the shop for justice; besides which, my attorney is a-breakfasting this morning with the Wice-President of the House of Commons; but I shall have something to say elsewhere, and so will he, and so will a wery numerous and 'spectable circle of acquaintance as'll make them beaks wish they'd never been born, or that they'd got their footmen to hang 'em up to their own hat-pegs afore they let 'em come out this morning to try it on upon me. I'll——'

'There! He's fully committed!' interposed the clerk. 'Take him away.'

'Come on,' said the jailer.

'Oh, ah! I'll come on,' replied the Dodger, brushing his hat with the palm of his hand. 'Ah! (to the Bench), it's no use your looking frightened; I won't show you no mercy, not a ha'porth of it. *You'll* pay for this, my fine fellers. I wouldn't be you for something! I wouldn't go free, now, if you was to fall down on your knees and ask me. Here, carry me off to prison! Take me away!'⁷

Now the point about the Dodger's defiance which is apt to escape our notice, so fantastic and uproarious is the scene and so used are we to regarding a Dickens novel simply in terms of a display of eccentric 'character', is the actual substance of his comments. Yet in fact, if we recall the court in which Mr Fang had heard Oliver's case, we must realise the justice of the Dodger's complaints, which strike at the very heart of the judicial system that is doing its worst on him. Where *are* the Englishman's privileges? Where *is* the law that allows the jailer to say what he does? What, in sober fact, *are* these magistrates? What comment could be more relevant than the contemptuous 'this ain't the shop for justice'? The importance of the Artful Dodger in the pattern of the novel is that he, almost alone of the characters of the underworld, does stick up for himself, does continue and develop the conflict that Oliver had begun when he asked for more.

The final section of the book (the murder of Nancy, the flight and end of Sikes, the death of Fagin and the tying-up of the plot) is an extraordinary mixture of the genuine and the bogus. The violence which has run right through the novel reaches its climax with the murder of Nancy; and the sense of terror is remarkably well sustained right up to the death of Sikes.

Here again Dickens's instinct for the symbolic background is what grips our imagination. The atmosphere of squalid London, powerfully present in so much of the novel, is here immensely effective, especially the description of Folly Ditch and Jacob's Island, sombre and decayed, 'crazy wooden galleries common to the backs of half a dozen houses, with holes from which to look upon the slime beneath; windows broken and patched, with poles thrust out on which to dry the linen that is never there ... chimneys half crushed, half hesitating to fall. . . .'[8] The scene itself ceases to be a mere backcloth and becomes a sculptured mass making an integral part of the novel's pattern. So that in the end it is not Sikes's conscience that we remember but a black picture of human squalor and desolation. Sikes is gathered into the world that has begotten him and the image of that world makes us understand him and even pity him, not with an easy sentimentality, but through a sense of all the hideous forces that have made him what he is.

The end of Fagin is a different matter. It is sensational in the worst sense, with a *News of the World* interest which touches nothing adequately and is worse than inadequate because it actually coarsens our perceptions. It is conceived entirely within the terms of the plot (Oliver is taken—in the name of morality—to the condemned cell to find out where the missing papers are hidden) and the whole debasing effect of the plot on the novel is immediately illustrated; for it is because he is working within the moral framework of the plot—in which the only standards are those of the sanctity of property and complacent respectability—that Dickens *cannot* offer us any valuable human insights, *cannot* give his characters freedom to live as human beings.

That is why the struggle throughout *Oliver Twist* between the plot and the pattern is indeed a life and death struggle, a struggle as to whether the novel shall live or not. And in so far as the plot succeeds in twisting and negating the pattern the value of the novel is in fact weakened. To a considerable degree the novel *is* thus ruined; the loss of tension in the third quarter and the dubious close are the testimony. But the total effect is not one of disaster. The truth and depth of the central vision are such that a vitality is generated which struggles against and survives the plot. Oliver himself does not survive; but the force he has set in motion does. This force—let us call it the sense of the doom and aspirations of the oppressed—is too strong to be satisfied with the dream-solution of Oliver's metamorphosis, too enduring to let us forget the fat gentleman in the white waistcoat who has so conveniently faded from the picture till he is recalled by the Artful Dodger.

Confused, uneven, topsy-turvy as the effect of the novel is we would yet be doing it great injustice to discuss it, as it is often discussed, simply in terms of random moments and exuberant caricature. There is pattern behind that power, art behind the vitality, and if we recognise this in *Oliver Twist* we shall not come unarmed to Dickens's later, more mature and greater books: *Bleak House, Little Dorrit, Great Expectations, Our Mutual Friend.*

5

EMILY BRONTË: *WUTHERING HEIGHTS*

(1847)

Wuthering Heights, like all the greatest works of art, is at once concrete and yet general, local and yet universal. Because so much nonsense has been written and spoken about the Brontës and because Emily in particular has been so often presented to us as a ghost-like figure surrounded entirely by endless moorland, cut off from anything so banal as human society, not of her time but of eternity, it is necessary to emphasise at the outset the local quality of the book.

Wuthering Heights is about England in 1847 and the years before. The people it reveals live not in a never-never land but in Yorkshire. Heathcliff was born not in the pages of Byron, but in a Liverpool slum. The language of Nelly, Joseph and Hareton is the language of Yorkshire people. The story of *Wuthering Heights* is concerned not with love in the abstract but with the passions of living people, with property-ownership, the attraction of social comforts, the arrangement of marriages, the importance of education, the validity of religion, the relations of rich and poor.

There is nothing vague about this novel; the mists in it are the mists of the Yorkshire moors; if we speak of it as having an elemental quality it is because the very elements, the great forces of nature are evoked, which change so slowly that in the span of a human life they seem unchanging. But in this evocation there is nothing sloppy or uncontrolled. On the contrary the realisation is intensely concrete: we seem to smell the kitchen of Wuthering Heights, to feel the force of the wind across the moors, to sense the very changes of the seasons. Such concreteness is achieved not by mistiness but by precision.

It is necessary to stress this point but not, of course, to force it to a false conclusion. The power and wonder of Emily Brontë's novel does not lie in naturalistic description, nor in a detailed analysis of the hour-by-hour issues of social living. Her approach is, quite obviously, not the approach of Jane Austen; it is much nearer to the approach of Dickens. Indeed, *Wuthering Heights* is essentially the same kind of novel as *Oliver Twist*. It is not a romance, not (despite the film bearing the same title) an escape from life to the wild moors and romantic lovers. It is certainly not a picaresque novel and it cannot adequately be described as a moral fable, though it has a strong, insistent pattern. But the pattern, like that of Dickens's novel, cannot be abstracted as a neat sentence: its germ is not an intellectualised idea or concept.

Emily Brontë works not in ideas but in images, that is to say concepts which have a significance and validity on a level different from that of logical thought. Just as the significance of the work-house in *Oliver Twist* cannot adequately be conceived in merely logical terms but depends on a host of associations—including its physical shape and colour—which logical analysis may penetrate but is unlikely adequately to convey, so the significance of the moors in *Wuthering Heights* cannot be suggested in the cold words of logic (which does not mean that it is illogical). The symbolic novel is an advance on the moral fable just in the sense that a symbol can be richer—can touch on more of life—than an abstract moral concept.

The opening sentence of the *Social Contract* gives a simple example: 'Man was born free, but everywhere he is in chains.' Of the two statements in this sentence the first is abstract, the second symbolic. And the impact of the second on our imagination is greater than that of the first for this very reason. (If one were concerned to go deeper into the matter one might suggest that Rousseau *knew* that man was in chains but merely speculated that he had been born free.) Now, whereas the symbolism of the moral fable (and the fable is itself a kind of extended symbol) is inherently limited by the abstract concept behind it, the symbolism of *Wuthering Heights* or the good part of *Oliver Twist* is the expression of the very terms in which the novel has been conceived.* In fact, it *is* the

---

* A simple, though not infallible, indication of the kind of novel one is dealing with is given by the naming of characters. In allegory and the novel of 'humours' names always denote character—e.g. Faithful and Squire Allworthy. In totally non-symbolic novelists like Jane Austen the names are quite without significance: Emma Woodhouse might equally well be called Anne Elliot. In novels which have a certain symbolic quality the names of characters generally have a peculiar rightness of their own: Heathcliff, Noah Claypole, Henry James's characters.

novel and the novel stands or falls by its validity, its total adequacy to life.

Wuthering Heights is a vision of what life in 1847 was like. Whether it can be described as a vision of what life as such—all life—is like is a question we will consider later. It is, for all its appearance of casualness and the complexity of its family relationships, a very well-constructed book, in which the technical problems of presentation have been most carefully thought out. The roles of the two narrators, Lockwood and Nelly Dean, are not casual. Their function (they the two most 'normal' people in the book) is partly to keep the story close to the earth, to make it believable, partly to comment on it from a common-sense point of view and thereby to reveal in part the inadequacy of such common sense. They act as a kind of sieve to the story, sometimes a double sieve, which has the purpose not simply of separating off the chaff, but of making us aware of the difficulty of passing easy judgments. One is left always with the sense that the last word has not been said.

The narrators do not as a rule talk realistically, though sometimes Nelly's part is to slip into a Yorkshire dialect that 'places' what she is describing and counteracts any tendency (inherent in symbolic art) to the pretentious. At critical points in the narrative we are not conscious of their existence at all; there is no attempt at a limiting verisimilitude of speech. They do not impose themselves between us and the scene. But at other times their attitudes are important.

One of the subtleties of the book is the way these attitudes change and develop; Lockwood and Nelly, like us, learn from what they experience, though at first their limitations are made use of, as in the very first scene when the expectations of the conventional Lockwood are so completely shocked by what he finds at Wuthering Heights. He goes there, he the normal Victorian gentleman, expecting to find the normal Victorian middle-class family. And what he finds—a house seething with hatred, conflict, horror—is a shock to us, too. The attack on our complacency, moral, social and spiritual, has already begun.

The centre and core of the book is the story of Catherine and Heathcliff. It is a story which has four stages. The first part, ending in the visit to Thrushcross Grange, tells of the establishing of a special relationship between Catherine and Heathcliff and of their common rebellion against Hindley and his régime in Wuthering Heights. In the second part is revealed Catherine's betrayal of

Heathcliff, culminating in her death. The third part deals with Heathcliff's revenge, and the final section, shorter than the others, tells of the change that comes over Heathcliff and of his death. Even in the last two sections, after her death, the relationship with Catherine remains the dominant theme, underlying all else that occurs.

It is not easy to suggest with any precision the quality of feeling that binds Catherine and Heathcliff. It is not primarily a sexual relationship. Emily Brontë is not, as is sometimes suggested, afraid of sexual love; the scene at Catherine's death is proof enough that this is no platonic passion, yet to describe the attraction as sexual is surely quite inadequate. Catherine tries to express her feelings to Nelly (she is about to marry Linton):

'My great miseries in this world have been Heathcliff's miseries, and I watched and felt each from the beginning: my great thought in living is himself. If all else perished, and *he* remained, *I* should still continue to be; and if all else remained, and he were annihilated, the universe would turn to a mighty stranger: I should not seem a part of it. My love for Linton is like the foliage in the woods: time will change it, I'm well aware, as winter changes the trees. My love for Heathcliff resembles the eternal rocks beneath : a source of little visible delight, but necessary. Nelly, I *am* Heathcliff! He's always, always in my mind: not as a pleasure, any more than I am always a pleasure to myself, but as my own being.'[1]

and Heathcliff cries, when Catherine is dying: 'I *cannot* live without my life, I *cannot* live without my soul.'[2] What is conveyed to us here is the sense of an affinity deeper than sexual attraction, something which it is not enough to describe as romantic love.

This affinity is forged in rebellion and, in order to grasp the concrete and unromantic nature of this book, it is necessary to recall the nature of that rebellion. Heathcliff, the waif from the Liverpool slums, is treated kindly by old Mr Earnshaw but insulted and degraded by Hindley. After his father's death Hindley reduces the boy to the status of a serf. 'He drove him from their company to the servants, deprived him of the instructions of the curate, and insisted that he should labour out of doors instead; compelling him to do so as hard as any other hand on the farm.'[3] The situation at Wuthering Heights is wonderfully evoked in the passage from Catherine's journal, which Lockwood finds in his bedroom:

'An awful Sunday!' commenced the paragraph beneath. 'I wish my father were back again. Hindley is a detestable substitute—his conduct

to Heathcliff is atrocious—H. and I are going to rebel—we took our
initiatory step this evening.

'All day had been flooding with rain; we could not go to church, so
Joseph must needs get up a congregation in the garret, and, while Hindley
and his wife basked downstairs before a comfortable fire—doing anything but reading the Bibles, I'll answer for it—Heathcliff, myself, and
the unhappy plough-boy, were commanded to take our Prayer-books,
and mount: were ranged in a row, on a sack of corn, groaning and
shivering, and hoping that Joseph would shiver too, so that he might
give us a short homily for his own sake. A vain idea! The service lasted
precisely three hours: and yet my brother had the face to exclaim, when
he saw us descending, "What, done already?" On Sunday evenings we
used to be permitted to play, if we did not make much noise; now a mere
titter is sufficient to send us into corners!

' "You forget you have a master here,' 'says the tyrant. 'I'll demolish
the first who puts me out of temper! I insist on perfect sobriety and
silence. Oh, boy! was that you? Frances darling, pull his hair as you go
by: I heard him snap his fingers." Frances pulled his hair heartily, and
then went and seated herself on her husband's knee: and there they were,
like two babies, kissing and talking nonsense by the hour—foolish
palaver that we should be ashamed of. We made ourselves as snug as our
means allowed in the arch of the dresser. I had just fastened our pinafores
together, and hung them up for a curtain, when in comes Joseph on an
errand from the stables. He tears down my handiwork boxes my ears
and croaks—

' "T' maister nobbut just buried, and Sabbath no o'ered, and t' sound
o' t' gospel still i' yer lugs, and ye darr be laiking! Shame on ye! Sit ye
down, ill childer! There's good books enough if ye'll read 'em! Sit ye
down, and think of yer sowls!"

'Saying this, he compelled us so to square our positions that we might
receive from the far-off fire a dull ray to show us the text of the lumber he
thrust upon us. I could not bear the employment. I took my dingy volume
by the scroop, and hurled it into the dog-kennel, vowing I hated a good
book. Heathcliff kicked his to the same place. Then there was a hubbub!

' "Maister Hindley!" shouted our chaplain. "Maister, coom hither!
Miss Cathy's riven th' back of 'Th' Helmet O' Salvation,' un Heathcliff's
pawsed his fit into t' first part o' 'T' Brooad Way to Destruction.' It's
fair flaysome, that ye let 'em go on this gait. Ech! th' owd man wad ha'
laced 'em properly—but he's goan!"

'Hindley hurried up from his paradise on the hearth, and seizing one
of us by the collar, and the other by the arm, hurled both into the back
kitchen, where, Joseph asseverated, "owd Nick" would fetch us as sure
as we were living, and, so comforted, we each sought a separate nook to
await his advent.'[4]

This passage reveals, in itself, a great deal of the extraordinary quality of *Wuthering Heights*. It is a passage which, in the typical manner of the novel, evokes, in language which involves the kind of attention we give to poetry, a world far larger than the scene it describes, and evokes it through the very force and concreteness of the particular scene. The rebellion of Catherine and Heathcliff is made completely concrete. They are not vague romantic dreamers. Their rebellion is against the régime in which Hindley and his wife sit in fatuous comfort by the fire whilst they are relegated to the arch of the dresser and compelled for the good of their souls to read the *Broad Way to Destruction* under the tutelage of the canting hypocrite Joseph. It is a situation not confined, in the year 1847, to the more distant homesteads of the Yorkshire moors.

Against this degradation Catherine and Heathcliff rebel, hurling their pious books into the dog-kennel. And in their revolt they discover their deep and passionate need of each other. He, the outcast slummy, turns to the lively, spirited, fearless girl who alone offers him human understanding and comradeship. And she, born into the world of Wuthering Heights, senses that to achieve a full humanity, to be true to herself as a human being, she must associate herself totally with him in his rebellion against the tyranny of the Earnshaws and all that tyranny involves.

It is this rebellion that immediately, in this early section of the book, wins over our sympathy to Heathcliff. We know he is on the side of humanity and we are with him just as we are with Oliver Twist, and for much the same reasons. But whereas Oliver is presented with a sentimental passivity, which limits our concern, Heathcliff is active and intelligent and able to carry the positive values of human aspiration on his shoulders. He is a conscious rebel. And it is from his association in rebellion with Catherine that the particular quality of their relationship arises. It is the reason why each feels that a betrayal of what binds them together is in some obscure and mysterious way a betrayal of everything, of all that is most valuable in life and death.

Yet Catherine betrays Heathcliff and marries Edgar Linton, kidding herself that she can keep them both, and then discovering that in denying Heathcliff she has chosen death. The conflict here is, quite explicitly, a social one. Thrushcross Grange, embodying as it does the prettier, more comfortable side of bourgeois life, seduces Catherine. She begins to despise Heathcliff's lack of 'culture'. He has no conversation, he does not brush his hair, he is dirty, whereas Edgar, besides being handsome, 'will be rich and

I shall like to be the greatest woman of the neighbourhood, and I shall be proud of having such a husband'.[5] And so Heathcliff runs away and Catherine becomes mistress of Thrushcross Grange.

Heathcliff returns, adult and prosperous, and at once the social conflict is re-emphasised. Edgar, understandably, does not want to receive Heathcliff, but Catherine is insistent:

> 'I know you didn't like him,' she answered, repressing a little the intensity of her delight. 'Yet, for my sake, you must be friends now. Shall I tell him to come up?'
> 'Here,' he said, 'into the parlour?'
> 'Where else?' she asked.
> He looked vexed, and suggested the kitchen as a more suitable place for him. Mrs Linton eyed him with a droll expression—half angry, half laughing at his fastidiousness.
> 'No,' she added after a while; 'I cannot sit in the kitchen. Set two tables here, Ellen: one for your master and Miss Isabella, being gentry, the other for Heathcliff and myself, being the lower orders. Will that please you, dear? . . .'[6]

And from the moment of Heathcliff's reappearance Catherine's attempts to reconcile herself to Thrushcross Grange are doomed. In their relationship now there is no tenderness, they trample on each other's nerves, madly try to destroy each other; but, once Heathcliff is near, Catherine can maintain no illusions about the Lintons. The two are united only in their contempt for the values of Thrushcross Grange. 'There it is,' Catherine taunts Edgar, speaking of her grave, 'not among the Lintons, mind, under the chapel roof, but in the open air, with a headstone.'[7] The open air, nature, the moors are contrasted with the world of Thrushcross Grange. And the contempt for the Lintons is a *moral* contempt, not a jealous one. When Nelly tells Heathcliff that Catherine is going mad, his comment is:

> 'You talk of her mind being unsettled. How the devil could it be otherwise in her frightful isolation? And that insipid paltry creature attending her from *duty* and *humanity*! From *pity* and *charity*! He might as well plant an oak in a flower pot, and expect it to thrive, as imagine he can restore her to vigour in the soil of his shallow cares!'[8]

The moral passion here is so intense, so deeply imbedded in the rhythm and imagery of the prose, that it is easy to be swept along without grasping its full and extraordinary significance. Heathcliff at this point has just perpetrated the first of his callous and ghastly acts of revenge, his marriage to Isabella. It is an act so morally repulsive that it is almost inconceivable that we should be able now to take seriously his attack on Edgar Linton, who has, after all, by conventional, respectable standards, done nobody any harm. And yet we *do* take the attack seriously because Emily Brontë makes us. The passion of the passage just quoted has the quality of great poetry. Why?

We continue to sympathise with Heathcliff, even after his marriage with Isabella, because Emily Brontë convinces us that what Heathcliff stands for is morally superior to what the Lintons stand for. This is, it must be insisted, not a case of some mysterious 'emotional' power with which Heathcliff is charged. The emotion behind his denunciation of Edgar is *moral* emotion. The words 'duty' and 'humanity', 'pity' and 'charity' have precisely the kind of force Blake gives such words in his poetry.*

They are used not so much paradoxically as in a sense inverted but more profound than the conventional usage. Heathcliff speaks, apparently paradoxically, of Catherine's 'frightful isolation', when to all appearances she is in Thrushcross Grange less isolated, more subject to care and society, than she could possibly be with him. But in truth Heathcliff's assertion is a paradox only to those who do not understand his meaning. What he is asserting with such intense emotional conviction that we, too, are convinced, is that what he stands for, the alternative life *he* has offered Catherine, is more natural (the image of the oak enforces this), more social and more moral than the world of Thrushcross Grange. Most of those who criticise Heathcliff adversely (on the grounds that he is unbeliev- able, or that he is a neurotic creation, or that he is merely the Byronic satan-hero revived) fail to appreciate his significance because they fail to recognise this moral force. And as a rule they fail to recognise the moral force because they are themselves, consciously or not, of the Linton party.

The climax of this inversion by Heathcliff and Catherine of the common standards of bourgeois morality comes at the death of Catherine. To recognise the revolutionary force of this scene one

---

* e.g. Pity would be no more
    If we did not make somebody Poor;
    And Mercy no more could be
    If all were as happy as we

or

    Was Jesus humble? or did he
    Give any proofs of Humility.

has only to imagine what a different novelist might have made of it.

The stage is all set for a moment of conventional drama. Catherine is dying, Heathcliff appears out of the night. Two possibilities present themselves: either Catherine will at the last reject Heathcliff, the marriage vow will be vindicated and wickedness meets its reward; or true love will triumph and reconciliation proclaim the world well lost. It is hard to imagine that either possibility ever crossed Emily Brontë's mind, for either would destroy the pattern of her book, but her rejection of them is a measure of her moral and artistic power. For instead of its conventional potentialities the scene acquires an astonishing moral power. Heathcliff confronted with the dying Catherine, is ruthless, morally ruthless: instead of easy comfort he offers her a brutal analysis of what she has done.

'You teach me now how cruel you've been—cruel and false. _Why_ did you despise me? _Why_ did you betray your own heart Cathy? I have not one word of comfort. You deserve this. You have killed yourself. Yes, you may kiss me, and cry: and wring out my kisses and tears: they'll blight you—they'll damn you. You loved me—then what _right_ had you to leave me? What right—answer me—for the poor fancy you felt for Linton? Because misery and degradation, and death, and nothing that God or Satan could inflict would have parted us, _you_, of your own will, did it. I have not broken your heart—_you_ have broken it; and in breaking it you have broken mine. So much the worse that I am strong. Do I want to live? What kind of living will it be when you—oh, God! would _you_ like to live with your soul in the grave?'[9]

It is one of the harshest passages in all literature, but it is also one of the most moving. For the brutality is not neurotic, nor sadistic, nor romantic. The Catherine–Heathcliff relationship, standing as it does for a humanity finer and more morally profound than the standards of the Lintons and Earnshaws, has to undergo the kind of examination Heathcliff here brings to it. Anything less, anything which smudged or sweetened the issues involved, would be inadequate, unworthy. Heathcliff knows that nothing can save Catherine from death but that one thing alone can give her peace, a full and utterly honest understanding and acceptance of their relationship and what it implies. There is no hope in comfort or compromise. Any such weakness would debase them both and make a futile waste of their lives and death. For Heathcliff and Catherine, who reject the Lintons' chapel roof and the consolations of Christianity, know, too, that their relationship is more important than death.

In the section of the book that follows Catherine's death Heathcliff continues the revenge he has begun with his marriage to Isabella. It is the most peculiar section of the novel and the most difficult because the quality of Heathcliff's feeling is of a kind most of us find hard to comprehend. All normal and healthy human feeling is rejected. He cries:

'I have no pity! I have no pity! The more the worms writhe, the more I yearn to crush out their entrails! It is a moral teething; and I grind with greater energy, in proportion to the increase of pain.'[10]

'It is a moral teething'—the phrase is both odd and significant, giving as it does the answer to our temptation to treat this whole section as a delineation of pathological neurosis. Heathcliff becomes a monster: what he does to Isabella, to Hareton, to Cathy, to his son, even to the wretched Hindley, is cruel and inhuman beyond normal thought. He seems concerned to achieve new refinements of horror, new depths of degradation. And we tend to feel, perhaps, unless we read with full care and responsiveness, that Emily Brontë has gone too far, that the revenge (especially the marriage of Cathy and Linton Heathcliff) had o'erflown the measure.

And yet it is only one side of our minds, the conscious, limited side that refers what we are reading to our everyday measures of experience that makes this objection. Another side, which is more completely responding to Emily Brontë's art, is carried on. And the astonishing achievement of this part of the book is that, despite our protests about probability (protests which, incidentally, a good deal of twentieth-century history makes a little complacent), despite everything he does and is, we continue to sympathise with Heathcliff—not, obviously, to admire him or defend him, but to give him our inmost sympathy, to continue in an obscure way to identify ourselves with him *against* the other characters.

The secret of this achievement lies in such a phrase as 'it is a moral teething' and in the gradually clarifying pattern of the book. Heathcliff's revenge may involve a pathological condition of hatred, but it is not at bottom merely neurotic. It has a moral force. For what Heathcliff does is to use against his enemies with complete ruthlessness their own weapons, to turn on them (stripped of their romantic veils) their own standards, to beat them at their own game. The weapons he uses against the Earnshaws and Lintons are their own weapons of money and arranged marriages. He gets power over them by the classic methods of the ruling class, expropriation and property deals. He buys out Hindley and reduces him to drunken impotency, he marries Isabella and then organises the marriage of his son to Catherine Linton, so that the entire property of the two families shall be controlled by himself. He systematically degrades Hareton Earnshaw to servility and illiteracy. 'I want the triumph of seeing *my* descendant fairly lord of *their* estates! My child hiring their children to till their father's lands for wages.'[11] (This is a novel which, some critics will tell you, has nothing to do with anything as humdrum as society or life as it is actually lived.) And what particularly tickles Heathcliff's fancy is his achievement of the supreme ruling-class triumph of making Hareton, the boy he degrades, feel a deep and even passionate attachment towards himself.

Heathcliff retains our sympathy throughout this dreadful section of the book because instinctively we recognise a rough moral justice in what he has done to his oppressors and because, though he is inhuman, we understand *why* he is inhuman. Obviously we do not approve of what he does, but we understand it; the deep and complex issues behind his actions are revealed to us. We recognise that the very forces which drove him to rebelling for a higher freedom have themselves entrapped him in their own values and determined the nature of his revenge.

If *Wuthering Heights* were to stop at this point it would still be a great book, but a wholly sombre and depressing one. Man would be revealed as inevitably caught up in the meshes of his own creating; against the tragic horror of Heathcliff's appalling rebellion the limited but complacent world of Thrushcross Grange would seem a tempting haven and the novel would resolve itself into the false antithesis of Thrushcross Grange–Wuthering Heights, just as in *Oliver Twist* the real antithesis becomes sidetracked into the false one of Brownlow/Fagin. But *Wuthering Heights*, a work of supreme and astonishing genius, does not stop here. We have not done with Heathcliff yet.

For at the moment of his horrible triumph a change begins to come over Heathcliff.

'It is a poor conclusion, is it not?' he observed, having brooded a while on the scene he had just witnessed: 'an absurd termination to my violent exertions? I get levers and mattocks to demolish the two houses, and train myself to be capable of working like Hercules, and when everything

is ready and in my power, I find the will to lift a slate off either roof has
vanished! My old enemies have not beaten me; now would be the precise
time to revenge myself on their representatives: I could do it, and none
could hinder me. But where is the use? I don't care for striking; I can't
take the trouble to raise my hand! That sounds as if I had been labouring
the whole time only to exhibit a fine trait of magnanimity. It is far from
being the case: I have lost the faculty of enjoying their destruction, and
I am too idle to destroy for nothing.

'Nelly, there is a strange change approaching: I'm in its shadow at
present.'[12]

and he goes on to speak of Cathy and Hareton, who 'seemed a
personification of my youth, not a human being'. 'Hareton's aspect
was the ghost of my immortal love; of my wild endeavour to hold
my right; my degradation, my pride, my happiness and my anguish.' When Nelly asks 'But what do you mean by a *change*,
Mr Heathcliff?' he can only answer 'I shall not know that till it
comes,' he said. 'I'm only half conscious of it now.' Once more the
stage is set for a familiar scene, the conversion of the wicked who
will in the final chapter turn from his wickedness. And once more
the conventional must look again.

The change that comes over Heathcliff and the novel and leads
us on to the wonderful, quiet, gentle, tentative evocation of nature
in the final sentence, is a very subtle one. It has something of the
quality of the last two acts of *The Winter's Tale* but is much less
complete, less confident. Mr Klingopulos in his interesting essay on
Wuthering Heights[13] has commented on the ambiguous nature of
this final tranquillity. I do not agree with his analysis but he has
caught the tone most convincingly. Heathcliff, watching the love
of Cathy and Hareton grow, comes to understand something of the
failure of his own revenge. As Cathy teaches Hareton to write and
stops laughing at his ignorance we too are taken back to the first
Catherine.

Cathy and Hareton are not in the novel an easy re-creation of
Catherine and Heathcliff; they are, as Mr Klingopulos remarks,
different people, even lesser people, certainly people conceived on
a less intense and passionate scale than the older lovers. But they
do symbolise the continuity of life and human aspirations, and it is
through them that Heathcliff comes to understand the hollowness
of his triumph. It is when Hareton, who loves him, comes to
Cathy's aid when he strikes her that the full meaning of his own
relationship with Catherine comes back to him and he becomes
aware that in the feeling between Cathy and Hareton there is

something of the same quality. From the moment that Cathy and Hareton are drawn together as rebels the change begins. For now for the first time Heathcliff is confronted not with those who accept the values of Wuthering Heights and Thrushcross Grange but with those who share, however remotely, his own wild endeavours to hold his right.

Heathcliff does not repent. Nelly tries to make him turn to the consolations of religion.

'You are aware, Mr Heathcliff,' I said, 'that from the time you were thirteen years old, you have lived a selfish, unchristian life; and probably hardly had a Bible in your hands during all that period. You must have forgotten the contents of the Book, and you may not have space to search it now. Could it be hurtful to send for someone—some minister of any denomination, it does not matter which—to explain it, and show you how very far you have erred from its precepts; and how unfit you will be for its heaven, unless a change takes place before you die?'

'I'm rather obliged than angry, Nelly,' he said, 'for you remind me of the manner in which I desire to be buried. It is to be carried to the church-yard in the evening. You and Hareton may, if you please, accompany me: and mind, particularly, to notice that the sexton obeys my directions concerning the two coffins! No minister need come; nor need anything be said over me.—I tell you I have nearly attained my heaven, and that of others is altogether unvalued and uncoveted by me.'[14]

One sentence here, in its limpid simplicity, especially evokes the state of mind Heathcliff has come to. He speaks of the manner in which he wishes to be buried. 'It is to be carried to the churchyard in the evening.' The great rage has died in him. He has come to see the pointlessness of his fight to revenge himself on the world of power and property through its own values. Just as Catherine had to face the full moral horror of her betrayal of their love, he must face the full horror of his betrayal too. And once he has faced it he can die, not nobly or triumphantly, but at least as a man, leaving with Cathy and Hareton the possibility of carrying on the struggle he has begun, and in his death he will achieve again human dignity, 'to be carried to the churchyard in the evening'.

It is this re-achievement of manhood by Heathcliff, an under-standing reached with no help from the world he despises, which, together with the developing relationship of Cathy and Hareton and the sense of the continuity of life in nature, gives to the last pages of *Wuthering Heights* a sense of positive and unsentimental hope. The Catherine–Heathcliff relationship has been vindicated.

Life will go on and others will rebel against the oppressors. Nothing has been solved but much has been experienced. Lies, complacencies and errors, appalling errors, have been revealed. A veil has been drawn from the conventional face of bourgeois man; he has been revealed, through Heathcliff, without his mask.

Above all, the quality of the feeling that binds Catherine and Heathcliff has been conveyed to us. Their love, which Heathcliff can without idealism call immortal, is something beyond the individualist dream of two soul-mates finding full realisation in one another; it is an expression of the necessity of man, if he is to choose life rather than death, to revolt against all that would destroy his inmost needs and aspirations, of the necessity of all human beings to become, through acting together, more fully human. Catherine, responding to this deep human necessity, rebels with Heathcliff but in marrying Edgar (a 'good' marriage if ever there was one) betrays her own humanity; Heathcliff, by revenging himself on the tyrants through the adoption of their own standards, makes more clear those standards but betrays too his humanity and destroys his relationship with the dead Catherine whose spirit must haunt the moors in terror and dismay.

Only when the new change has come over Heathcliff and he again recognises through Hareton (and remotely, therefore, through Catherine herself) the full claims of humanity can Catherine be released from torment and their relationship re-established. Death is a matter of little importance in *Wuthering Heights* because the issues the novel is concerned with are greater than the individual life and death. The deaths of Catherine and Heathcliff are indeed a kind of triumph because ultimately each faces death honestly, keeping faith. But there is no suggestion that death itself is a triumph: on the contrary it is life that asserts itself, continues, blossoms again.

Mr David Wilson in his excellent essay on Emily Brontë [15] to which I am deeply indebted (though I do not agree with all of his interpretation) suggests an identification, not necessarily conscious in Emily Brontë's mind, of Heathcliff with the rebellious working men of the hungry 'forties' and of Catherine with that part of the educated class which felt compelled to identify itself with their cause. Such a formulation, suggestive as it is, seems to me to be too far removed from the actual impact of *Wuthering Heights* as a novel to be satisfactory. But Mr Wilson has done a valuable service in rescuing *Wuthering Heights* from the transcendentalists and in insisting on the place of Haworth (generally assumed to be a remote country village) in the industrial revolution and its attendant social unrest.* The value of his suggestion with regard to Heathcliff and Catherine seems to me in the emphasis it gives to the concrete, local particularity of the book.

It is very necessary to be reminded that just as the values of Wuthering Heights and Thrushcross Grange are not simply the values of *any* tyranny but specifically those of Victorian society, so is the rebellion of Heathcliff a particular rebellion, that of the worker physically and spiritually degraded by the conditions and relationships of this same society. That Heathcliff ceases to be one of the exploited is true, but it is also true that just in so far as he adopts (with a ruthlessness that frightens even the ruling class itself) the standards of the ruling class, so do the human values implicit in his early rebellion and in his love for Catherine vanish. All that is involved in the Catherine–Heathcliff relationship, all that it stands for in human needs and hopes, can be realised only through the active rebellion of the oppressed.

Wuthering Heights then is an expression in the imaginative terms of art of the stresses and tensions and conflicts, personal and spiritual, of nineteenth-century capitalist society. It is a novel without idealism, without false comforts, without any implication that power over their destinies rests outside the struggles and actions of human beings themselves. Its powerful evocation of nature, of moorland and storm, of the stars and the seasons is an essential part of its revelation of the very movement of life itself. The men and women of *Wuthering Heights* are not the prisoners of nature; they live in the world and strive to change it, sometimes successfully, always painfully, with almost infinite difficulty and error.

This unending struggle, of which the struggle to advance from class society to the higher humanity of a classless world is but an episode, is conveyed to us in *Wuthering Heights* precisely because the novel is conceived in actual, concrete, particular terms, because the quality of oppression revealed in the novel is not abstract but concrete, not vague but particular. And that is why Emily Brontë's novel is at the same time a statement about the life she knew, the life of Victorian England, and a statement about life as such. Virginia Woolf, writing about it, said:

* One of the most interesting exhibits in the Haworth museum today is a proclamation of the Queen ordering the reading of the Riot Act against the rebellious workers of the West Riding.

That gigantic ambition is to be felt throughout the novel, a struggle half thwarted but of superb conviction, to say something through the mouths of characters which is not merely 'I love' or 'I hate' but 'we, the whole human race' and 'You; the eternal powers . . .' the sentence remains unfinished.[16]

I do not think it remains unfinished.

6

THACKERAY: *VANITY FAIR*

(1847–8)

Thackeray's method in *Vanity Fair* is in all essentials the method of Fielding in *Tom Jones*. To call the method panoramic, as many critics do (and in particular Mr Percy Lubbock in *The Craft of Fiction*), is true but can be misleading. It is true in the sense that Thackeray's vision shifts about, that he surveys a broad field of territory and that the reader is kept at a certain distance from the scene.

The core of *Vanity Fair* is not a developing emotional situation involving the intense experience of a limited number of characters. We do not get 'inside' one particular character and see the action through the imprint upon his consciousness, nor do we become so closely involved in a concrete situation (seeing it, so to speak, backward and forward and from many angles) that we have a sense of encompassing the whole complex of forces that makes such a situation vital. Even at a big dramatic moment, such as the famous scene when Rawdon Crawley returns from the spunging-house and finds Becky and Lord Steyne together, we do not have the effect of a vital clash of conflicting forces.

We wonder what is going to happen, we relish the theatrical quality of the scene; but our emotions are not deeply engaged because we know that nothing truly disturbing or exquisitely comic will be revealed; nothing will be changed, neither Becky nor Rawdon nor Steyne nor us. Even the ambiguity which Thackeray is at pains to achieve—'was Becky innocent?'—does not succeed in making us look at the scene in a fresh way, because the issue is morally a false one. Whether Becky is actually Steyne's mistress or not scarcely matters. And Thackeray knows it scarcely matters; with the result that the raising of the issue gives the impression of a sexual archness rather than that of a genuine ambiguity, the effect of which would be, by raising an important doubt in our mind, to make us suddenly see the episode in a new way, with a new flash of insight.

Everything in *Vanity Fair* remains at a distance because between the scene and the reader there always stands, with an insistent solidity, Thackeray himself. Of course it is true that every novelist stands between the scene of his novel and the reader, controlling and directing our attention. But by a Jane Austen or an Emily Brontë or a Dickens the directing is done, not necessarily un-obtrusively (we are always aware of Dickens especially), but with an eye primarily on the object or the scene that is being revealed, whereas with Thackeray one has constantly the sense that the scene itself is less important than something else.

Take, for instance, the very first episode of *Vanity Fair*, the great scene of the departure of Amelia and Becky from Miss Pinkerton's academy in Chiswick Mall, at the climax of which Becky throws the dictionary out of the coach window into the garden. It is a beautifully and dramatically conceived scene, an episode that is to tell us more about Becky than fifty pages of reminiscence; but notice how Thackeray handles the climax:

Sambo of the bandy legs slammed the carriage-door on his young weeping mistress. He sprang up behind the carriage. 'Stop!' cried Miss Jemima, rushing to the gate with a parcel.

'It's some sandwiches, my dear,' said she to Amelia. 'You may be hungry, you know; and Becky, Becky Sharp, here's a book for you that my sister—that is, I,—Johnson's Dictionary, you know; you mustn't leave us without that. Good-bye. Drive on, coachman. God bless you!'

And the kind creature retreated into the garden, overcome with emotions.

But, lo! and just as the coach drove off, Miss Sharp put her pale face out of the window, and actually flung the book back into the garden.

This almost caused Jemima to faint with terror.

'Well, I never,' said she; 'what an audacious—' Emotion prevented her from completing either sentence. The carriage rolled away. . . .[1]

This is excellent, but there is one word in the passage that prevents the scene from being fully dramatic and stops it achieving its potential force—the word 'actually' in the sentence describing the flinging of the book. This one word colours the scene, investing it with a sense of scandalised amazement which may well reflect Miss Jemima's feelings but which weakens (not disastrously, of course, but appreciably) the objective force of the episode. After all, we know without that adverb what Miss Jemima's feelings are; its only function in the description is in fact to bring a particular colouring to the scene. It is Thackeray who steps in and in stepping in reduces the whole episode. The tone of that 'actually' is the tone that puts almost everything in *Vanity Fair* at a distance.

Does it necessarily matter, this distancing of a novel by its author? I do not think it matters at all if it is a successful part of a consistent plan. Fielding achieves it very successfully in *Tom Jones*, so does Samuel Butler in the greater part of *The Way of All Flesh*. But the method, it must be recognised, puts an enormous strain on the author. If we are to be constantly seeing a novel through a kind of haze of reflectiveness spread around it by the author, then the comments, the reflections, the qualities of mind of the writer have got to be distinguished by quite remarkable understanding and control. We have seen how, in *Oliver Twist*, the conscious attitudes of Dickens are very frequently inadequate to what he is portraying. With Dickens this does not matter very much because his dramatic method concentrates the whole attention on the developing scene and makes the comment unimportant (one can mentally skip it without doing violence to the novel).

But with Thackeray's method the opposite holds. Everything depends on the capacity of the novelist to encompass in his own personality an adequate attitude to what he is describing. If he succeeds he will indeed cast around his puppets that understanding and humanity which (in Henry James's words about Fielding) do 'somehow really enlarge, make everyone and everything important'. But if his attitudes are less than adequate, then by driving his characters into the distance he will be weakening his whole effect.

The description 'panoramic' may become misleading when applied to *Vanity Fair* if the word suggests that the individual characters in Thackeray's novel are not important, that the book has anything of the nature of the documentary. Mr Lubbock (whose pages on Thackeray are consistently stimulating) seems to me on rather dangerous ground when he writes:

Not in any single complication of incident, therefore, nor in any single strife of will, is the subject of *Vanity Fair* to be discerned. It is nowhere but in the impression of a world, a society, a time—certain manners of life within a few square miles of London, a hundred years ago. Thackeray flings together a crowd of the people he knows so well, and it matters not at all if the tie that holds them to each other is of the slightest; it may easily chance that his good young girl and his young adventuress set out together on their journey, their paths may even cross from time to time later on. The light link is enough for the unity of his tale, for that unity does not depend on an intricately woven intrigue. It depends in truth upon one fact only, the fact that all his throng of men and women are strongly, picturesquely typical of the world from which they are taken, that all in their different ways can add to the force of its effect. The book is not the story of any one of them, it is the story that they unite to tell, a chapter in the notorious career of well-to-do London.[2]

There is so much that is true here that it may seem a little pedantic and ungenerous to insist that it is not altogether helpful. It is indeed true that the subject of *Vanity Fair* is a society—the world of well-to-do Britain (not merely London) at the beginning of the last century. But it is also true that this subject is seen in terms not of a general impression but of specific human relationships. 'An impression of manners' is not an accurate description. As we look back on Thackeray's novel we recall a whole world, a bustling, lively, crowded world; but we recall it in terms of individual people and their relationships. These people are presented to us, by and large, in the tradition of the comedy of humours. That is to say each has particular characteristics, somewhat exaggerated and simplified, by which they are easily comprehensible.

These characters are almost always static [Mr Edwin Muir has said]. They are like a familiar landscape, which now and then surprises us when a particular effect of light or shadow alters it, or we see it from a new prospect. Amelia Sedley, George Osborne, Becky Sharp, Rawdon Crawley—these do not change as Eustacia Vye and Catherine Earnshaw do; the alteration they undergo is less a temporal one than an unfolding in a continuously widening present. Their weaknesses, their vanities, their foibles, they possess from the beginning and never lose to the end; and what actually does change is not these, but our knowledge of them.[3]

This is, broadly speaking, true, but not quite fair. Some of the characters in *Vanity Fair* do change; Pitt Crawley, for instance, who begins as a simple unworldly prig, blossoms out with a fortune into an ambitious worldly idiot, and yet remains the same person, and particularly Amelia who, in her infuriating way, develops a

good deal in the course of the novel.* The important point, however, is that Thackeray's puppets (it is a pity he used the word, for
it has encouraged an underestimation of his subtlety) are all involved in human relationships which, though not presented with
much intimacy or delicacy of analysis, are for the most part true
and convincing relationships.

We know, for instance, quite precisely enough the quality of
George Osborne's feeling for Amelia or of Rawdon's for Becky.
The latter relationship could scarcely be better illustrated than by
the letter Rawdon writes from the spunging-house:

'Dear Becky' [Rawdon wrote],—'*I hope you slept well.* Don't be
frightened if I don't bring you in your *coffy.* Last night as I was coming
home smoaking, I met with an *accadent.* I was *nabbed* by Moss of Cursitor
Street—from whose *gilt and splendid parler* I write this—the same that
had me this time two years. Miss Moss brought in my tea—she is grown
very *fat,* and as usual, had *her stockens down at heal.*

'It's Nathan's business—a hundred and fifty—with costs, hundred and
seventy. Please send me my desk and some *cloths*—I'm in pumps and a
white tye (something like Miss M's stockings)—I've seventy in it. And
as soon as you get this, Drive to Nathan's —offer him seventy-five down,
and ask *him to renew*—say I'll take wine—we may as well have some
dinner sherry; but not *picturs,* they're too dear.

'If he won't stand it. Take my ticket and such of your things as you
can *spare,* and send them to *Balls*—we must, of coarse, have the sum
to-night. It won't do to let it stand over, as to-morrow's Sunday; the
beds here are not very *clean,* and there may be other things out against
me—I'm glad it an't Rawdon's Saturday for coming home. God bless
you.

'Yours in haste,
'R.C.

'*P.S.*—Make haste and come.'[4]

Every sentence of this is masterly. Thackeray is marvellously good
at depicting typical upper-class young men—the sketch of James
Crawley with his 'dawgs' is a delightful minor example—the kind
of people of whom Matthew Arnold wrote: 'One has often wondered whether upon the whole earth there is anything so un-
intelligent, so unapt to perceive how the world is really going,

* One or two characters change quite unconvincingly, not because they develop
organically but because Thackeray seems to change his plans for them half-way
through. Lady Jane Sheepshanks (who marries Pitt Crawley) is one of these. Some
critics consider that Amelia changes in this way only, but I think the evidence is
against them.

as an ordinary young Englishman of our upper class.'[5] Now it is
true that we do not enter intimately into the feelings of any of these
characters, but it would be wrong to suppose they are any the less
human. When we say we know the quality of their feelings what
we mean is that we know all *about* those feelings, not that we share
them in the way we share Emma's responses. But it is not, even in
the very broadest sense, their manners that are the subject of the
book.

The central relationship with which Thackeray, like Fielding
and Richardson and Jane Austen, is concerned is marriage. *Vanity
Fair* is about the difficulties of personal relationships, particularly
marriage relationships, in nineteenth-century, upper-class English
society. It is a well-organised novel despite its discursiveness and
some lapses in construction (the most clumsy being the return to
England of Dobbin and Joseph Sedley; the chronology and therefore what has been well called the choreography is very confused
here). The planning of the double story of Becky and Amelia is by
no means as casual as Mr Lubbock would seem to suggest. Not
only do the two girls stand in a complementary relation to each
other—the one active and 'bad', the other passive and 'good'—but
their careers are juxtaposed in contrasting curves of development,
Becky's curve rising in the centre of the book, Amelia's declining.
The fact that from the death of George at Waterloo to the reunion
at Pumpernickel the two women scarcely meet does not weaken the
pattern of the book nor blur the underlying contrast between them,
for each is playing her necessary part.

Lord David Cecil in his essay on Thackeray notices the strong
pattern of the book but seems curiously imperceptive as to its
significance.

The characters of the two girls are designed to illustrate the laws
controlling *Vanity Fair* as forcibly as possible. And in order to reveal
how universally these laws work, they are of strongly-contrasted types.

Amelia is an amiable character, simple, modest and unselfish. But, says
Thackeray, in *Vanity Fair* such virtue always involves as a corollary a
certain weakness. Amelia is foolish, feeble and self-deceived. She spends
a large part of her youth in a devotion, genuine enough to begin with,
later merely a sentimental indulgence in her emotions, to a man unworthy
of her. For him she rejects a true lover; and though she is ultimately
persuaded to marry this lover, it is only ironically enough, through the
chance caprice of the woman for whom her first love had rejected her.
Nor is she wholly saved from the punishment of her error. By the time
he marries her, her true lover has learnt to see her as she is.

Becky, the second 'heroine' is not weak and self-deceived; she is a
'bad' character, a wolf not a lamb, artful, bold and unscrupulous. But she,
no more than Amelia, can escape the laws governing the city of her
nativity. By nature a Bohemian, she is beguiled, by the false glitter surrounding the conventional rank and fashion which are the vulgar and
predominant idols of *Vanity Fair* to spend time and energy in trying to
attain them. She succeeds, but she is not satisfied. Nor is she able to maintain her success. She is too selfish to treat the husband, who is necessary
to her position, with the minimum of consideration necessary to keep
him. She sinks to the underworld of society. But her eyes are not opened;
and the rest of her life is spent in trying to retrieve herself, so far successfully that we see her last as a charitable dowager, a pattern of respectability, a final flamboyant example of the deceptiveness of outward appearances in *Vanity Fair*.

This parallel structure extends to the men who enter Amelia's and
Becky's lives; they are similarly contrasted, similarly self-deceived. . . .[6]

This appears to me a remarkable example of criticism gone
wrong, missing the essential part of the novel under consideration.
To write of Becky as 'beguiled by the false glitter surrounding the
conventional rank and fashion, etc.' is surely to miss the vital
question: what else could Becky do? And once we ask that question
it becomes irrelevant to talk of self-deception. Lord David Cecil,
having insisted that the book is about a society, Vanity Fair, then
proceeds to abstract the characters morally from that society and
discuss them as though they had any existence outside it. Because
he sees the individual and society as separate entities and social
'laws' as something abstract and distinct from personal moral
standards he misses the vital motive-force of the novel.

The trouble with Becky is not that 'she is too selfish, etc.' (It is
not selfishness of that type that leads to the intrigue with Lord
Steyne, nor is the keeping of a husband in that sense Becky's
greatest necessity.) Becky's dilemma—and Amelia's for that
matter—is the dilemma of Jane Fairfax in *Emma* and of almost all
the heroines of English fiction from Moll Flanders onwards. What
is a young woman of spirit and intelligence to do in the polite but
barbarous world of bourgeois society? Only two courses are open
to her, the passive one of acquiescence to subjugation or the active
one of independent rebellion.* The only hope of a compromise

* It is interesting to note how in *Vanity Fair* as in the eighteenth-century novels
the one thing that none of the important characters (however hard pressed) ever
contemplates doing is physical work. For a woman the job of governess or companion
is degradation enough, below that is unthinkable, however critical one's situation,
and as a last resort prostitution is a greatly preferable alternative to labour. As for

solution is the lucky chance of finding an understanding man like Mr Darcy or Mr Knightley, rich enough to buy certain civilised values and kind enough to desire them; but the snag is that the Mr Knightleys require something Becky by her very fate (she has had a harder fight than Jane Fairfax) can never have—'true elegance of mind'. You cannot pick that up in Soho or slaving for Miss Pinkerton.

Becky, like Moll and Clarissa and Sophia (each after her own fashion) before her, rebels. She will not submit to perpetual slavery and humiliation within the governess trade. And so she uses consciously and systematically all the men's weapons plus her one natural material asset, her sex, to storm the men's world. And the consequence is of course morally degrading and she is a bad woman all right. But she gains our sympathy nevertheless—not our approving admiration but our human fellow-feeling—just as Heathcliff does, and she too gains it not in spite but because of her rebellion. She gains it from the moment she flings kind Miss Jemima's dictionary out of the window and thereby rejects the road that would have led her to become a Miss Jemima herself. It is this act that sets in motion the vital vibrations of the book, and it is interesting to compare it with that other act of rebellion that sets off so vastly different a book as *Wuthering Heights*.

There is no mystery about the vitality and fascination of Becky Sharp. It is not a sentimental sympathy that she generates. Thackeray, the Victorian gentleman, may tone down her rebellion by ambiguous adverbs and a scandalised titter, but the energy he has put into her is more profound than his morals or his philosophy and she sweeps him along. Of course Becky is unadmirable (though for the moment when she tells Amelia the truth about George Osborne, 'that selfish humbug, that low-bred cockney-dandy, that padded booby, etc.', one can forgive her much), but what else could she have been?

'It isn't difficult to be a country gentleman's wife,' Rebecca thought. 'I think I could be a good woman if I had five thousand a year. I could dawdle about in the nursery, and count the apricots on the wall. I could

men, the typical solution—credit and the generosity of relatives breaking down—is a commission in the Army. This failing, Newgate, or the spunging-house is the next step, with the extreme possibility of a life of crime. But no one ever becomes a worker and the reason is obvious. Once one had passed from the owning to the labouring class one was lost. One never got back and life, to one who had once known the standards of the civilised world, was simply not worth living. George Osborne found he could not possibly live on two thousand a year; but it is left to Amelia to discover that 'women are working hard, and better than she can, for twopence a day'. (ch. L) water plants in a green-house, and pick off dead leaves from the geraniums. I could ask old women about their rheumatisms, and order half-a-crown's worth of soup for the poor. I shouldn't miss it much, out of five thousand a year. I could even drive out ten miles to dine at a neighbour's, and dress in the fashions of the year before last. I could go to church and keep awake in the great family pew; or go to sleep behind the curtains and with my veil down, if I only had practice. I could pay everybody, if I had but the money . . .'[7]

In other words she could have been, with luck, someone not unlike Mrs Elton in *Emma*, though she would have played her cards a good deal better. She could alternatively, of course, have had a shot at being Amelia. Amelia also could be a very good woman (by Victorian standards) on five thousand a year and at the conclusion of the book is in this happy condition. But not before the consequences of being Amelia have been pretty thoroughly shown up, even to the wooden old war-horse, Dobbin.

Amelia is often regarded as one of Thackeray's failures, the weak link in *Vanity Fair*. I think this is because too many readers want her to be something she cannot be within the pattern of the book— a heroine. Certainly as a heroine she cuts a very feeble figure. Certainly, too, there is a recurring ambiguity in Thackeray's attitude to her. If we tend to think of her as a heroine *manquée* it is largely his fault, for in the first part of the novel it is hard to believe that his comments on poor, tender, abused little Amelia are in any deep sense ironical. And yet if we expect too much of Amelia we cannot put all the blame on Thackeray. We are warned in the first chapter by the tone of: 'She had twelve intimate and bosom friends out of the twenty-four young ladies . . .' And by chapter XII we should realise that Amelia is not being produced for our uncritical approval:

. . . in the course of a year (love) turned a good young girl into a good young woman—to be a good wife presently when the happy time should come. This young person (perhaps it was very imprudent in her parents to encourage her, and abet her in such idolatry and silly, romantic ideas), loved, with all her heart, the young officer in his Majesty's service with whom we have made a brief acquaintance. She thought about him the very first moment on waking; and his was the very last name mentioned in her prayers. She never had seen a man so beautiful or so clever; such a figure on horseback: such a dancer: such a hero in general. Talk of the Prince's bow! what was it to George's? She had seen Mr Brummell, whom everybody praised so. Compare such a person as that to her

George! . . . He was only good enough to be a fairy prince; and oh, what magnanimity to stoop to such a humble Cinderella! . . .⁸

(Here again Thackeray does not play quite fair. It is pretty clear that the 'goods' of the first sentence are not to be taken quite at their face-value, but the tone of 'silly, romantic ideas' is highly ambiguous. Against whom is the irony directed?) Certainly after fifteen years of self-deception as widow no one can go on taking Amelia as deserving our unqualified sympathy. And indeed the whole section dealing with the Sedleys' life at Fulham is done with a realism that precludes uncritical attitudes. Had Thackeray been by this time wallowing in the kind of sentimentality which many readers feel is implicit in his attitude to Amelia, he would scarcely have permitted himself the realism of allowing young George to leave his mother with barely a regret. Nor would he have risked the final description of his heroine as a 'tender little parasite'.

No, Amelia is no more the heroine of *Vanity Fair* than Becky. She is, rather, the opposite possibility, the image that Becky might have chosen to become. And it is Thackeray's merit that he shows us Amelia as she is, a parasite, gaining life through a submission that is not even an honest submission, exploiting her weakness, deceiving even herself.

The weakness in the pattern of *Vanity Fair* lies not in Amelia (despite the ambiguities I have referred to) but in Dobbin. It is he who lets down the novel, not merely because he is in the psychological sense unconvincing, but because he fails to bear the weight of the positive values implicit in the pattern of the book, values which, had they been successfully embodied, would have made of this novel a greater *Tom Jones*, a real comic epic in prose.

Dobbin begins as a sheepish but sensitive schoolboy fighting the snobs, but as the novel proceeds he becomes a sort of clothes-horse of the respectable middle-class virtues. He is shrewd and cultured (young George Osborne finds him a mine of information during their trip through Europe) but simple and steadfast. How any man of such sense and character could remain utterly in love, in quite an adolescent way, with Amelia all those years Thackeray can neither explain nor convince us. Perhaps his is a case of arrested development in the emotional sphere? But no, there is no such suggestion to be found. We are to take Dobbin seriously. He is not a hero but he is a rock, or rather an oak, the rugged old oak around which the tender parasite clings.

The effect of Dobbin is to keep, obscurely but nevertheless quite definitely, in the background of the novel a wooden sort of norm, an average but good man, certainly not a rebel yet just as certainly untainted by the values of Vanity Fair. It is because he is thus untainted that Dobbin is psychologically unconvincing as a character and useless to the pattern of the book. For Thackeray's great strength, by and large, is his ability to see his characters as parts of a concrete social situation. His concern, for instance, with financial details in his novel is an example not of a trivial naturalism but of his power of setting his people so firmly in the world that we believe in them completely even though we know comparatively little about them.

We do not know very much, when all is said, about Becky herself. We can only guess how happy she is, what qualms she may have, precisely what emotions drive her to act as she does. We do not know how much she likes Rawdon and her unkindness to her child is not quite convincing. She is, as we have noticed, always at a distance. And yet she is emphatically there, alive beyond a doubt, one of the great characters in all fiction. How does Thackeray do it? Fundamentally, I suggest, by this precise and firm placing of a character in a concrete social situation. We may not be told very much about what Becky *feels* but we know exactly what her situation is. We know her relationship, financial and social (in the broadest sense), with every other character in the book and we know the guiding principle of her conduct, that she wants to be mistress of her own life.

And so the psychological gaps, the gaps in analysis, the ambiguities surrounding her do not matter much. Indeed there is a sense in which their absence is a positive strength, for most such analysis in novels involves unreal abstraction, presents problems of character in a static way and diverts attention from the reality of the character's actions by an exclusive concentration on his motives. In a very important sense we know more about Becky than about, say, Proust's hero. Like Oliver Twist and Jeanie Deans she has a typical, symbolic quality which makes her an individual and yet more than an individual.

This sort of typicality is regarded by some critics as a weakness in art. To say of a character that he is a type is supposed to show a deficiency, a failure to individualise on the part of the author. But in fact characters in literature who are in no sense typical cannot well be artistically interesting. If Hamlet were an isolated creature, a being whose individuality made him essentially and utterly different from other individuals, a neurotic who had lost touch with the typical contours of human existence and relationships, he would not be a great artistic character. He is in fact no less an individual for being a type, a fact which Shakespeare recognised well enough when he presented him in the convention of the melancholic man, a class of character easily recognisable by and significant to the Elizabethan audience.

The artistic type (and here we see the value of the old theory of 'humours' despite its psychological crudity) is not an average, not a lowest common multiple of human characteristics, but rather the embodiment of certain forces which come together in a particular social situation to create a peculiar kind of vital energy. Molière's miser is not a typical man in the sense of being an average man, but he is a type, a more-than-individual as well as a very definite, unique individual. Charlie Chaplin on the screen is not an average man (no one has ever seen anybody quite like him) and yet he is unmistakably typical, not just an oddity for all his uniqueness, but somehow more typical of the 'little man', the individual worker in our industrial society, than any little man we actually know; and in this lies his greatness.

Thackeray's best characters seem to me types in just this sense, and it is this quality that gives them their vitality despite their distance from the reader, the limits to our knowledge about them and the crippling inadequacy of Thackeray's comments. Becky is an unmistakable individual, yet she is every woman of spirit rebelling against the humiliations forced on her by certain social assumptions. Old Osborne, similarly, is every successful nineteenth-century business man, encased in a gloomy, luxurious ugliness in that big house in Russell Square. How solid he is! How all respectable England trembles at the horror of his anger when he hears his son has married a bankrupt's daughter! How a whole world and its values come crowding up as he leans over and speaks to his grandson when he hears of old John Sedley's death:

'You see,' said old Osborne to George, 'what comes of merit and industry, and judicious speculations, and that. Look at me and my banker's account. Look at your poor grandfather, Sedley, and his failure. And yet he was a better man than I was, this day twenty years—a better man, I should say, by ten thousand pound.'[9]

Thackeray himself does his best to destroy his picture of the ruling-class world. Only at certain moments will he remove him-

self from the position of chorus and allow the scene to make its full
effect. Then his talent for the extreme and the bizarre is given full
scope. Old Osborne reacting to George's death; the wicked old
Sir Pitt Crawley, helpless, dumb and half-insane, sobbing pitifully
when left in the charge of a servant-girl; Lady Bareacres sitting in
her horseless carriage in Brussels; the description of Lord Steyne's
house and family: such episodes are extraordinarily successful. But
constantly, throughout the whole novel, the effect produced by
what the characters do is weakened or dissipated by the author's
comments.

It is not so much the sense of these comments as their tone that
is disastrous. It is an ambiguous tone. In the worst of senses it is
vulgar. Thackeray's attitude to nearly all his main characters—and
especially Amelia and Becky—is ambiguous. And the ambiguity
does not arise from subtlety, a sense that the whole truth can never
be told, that there is always a complicating factor in every judgment;
it comes from pusillanimity, from a desire to expose illusions and
yet keep them.

The artistic motive-force of *Vanity Fair* is Thackeray's vision
of bourgeois society and of the personal relationships engendered
by that society. That is what his novel is about. And the sweep and
vividness of it, the vitality of Becky, the rich and teeming comic
life of the panorama, all derive from the insight and honesty of
Thackeray's vision. He pierces the hypocrisies of Vanity Fair,
reveals the disgusting, brutal, degrading sordidness behind and
below its elegant glitter. It is the heyday of bourgeois society that
he paints, the days when an expanding economy could for a while
carry along the hangers-on through the credit it generated (this is
how Becky and Rawdon manage to live well on nothing a year)
despite its pitiless rejection of its failures like old John Sedley. And
the human feeling of Thackeray rebels at this society. And yet . . .
and yet . . . doesn't he rather like it? To put the doubt in literary
terms: is *Vanity Fair* a novel of utter integrity, as *Wuthering
Heights* is?

The human indignation is constantly diluted by the clubman's
bogus mellowness, not the mellowness of Fielding which is based
on the real (though limited) security of the English revolution, but
the mellowness of the successful novelist who has looked the world
in the face and doesn't care to go on looking. He turns to a loose
and general cynicism:

Ah! *Vanitas Vanitatum!* Which of us is happy in this world? Which of us has his desire? or, having it, is satisfied?—Come, children, let us shut up the box and the puppets, for our play is played out.[10]

It is the feeblest of endings, the flattest of statements of faith. And one doesn't even feel that Thackeray means it.

7

GEORGE ELIOT: MIDDLEMARCH

(1871–2)

This is so large a novel, spacious, unhurried, broad in scope and attitude, that to insist that it is the same *kind* of novel as *Emma* may seem at first a little perverse. The range of interest, obviously, is far greater. A concern which includes such issues as the relation of art to life, the progress of the biological sciences, the social consequences of the Reform Bill of 1832, the problems of the scholar's vocation, the psychology of martyrdom, such a concern would not appear superficially to be usefully comparable with the interests of Jane Austen. Yet the range of interest, wonderfully impressive as it is, does not reveal any basically new attitude to the art of fiction. George Eliot extends the method of Jane Austen but does not substantially alter it.

The world of Middlemarch is bigger and more various than that of Highbury, the interests of its inhabitants take different forms and lead us to issues which can justly be called wider; but *Middlemarch*, though it is in some respects the most impressive novel in our language, and one which it is not ridiculous to compare with the novels of Tolstoy, is not in any sense a revolutionary work.

The comparison with Jane Austen is worth developing. In the very first chapter of the novel we come upon the description of Mr Brooke:

A man nearly sixty, of acquiescent temper, miscellaneous opinions, and uncertain vote. He had travelled in his younger years, and was held in this part of the country to have contracted a too rambling habit of mind. Mr Brooke's conclusions were as difficult to predict as the weather:

it was only safe to say that he would act with benevolent intentions, and he would spend as little money as possible in carrying them out.[1]

Apart perhaps from an already apparent interest in her characters' 'opinions', an interest which on this level Jane Austen anyway shares, there is nothing whatever to distinguish this passage, even in its diction, from similar descriptions in *Emma*. The same quality of wit is there, dependent on a poise which in its turn depends on a precise and highly conscious set of social values which emanate from full participation in the life of a particular community. The next sentence, however, marks a change:

For the most glutinously indefinite minds enclose some hard grains of habit; and a man has been seen lax about all his own interests except the retention of his snuff-box, concerning which he was watchful, suspicious, and greedy of clutch.

It is not merely that with the introduction of the word glutinously we sense a lack of 'elegance' which in *Emma* would never do; the whole sentence has a heaviness, almost a clumsiness, which corresponds to a habit of mind in George Eliot quite distinct from that of the earlier novelist. A certain forcing of the issue, one might call it, a tendency to illustrate a shade too often the moral generalisation. From a description, witty and certainly not morally uncritical, of Mr Brooke, a description in which *his* vitality as a character and *our* view of him are developed together, we pass immediately to the generalisation which has the effect of putting Mr Brooke away at a distance again. Almost imperceptibly, with the 'has been seen', we have passed from Mr Brooke's 'mind' (such as it is) to 'minds' in general. The transition is not offensive and it marks one of the great strengths of George Eliot as a novelist, her insistence that we should continuously relate her fiction to our lives, that we should not lose ourselves in the fantastic world of the novel; but it illustrates the direction of the modification she brings to Jane Austen's method. When Jane Austen in *Emma* offers us a generalised comment, such as her remarks about dancing and the holding of dances, we feel no temptation to apply her irony as a thought on the meaning of Life; with George Eliot the more presumptuous claim implicit in the capital letter is for ever being made.

That the claim is not fatuous is ensured by the breadth of her interest and the inclusiveness of her prodigious intelligence. Let us turn to another of her minor characters, Mrs Cadwallader:

Her life was rurally simple, quite free from secrets either foul, dangerous, or otherwise important, and not consciously affected by the great affairs of the world. All the more did the affairs of the great world interest her when communicated in the letters of high-born relations: the way in which fascinating younger sons had gone to the dogs by marrying their mistresses, the fine old-blooded idiocy of young Lord Tapir, and the furious gouty humours of old Lord Megatherium; the exact crossing of genealogies which had brought a coronet into a new branch and widened the relations of scandal,—these were topics of which she retained details with the utmost accuracy, and reproduced them in an excellent pickle of epigrams, which she herself enjoyed the more because she believed as unquestioningly in birth and no-birth as she did in game and vermin. She would never have disowned any one on the ground of poverty: a De Bracy reduced to take his dinner in a basin would have seemed to her an example of pathos worth exaggerating, and I fear his aristocratic vices would not have horrified her. But her feeling towards the vulgar rich was a sort of religious hatred; they had probably made all their money out of high retail prices, and Mrs Cadwallader detested high prices for everything that was not paid in kind at the Rectory: such people were no part of God's design in making the world; and their accent was an affliction to the ears. A town where such monsters abounded was hardly more than a sort of low comedy, which could not be taken account of in a well-bred scheme of the universe. Let any lady who is inclined to be hard on Mrs Cadwallader inquire into the comprehensiveness of her own beautiful views, and be quite sure that they afford accommodation for all the lives which have the honour to coexist with hers.

With such a mind, active as phosphorous, biting everything that came near into the form that suited it, how could Mrs Cadwallader feel that the Miss Brookes and their matrimonial prospects were alien to her?[2]

George Eliot is sometimes regarded as a worthy but essentially forbidding writer; her Puritanism is too easily associated with a moral narrowness. It is a very unfair criticism. The vivacity of the passage just quoted has nothing narrow about it. The wit is 'deeper' than Jane Austen's wit only in the sense that a more variously stocked consciousness is involved. 'Rurally simple' places the parish of Tipton in a world larger than anyone in *Emma* contemplates. The play on 'the great affairs of the world' and 'the affairs of the great world', involves a knowledge of 'affairs' to which Jane Austen would make no claim—and it is not a bogus knowledge. On the contrary George Eliot's urbanity is quite without the shallowness of a superficial sophistication and it gives a wonderful breadth and solidity to her criticism. 'Fine old-blooded idiocy': the phrase might easily be shrill, the criticism crude, but in fact it adequately encompasses a whole stratum of society. Mrs Cadwallader's 'excellent pickle of epigrams' is backed by her creator's own wit, just as the force of 'active as phosphorous' is backed by George Eliot's awareness of scientific processes. The point is not, of course, that George Eliot is more intelligent than Jane Austen but that her intelligence has encompassed a larger field.

In the passage on Mrs Cadwallader, as in that on Mr Brooke, a tell-tale sentence intrudes. 'Let any lady who is inclined to be hard on Mrs Cadwallader inquire into the comprehensiveness of her own beautiful views, and be quite sure that they afford accommodation for all the lives which have the honour to coexist with hers.' Again we have the direct thrust at the reader's conscience, not offensive in itself, yet less than fully incorporated in George Eliot's overall purposes. The adjective 'beautiful' is clumsy and inadequate, the irony implicit in it crude, not on the level of the use of previous adjectives. And the phrase 'all the lives which have the honour, etc.' is an uncertain one. In what sense is 'honour' to be read? Against what is the irony directed? The ambiguity betrays a weakness. Why is the sentence there at all?

Can we, perhaps, in these sentences in which George Eliot turns her moral gaze direct upon the reader and beckons to his personal conscience, isolate a weakness in her method and put our finger on a note in *Middlemarch* which may justly be described as a shade flat? It is a complicated question to which we shall have to return.

Meanwhile let us turn to another description in *Middlemarch*, that scene when Dorothea, six weeks after her marriage, is disclosed weeping in her apartment in Rome.

To those who have looked at Rome with the quickening power of a knowledge which breathes a growing soul into all historic shapes, and traces out the suppressed transitions which unite all contrasts, Rome may still be the spiritual centre and interpreter of the world. But let them conceive one more historical contrast: the gigantic broken revelations of that Imperial and Papal city thrust abruptly on the notions of a girl who had been brought up in English and Swiss Puritanism, fed on meagre Protestant histories and an art chiefly of the hand-screen sort; a girl whose ardent nature turned all her small allowance of knowledge into principles, fusing her actions into their mould, and whose quick emotions gave the most abstract things the quality of pleasure or pain, a girl who had lately become a wife, and from the enthusiastic acceptance of untried duty found herself plunged in tumultuous preoccupation with her personal lot. The weight of unintelligible Rome might lie easily on bright nymphs to whom it formed a background for the brilliant picnic of

Anglo-Foreign society: but Dorothea had no such defence against deep impressions. Ruins and basilicas, palaces and collossi, set in the midst of a sordid present, where all that was living and warm-blooded seemed sunk in the deep degeneracy of a superstition divorced from reverence; the dimmer but yet eager Titanic life gazing and struggling on walls and ceilings; the long vistas of white forms whose marble eyes seemed to hold the monotonous light of an alien world: all this vast wreck of ambitious ideals, sensuous and spiritual, mixed confusedly with the signs of breathing forgetfulness and degradation, at first jarred her as with an electric shock, and then urged themselves on her with that ache belonging to a glut of confused ideas which check the flow of emotion. Forms both pale and glowing took possession of her young sense, and fixed themselves in her memory even when she was not thinking of them, preparing strange associations which remained through her after-years. Our moods are apt to bring with them images which succeed each other like the magic-lantern pictures of a doze; and in certain states of dull forlornness Dorothea all her life continued to see the vastness of St Peter's, the huge bronze canopy, the excited intention in the attitudes and garments of the prophets and evangelists in the mosaics above, and the red drapery which was being hung for Christmas spreading itself everywhere like a disease of the retina.

Not that this inward amazement of Dorothea's was anything very exceptional: many souls in their young nudity are tumbled out among incongruities and left to 'find their feet' among them, while their elders go about their business. Nor can I suppose that when Mrs Casaubon is discovered in a fit of weeping six weeks after her wedding, the situation will be regarded as tragic. Some discouragement, some faintness of heart at the new real future which replaces the imaginary, is not unusual and we do not expect people to be deeply moved by what is not unusual. That element of tragedy which lies in the very fact of frequency, has not yet wrought itself into the coarse emotion of mankind; and perhaps our frames could hardly bear much of it. If we had a keen vision and feeling of all ordinary human life, it would be like hearing the grass grow and the squirrel's heart beat, and we should die of that roar which lies on the other side of silence. As it is, the quickest of us walk about well wadded with stupidity.[3]

It is a passage which shows George Eliot, if not quite at her best, as the great novelist she is; and it shows very clearly the direction of her extension of Jane Austen's method. It is, for a piece of writing describing and analysing a peculiarly intimate personal emotion, a remarkably impersonal passage. Dorothea's own feelings, though we are persuasively made to understand them, are revealed as embedded within a generalised situation. George Eliot begins by recalling the Roman scene, not through anyone's sense-impressions, but in its historical, highly intellectualised context. The clash of Catholic and Protestant, pagan and Puritan, are evoked at first objectively and then made gradually to illuminate Dorothea's mental state.

Only very occasionally are we brought into contact with her actual feelings. We do not feel *closer* to her as we read on, but we understand her better and the understanding is not a purely objective one. George Eliot has here herself the power to give 'the most abstract things the quality of a pleasure or a pain' because under her contemplation of the particular, concrete situation (Dorothea's state of mind at this moment) the generalised experience and abstract thought cease to be abstract and become symbolic—the squirrel's heart-beat and the roar which lies on the other side of silence.

The achievement of the symbolic moment, the instant in which through our gained insight into the particular situation a new apprehension of the processes of life is reached, is not frequent in *Middlemarch*. By and large the novel is no more symbolic than *Emma*. It works on our consciousness through the presentation of very real, rounded characters in a very real, solidly constructed social situation.

George Eliot takes a great deal of pains with her 'background' and the question arises as to whether background is the right word to use. What, we have to ask ourselves, is the central theme, the unifying subject of this *Study of Provincial Life?*

From the Prelude one gathers that this is to be a novel about latter-day Saint Theresas, about those whose flames, 'fed from within, soared after some illimitable satisfaction, some object which would never justify weariness, which would reconcile self-despair with the rapturous consciousness of life beyond self'; and we are given the hint that the problem of such modern saints is that they are 'helped by no coherent social faith and order which could perform the function of knowledge for the ardently willing soul'.[4]

This expectation is immediately justified by the introduction of Dorothea Brooke, the mention of the Blessed Virgin in the second sentence of the first chapter confirming all our anticipation. And the first movement of the novel, the whole of the first book up to the introduction of Lydgate, continues the development of the theme. Dorothea is the centre of it and Dorothea is presented to us wonderfully, her limitations, her immaturity, her 'theoretic' mind no less than her ardour, her yearning for a life more deeply satisfying than Tipton and Middlemarch can give.

Up to this point Middlemarch may be said to be to the novel what Highbury is to *Emma*, the world in which Dorothea and Casaubon and the surrounding characters live, and very subtly does George Eliot convey how Middlemarch has made them what they are. We feel no temptation to abstract these characters from the society that contains them. Dorothea is not Saint Theresa. She is an intelligent and sensitive girl born into the English landed ruling class of the early nineteenth century, full of half-formulated dissatisfactions with the fatuous, genteel life of the women of her class, seeking something beyond the narrow 'selfishness' of her acquaintances and turning towards a religious Puritanism and a high-minded philanthropy (cottages for the farm-labourers) to satisfy her unfulfilled potentialities; finally and disastrously imagining that in marriage to Casaubon she will find the fulfilment of her aspirations.

It is with the introduction of Lydgate, quickly followed by the Vincys and Bulstrode, that the basic structure of the novel changes. We know now that George Eliot in fact joined together in *Middlemarch* two novels originally planned separately—the story of *Miss Brooke* and the story of Lydgate. But even without this knowledge we should find, before the end of the first book, a change coming over *Middlemarch*. George Eliot forces the problem on our attention in chapter XI, just after the introduction of Lydgate and Rosamond.

Certainly nothing at present could seem much less important to Lydgate than the turn of Miss Brooke's mind, or to Miss Brooke than the qualities of the woman who had attracted this young surgeon. But any one watching keenly the stealthy convergence of human lots, sees a slow preparation of effects from one life on another, which tells like a calculated irony on the indifference or the frozen stare with which we look at our unintroduced neighbour. Destiny stands by sarcastic with our *dramatis personæ* folded in her hand.

Old provincial society had its share of this kind of subtle movement: had not only its striking downfalls, its brilliant young professional dandies who ended by living up an entry with a drab and six children for their establishment, but also those less marked vicissitudes which are constantly shifting the boundaries of social intercourse and begetting new consciousness of inter-dependence. Some slipped a little downward some got higher footing: people denied aspirates, gained wealth, and fastidious gentlemen stood for boroughs; some were caught in political currents, some in ecclesiastical, and perhaps found themselves surprisingly grouped in consequence; while a few personages or families that stood with rocky firmness amid all this fluctuation, were slowly presenting new

aspects in spite of solidity, and altering with the double change of self
and beholder. Municipal town and rural parish gradually made fresh
threads of connection—gradually, as the old stocking gave way to the
savings bank, and the worship of the solar guinea became extinct; while
squires and baronets, and even lords who had once lived blamelessly afar
from the civic mind, gathered the faultiness of closer acquaintanceship.
Settlers, too, came from distant counties, some with an alarming novelty
of skill, others with an offensive advantage in cunning. In fact, much the
same sort of movement and mixture went on in old England as we find
in older Herodotus, who also, in telling what had been, thought it well
to take a woman's lot for his starting point.[5]

It is a clumsy passage and its clumsiness comes from its function
as a bridge between what the novel started as and what it is becoming; but it is also a passage full of interest to an analysis of the
book. 'Destiny stands by sarcastic with our *dramatis personæ* folded
in her hand': It is a pretentious, unhelpful sentence, calling up a
significance it does not satisfy. Who, one feels tempted to ask, is
this Destiny, a character previously unmentioned by the author?
And, as a matter of fact, the figure of a sarcastic fate does not
preside over *Middlemarch*. On the contrary George Eliot is at pains
to dissociate herself from any such concept. Throughout the novel
with an almost remorseless insistence, each moral crisis, each
necessary decision is presented to the participants and to us with
the minimum of suggestion of an all-powerful Destiny. It is the
very core of George Eliot's morality and of the peculiar moral force
of the book that her characters, despite most powerful pressures,
and above all the prevailing pressure of the Middlemarch way of
life, are not impelled to meet each particular choice in the way they
do. Lydgate *need* not have married Rosamond, though we understand well enough why he did. Neither need Fred Vincy have
reformed; it is George Eliot's particular achievement here that
she convinces us of a transformation against which all the cards of
'Destiny' have been stacked.

My point here is that the appearance of this concept in chapter XI is not justified by the total organisation of the book and that
it betrays a weakness, a lack of control, which is intimately connected with the transformation of the novel from the story of
Dorothea to something else.

The something else is indicated in the sentence beginning 'Old
provincial society . . .' We realise as we read on that the centre of
attention of the novel is indeed being shifted, so that the story of
Miss Brooke is now not an end in itself but a starting-point. What

we are to contemplate is nothing less than the whole subtle movement of old provincial society. The background has become the
subject.

That it was bound to do so has already been hinted. So firmly
is the story of Dorothea in those early chapters 'set' in the society
of which she is a part, that it seems almost inevitable that an adequate examination of Dorothea must involve an examination of the
Middlemarch world more thorough than that so far contemplated,
and there is no doubt that it was under a sense of this compulsion
that George Eliot altered the plan of the book and called it *Middlemarch*. And the central question in our estimate of the novel is how
far she succeeds in this great, ambitious attempt thus to capture
and reveal the relation of each individual story, the stories of
Dorothea, of Lydgate, of Bulstrode, to the whole picture, the
Middlemarch world.

Dr Leavis, in his extremely interesting section on George Eliot
in *The Great Tradition*, writes:

> George Eliot had said in *Felix Holt*, by way of apology for the space
> she devoted to 'social changes' and 'public matters': 'there is no private
> life which has not been determined by a wider public life.' The aim im-
> plicit in this remark is magnificently achieved in *Middlemarch*, and it is
> achieved by a novelist whose genius manifests itself in a profound
> analysis of the individual.[6]

With the last statement—the emphasis on the profound analysis—
one must assuredly agree and one could not hope valuably to add
to Dr Leavis's remarks on Casaubon, Lydgate, Rosamond and
Bulstrode; nor is one disposed to quarrel with his estimate of the
treatment of Ladislaw and Dorothea.

Middlemarch is a wonderfully rich and intelligent book and its
richness lies in a consideration of individual characters firmly placed
in an actual social situation (it is because Ladislaw is never thus
placed but remains a romantic dream-figure that he is a failure). But
there seems to me a contradiction at the heart of *Middlemarch*, a
contradiction between the success of the parts and the relative
failure of the whole.

Middlemarch as a whole is not a deeply moving book. The total
effect is immensely impressive but not immensely compelling. Our
consciousness is modified and enriched but not much changed. We
are moved by particular things in the book: by the revelation of
Casaubon's incapacity; by the hideous quality of the Lydgate-

Rosamond impasse (certainly upon our pulses this), he unable to
find a chink in her smooth blonde armour and she incapable of
understanding the kind of man he could have been; by Dorothea's
disillusionment in Rome; by the scene in which Mrs Bulstrode
accepts her share in her husband's downfall. Mrs Bulstrode, conventional, unprofound, more than a little smug, a pillar of the
church and the Middlemarch bourgeoisie, learns of the black
disgrace of her husband through the revelation of his totally
discreditable past:

'But you must bear up as well as you can, Harriet. People don't blame
you. And I'll stand by you whatever you make up your mind to do,' said
the brother, with rough but well-meaning affectionateness.

'Give me your arm to the carriage, Walter,' said Mrs Bulstrode, 'I feel
very weak.'

And when she got home she was obliged to say to her daughter, 'I am
not well my dear; I must go and lie down. Attend to your papa. Leave
me in quiet. I shall take no dinner.'

She locked herself in her room. She needed time to get used to her
maimed consciousness, her poor lopped life, before she could walk
steadily to the place allotted her. A new searching light had fallen on her
husband's character, and she could not judge him leniently: the twenty
years in which she had believed in him and venerated him by virtue of
his concealments came back with particulars that made them seem an
odious deceit. He had married her with that bad past life hidden behind
him and she had no faith left to protest his innocence of the worst that
was imputed to him. Her honest ostentatious nature made the sharing of
a merited dishonour as bitter as it could be to any mortal.

But this imperfectly-taught woman, whose phrases and habits were
an odd patch-work had a loyal spirit within her. The man whose prosperity she had shared through nearly half a life, and who had unvaryingly
cherished her—now that punishment had befallen him it was not possible
to her in any sense to forsake him. There is a forsaking which still sits at
the same board and lies on the same couch with the forsaken soul,
withering it the more by unloving proximity. She knew, when she locked
her door, that she should unlock it ready to go down to her unhappy
husband and espouse his sorrow, and say of his guilt, I will mourn and
not reproach. But she needed time to gather up her strength; she needed
to sob out her farewell to all the gladness and pride of her life. When
she had resolved to go down, she prepared herself by some little acts
which might seem mere folly to a hard onlooker; they were her way of
expressing to all spectators visible or invisible that she had begun a new
life in which she embraced humiliation. She took off all her ornaments
and put on a plain black gown, and instead of wearing her much-
adorned cap and large bows of hair, she brushed her hair down and out

on a plain bonnet-cap, which made her look suddenly like an early
Methodist.

Bulstrode, who knew that his wife had been out and had come in
saying that she was not well, had spent the time in an agitation equal to
hers. He had looked forward to her learning the truth from others, and
had acquiesced in that probability, as something easier to him than any
confession. But now that he imagined the moment of her knowledge
come, he awaited the result in anguish. His daughters had been obliged
to consent to leave him, and though he had allowed some food to be
brought to him, he had not touched it. He felt himself perishing slowly
in unpitied misery. Perhaps he should never see his wife's face with
affection in it again. And if he turned to God there seemed to be no
answer but the pressure of retribution.

It was eight o'clock in the evening before the door opened and his
wife entered. He dared not look up at her. He sat with his eyes bent down,
and as she went towards him she thought he looked smaller—he seemed
so withered and shrunken. A movement of new compassion and old
tenderness went through her like a great wave, and putting one hand on
his which rested on the arm of the chair, and the other on his shoulder,
she said, solemnly but kindly—

'Look up, Nicholas.'

He raised his eyes with a little start and looked at her half amazed for
a moment: her pale face, her changed mourning dress, the trembling
about her mouth, all said 'I know': and her hands and eyes rested gently
on him. He burst out crying and they cried together, she sitting at his
side. They could not yet speak to each other of the shame which she was
bearing with him, or of the facts which had brought it down on them.
His confession was silent, and her promise of faithfulness was silent.
Open-minded as she was, she nevertheless shrank from the words which
would have expressed their mutual consciousness as she would have
shrunk from flakes of fire. She could not say, 'How much is only slander
and false suspicion?' and he did not say, 'I am innocent.'[7]

In such an episode as this the moral and emotional basis of a
personal relationship is explored with an insight and a sympathy
wholly admirable. And we are moved not simply because George
Eliot's moral concern is so profound and sure but because the scene,
with its many ramifications (including the implicit comparison with
the atittude of Rosamond), is presented with so deep a sense of the
social interpenetration that makes up life. And yet—it is the
paradox of the novel—this sense of social interpenetration, so
remarkably revealed in the exploration of the individual dilemma
and so consistently and consciously sought after by George Eliot
throughout the novel, does not in fact infuse the book as a whole.

Middlemarch taken in its completeness has almost everything except what is ultimately the most important thing of all, that final vibrant intensity of the living organism. Despite its superb achievements, despite the formidable intelligence which controls the whole book and rewards us, each time we return to it, with new insights, new richness of analysis and observation, there is something missing. We do not care about these people in the way in which, given the sum of human life and wisdom involved, we ought to care. What is lacking is not understanding, not sympathy, not warmth, certainly not seriousness.

George Eliot is the most intelligent of novelists; she always knows what she ought to do and she never shirks any issue. But she seems to lack what one might call a sense of the vital motion of things: she feels after this sense, but does not capture it. For all her intellect, all her human sympathy, all her nobility and generosity of mind, there is something of life that eludes her, that sense of the contradictions within every action and situation which is the motive-force of artistic energy and which perhaps Keats was seeking to express when he referred to Shakespeare's 'negative capability'.

George Eliot possesses this negative capability when she explores a particular situation, a concrete problem; *then* the conflicts within the essence are perforce accepted and in fighting themselves out breathe the breath of life into the scene. But it is as though in her philosophy, her consciously formulated outlook, there is no place for the inner contradiction. The word 'determined' in the sentence from *Felix Holt* quoted by Dr Leavis is, I think, significant.

I believe that most of the weaknesses of *Middlemarch* spring from this. It is behind the failure to impose an organic unity on the novel. The intention is, clearly, that Middlemarch itself should be the unifying factor, but in fact it is not. The 'subtle movement' of society which George Eliot herself refers to is not, in the achieved novel, caught. On the contrary the view of society presented is a static one. Nor is this simply because provincial society in the Midlands about 1832 was indeed comparatively unchanging (no society is really static when an artist looks at it), though it is perhaps significant that George Eliot, writing in the 1870s, should have set her novel forty years back. What is more important is the failure of the attempts to give 'historical colour' (like the surveying of the railroad and the election scenes) which are conscientious but not—on the artistic level—convincing, not integral to the novel's pattern.

More vital still is the fact that the various stories within the novel, though linked by the loose plot, have no organic unity. Many of the chief characters are related by blood, but their artistic relationship within the pattern of the novel is not fully realised. Between the story of Dorothea and that of Lydgate there is, it is true, an essential link. Lydgate's career (it is not by accident that he is a man) is the other side of the Saint Theresa theme. 'Lydgate and Dorothea together are the vehicle for the main theme in *Middlemarch*. The compromise each ultimately makes between the life to which they aspired and the life the conditions permit symbolises the conception at the heart of the book!'[8] Mrs Bennett's remark is to the point; and the phrase 'the life the conditions permit' is, I think, most significant.

For in such a phrase the limitation of the view of society implicit in *Middlemarch* is revealed and the reason for George Eliot's ultimate failure to capture its movement indicated. Society in this novel is presented to us as 'there'; that it is a part of a historical process is suggested intellectually only. And because the Middlemarch world is the given, static reality, the characters of the novel must be seen as at its mercy. They are free to make certain moral decisions within the bounds of the Middlemarch world, yet they are held captive by that world.

Hence the temptation of George Eliot, once she accepts the social implications of her story, to introduce an unconvincing, unrealised 'Destiny'. The artist in her does not believe in this Destiny and therefore when her imagination is fully engaged in the exploration of a concrete problem of individual relationships the concept of an impregnable social destiny disappears. But it is always lurking in the background and it eats into the overall vitality of the novel. In a sense it is a product of George Eliot's strength, her recognition of the complex social basis of morality. Had she not felt compelled to make Middlemarch the chief character of her book (a compulsion springing from her own honesty of analysis) she would not have needed the further social understanding which her later conception of the novel involved. She would not have attempted that advance on the art of Jane Austen which makes her at once a more impressive novelist and a less satisfactory one.

George Eliot's view of society is in the last analysis a mechanistic and determinist one. She has an absorbing sense of the power of society but very little sense of the way it changes. Hence her moral attitudes, like her social vision, tend to be static. 'We are all of us born in moral stupidity, taking the world as an udder to feed our supreme selves.'[9] The image, more than half ironical as it seems to be in the particular context, is significant, hinting as it does at a fully mechanistic outlook (not unlike Locke's conception of the mind as a blank sheet of white paper) in which the individual is essentially passive, a recipient of impressions, changed by the outside world but scarcely able to change it.

It is not by chance that human aspirations fare poorly in *Middlemarch*. All of the main characters, save Dorothea and Ladislaw and Mary and Fred, are defeated by Middlemarch, and Mary and Fred are undefeated only because they have never fought a thorough-going battle with the values of Middlemarch society. Mary and the Garths, it is true, reject the more distasteful aspects of nineteenth-century morality—the money-grabbing of old Featherstone, the hypocritical dishonesty of Bulstrode—but they accept as proper and inevitable the fundamental set-up of Middlemarch. Integrity and hard work within the framework of the *status quo* is the ideal of conduct that Mary demands of Fred, decent enough standards as far as they go but scarcely adequate (as one immediately realises if one applies them to Lydgate's dilemma) as an answer to the profound moral problems raised by the book as a whole or its central theme, and it is observable that the tensions of the book in the Garth–Vincy passages are considerably lower than in the Dorothea, Lydgate or Bulstrode sections.

It is George Eliot's mechanistic philosophy, too, which is at the root of the weakness, noted at the beginning of this essay, in her method of posing to us the moral issues at stake in the novel. The point here, it is worth insisting, is not that her moral concern should be consistent and explicit, not that she should continuously refer us back to our own consciences, but that she should do so in a way which weakens the tension of the scene she is describing and places her characters at a distance which makes an intimate conveying of their feelings difficult. Dr Leavis is, I am sure, quite right to stress as inadequate the view of George Eliot expressed in Henry James's words:

> We feel in her, always, that she proceeds from the abstract to the concrete; that her figures and situations are evolved, as the phrase is, from her moral consciousness, and are only indirectly the products of observation.[10]

I do not think that the continuous moral concern in *Middlemarch* is abstract or that George Eliot is trying to impose abstract concepts on a recalcitrant chunk of life. For all the deep moral preoccupation the novel has little of the moral fable about it.

On the contrary her method is to present most concretely a particular situation and then draw to our attention the moral issues involved in the choices which have to be made. The method is perhaps a little heavy-going; as we pass in the novel from moral crisis to moral crisis we feel a shade oppressed by the remorselessness of the performance. But what is oppressive is not any abstract plan lurking behind the screen but the very nature of George Eliot's moral judgments; there is too often a kind of flatness about them, which actually weakens the conflicts within the scene she is presenting. And the flatness comes, I think, from the assumptions implicit in her moral view of the world as an udder.

To put it in another way, her standards of right and wrong (perhaps her emphasis on Law and her sympathy for Judaism—not revealed in this particular book—are significant) are not quite adequate to the complexity of her social vision. Henry James's criticism that her figures and situations are not *seen* in the irresponsible plastic way is unfortunately expressed and invites the drubbing Dr Leavis rightly gives it, but it nevertheless hints at a genuine weakness. George Eliot's high-minded moral seriousness (which might in fact be described as Utilitarianism modified by John Stuart Mill, Comte and her early evangelical Christianity) does have an unfortunate effect on the novel, not because it is moral or serious, but because it is mechanistic and undialectical.

And like all mechanistic thinkers George Eliot ends by escaping into idealism. In this study of bourgeois society there are three rebels—Dorothea, Ladislaw and Lydgate—whose aspirations lead them to a profound dissatisfaction with the Middlemarch world. All three stand for, and wish to live by, values higher than the values of that world. They are the 'ardent spirits' who seek to serve humanity through science and art and common sympathy. Lydgate is defeated by Middlemarch through his marriage with Rosamond and the bitter story of his defeat is the finest and most moving thing in the novel. But it is significant that Lydgate, like all the other failures of the novel, fails not through his strength but through his weakness.

There is no heroism in *Middlemarch* (leaving aside for the moment Dorothea and Ladislaw), no tragic conflict and there cannot be, for the dialectics of tragedy, the struggle in which the hero is destroyed through his own strength, is outside George Eliot's scheme of things. Because her outlook is mechanistic and not revolutionary no one can fight Middlemarch or change it. The most that they can do is to improve it a little (as Farebrother does and perhaps Dorothea) by being a little 'better' than their neigh-bours. But the best that most can rise to—like Mary Garth and Mrs Bulstrode—is a sincere and unsentimental submission to its will. And therefore even the 'sympathetic' characters must either be passive or else be brought to their knees through their own faults. For though George Eliot hates Middlemarch she believes in its inevitability; it is the world and our udder.

Yet because she hates the values of the society she depicts and has a faith in men and women which her mechanistic philosophy cannot destroy, George Eliot has to find a way out of her dilemma. She, whose noble humanity informs the whole novel, even its weaknesses, cannot submit emotionally to a philosophy that binds her people for ever to the Middlemarch world. Hence the signifi-cance of the Saint Theresa theme, both as to its place in the novel and as to the rather breathless, uncontrolled, even embarrassing emotional quality which it exudes. Hence, too, the whole problem of Dorothea and Ladislaw. Dr Leavis has brilliantly indicated the nature of the unsatisfactoriness of Dorothea, the aspect of what he calls self-indulgence inherent in her conception.

> Dorothea . . . is a product of George Eliot's own 'soul-hunger'—another day-dream ideal self. This persistence, in the midst of so much that is so other, of an unreduced enclave of the old immaturity is dis-concerting in the extreme. We have an alternation between the poised impersonal insight of a finely tempered wisdom and something like the emotional confusions and self-importances of adolescence.[11]

And yet, for all the penetration of Dr Leavis's analysis, it is hard to agree entirely with his conclusion that 'the weakness of the book . . . is in Dorothea'. For although there is this weakness (which increases as the book goes on) it is also true that the strength of the book is in Dorothea. In spite of all our reservations it is Dorothea who, of all the characters of the novel, most deeply captures our imagination. It is her aspiration to a life nobler than the Middlemarch way of life that is the great positive force within the novel and the force which, above all, counteracts the tendency to present society as a static, invincible force outside the characters themselves. It is Dorothea alone who, with Ladislaw, successfully rebels against the Middlemarch values.

The word 'successfully' needs qualification. For one thing Dorothea herself has more of the Lady Bountiful about her than George Eliot seems prepared to admit, and there is always (though let us not overestimate the point) seven hundred a year between her and the full implications of her attitude. More important, the success of her rebellion is limited by the degree of artistic conviction which it carries. The 'day-dream' aspect of Dorothea which Dr Leavis has emphasised is a very basic limitation. But this quality, this sense we have of idealisation, of something incompletely realised, is due, I would suggest, not so much to any subjective cause, some emotional immaturity in George Eliot herself (it is hard to see how she could combine her remarkable total achievement in the novel with such immaturity) as to the limitations of her philosophy, her social understanding.

Dorothea represents that element in human experience for which in the determinist universe of mechanistic materialism there is no place—the need of man to change the world that he inherits. Dorothea is the force that she is in the novel precisely because she encompasses this vital motive-force in human life; and she fails ultimately to convince us because in George Eliot's conscious philosophy she has no place. The 'unreduced enclave' represented by the degree of George Eliot's failure here is the unreduced enclave of idealism in her world-outlook.

As for Ladislaw, he is far less successfully realised than Dorothea, far more than she a mere dream-figure, a romantic idealisation of the kind of man she deserves. Indeed it is only when she becomes involved with Ladislaw that we become seriously uneasy about Dorothea. And Ladislaw, interestingly enough, is an aesthete, a respectable dilettante, a Bohemian minus the sordid reality of Bohemianism. He is in fact almost everything into which the ineffectual rebels of the late Victorian era escaped, and he is saved from the degeneracy implicit in his way of life only by the convenient financial support of Casaubon, Mr Brooke and finally Dorothea herself. The artistic failure of George Eliot with Ladislaw, her failure to make him a figure realised on the artistic level of the other characters of the novel, is inseparable from the social unrealism in his conception. Artistically he is not 'there', not concrete, because socially he is not concrete, but idealised.

It is important, I think, to recognise the link between the weaknesses of *Middlemarch* and the limitations of George Eliot's philosophy. For there are two sorts of weakness in the novel which at first appear unrelated and even antithetical. In the first place there is the tendency towards a certain flatness or heaviness, a tendency which we have seen to be associated with her somewhat static view of society and mortality. In the second place there is

the element of unresolved emotionalism involved in the Dorothea–
Ladislaw relationship. The two weaknesses are not, in fact, contradictory; but rather two sides of the same coin. It is the very inadequacy of her mechanistic philosophy, its failure to incorporate
a dialectical sense of contradiction and motion, that drives George
Eliot to treat the aspirations of Dorothea idealistically.

Just as *War and Peace*—despite Tolstoy's enormous, pene-
trating sense of the dialectics of life, of birth, growth and development—is weakened by his mechanistic, determinist view of history,
so in *Middlemarch* does George Eliot's undialectical philosophy
weaken the total impact at which she aimed. And yet no novelist
before her had so consciously and conscientiously tried to convey
the inter-relatedness of social life or the changing nature of individuals and their relationships. She is a great, sincere and humane
writer and it may well be that—despite the ultimate weaknesses
within her work—the novelists of the future will turn to *Middlemarch* more often than to any other English novel.

NOTES AND REFERENCES

N.B. Owing to the great variety of editions I have given chapter rather than page references in the case of novels which are divided into chapters.

PART I

1. Henry James: *The Art of Fiction* (1948 ed.), p. 12, (my italics A. K.)
2. *Aspects of the Novel* (1947 ed.), p. 196
3. See below p. 48 ff.
4. *Scrutiny*, Vol. II, no. 4, p. 376
5. See Aldous Huxley: *Do What You Will* (Thinkers Library no.56, 1937)
6. Spanish picaresque novel, pub. 1554
7. *Guzman de Alfarache*, by Alemàn, 1599, trans. English 1622
8. By Thomas Nashe, 1594
9. See in particular H. M. and N. Chadwick: *The Growth of Literature* (1932–40); W. P. Ker: *Epic and Romance* (1897); Bertha Phillpotts: *Edda and Saga* (Home Univ. Library, 1931)
10. E. Vinaver: *Works of Thomas Malory* (1947). Introduction p. lxv
11. Christopher Caudwell: *Illusion and Reality* (1946 ed.) p. 26 ff.

PART II

1. *The Pilgrim's Progress*, 1st Part
2. Jack Lindsay: *Bunyan, Maker of Myths* (1937), p. 194
3. *Jonathan Wild*, Book I, ch. VIII
4. ibid., Book I, ch. IX
5. See especially F. R. Leavis's analyses of *Hard Times* (in *The Great Tradition*, 1948) and *The Europeans* (*Scrutiny*, Vol. XV, no. 3)
6. Henry Reed: *The Novel Since 1939* (British Council, 1946)
7. Godwin: *Fleetwood* (1832 ed.), Preface
8. Q. D. Leavis: *Fiction and the Reading Public* (1939), p. 102
9. See especially R. H. Tawney: *Religion and the Rise of Capitalism* (1926)
10. *Robinson Crusoe* (Everyman ed.), p. 6
11. Q. D. Leavis, op. cit., p. 104
12. *Colonel Jack* (Novel Library ed.), p. 62

13. *Clarissa* (Everyman ed.), Vol. I, letter XLIV
14. Brian W. Downs: *Richardson* (1928), p. 76
15. ibid., p. 76
16. *The Great Tradition* (1948), pp. 3–4
17. *Joseph Andrews*, Book III, ch. XIII
18. ibid., Book I, ch. XII
19. *Tom Jones*, Book IV, ch. II
20. ibid., Book IV, ch. XIV
21. Henry James: *The Princess Casamassima*, Preface
22. *Tristram Shandy*, Book I, ch. XXII
23. ibid., Book V, ch. VII

PART III

INTRODUCTION
1. G. Lukács: *Studies in European Realism* (1950), p. 150
2. Letter to Howard Sturgis, Aug. 5, 1914

EMMA
1. *Scrutiny*, Vol. X, nos. 1 and 2
2. *Emma*, Vol. III, ch. XV
3. ibid., Vol. II, ch. XIV
4. ibid., Vol. III, ch. XI
5. ibid., vol. II, ch. XVII
6. ibid., Vol. I, ch. X

THE HEART OF MIDLOTHIAN
1. *Heart of Midlothian*, ch. XLVII
2. ibid.
3. *The Living Novel* (1946), p. 52
4. *Sir Walter Scott, Bart.* (1938), p. 309
5. *Chronicles of the Canongate*, Introduction, ch. V
6. *Heart of Midlothian*, ch. IV
7. ibid., ch. IX
8. *Guy Mannering*, ch. VIII
9. *Heart of Midlothian*, ch. L
10. ibid., ch. LII
11. *Aspects of the Novel* (1947 ed.), p. 46 ff.
12. *The Novel and the People* (1937), p. 60

OLIVER TWIST
1. *Oliver Twist*, ch. XII
2. ibid., ch. V
3. ibid., ch. I
4. ibid., ch. IX
5. ibid., ch. I
6. ibid., ch. V
7. ibid., ch. XLIII
8. ibid., ch. L

WUTHERING HEIGHTS
1. *Wuthering Heights*, ch. IX
2. ibid., ch. XVI
3. ibid., ch. VI
4. ibid., ch. III
5. ibid., ch. IX
6. ibid., ch. X
7. ibid., ch. XII
8. ibid., ch. XIV
9. ibid., ch. XV
10. ibid., ch. XIV
11. ibid., ch. XX
12. ibid., ch. XXXIII
13. *Scrutiny*, Vol. XIV, no. 4
14. *Wuthering Heights*, ch. XXXIV
15. *Modern Quarterly*, Miscellany no. 1 (1947)
16. *The Common Reader* (Pelican ed.), p. 158

VANITY FAIR
1. *Vanity Fair*, ch. I
2. *The Craft of Fiction* (1921), p. 95
3. *The Structure of the Novel* (1946 ed.), p. 24
4. *Vanity Fair*, ch. LIII
5. *Culture and Anarchy* (1932 ed.), p. 84
6. *Early Victorian Novelists* (1945 ed.), p. 80
7. *Vanity Fair*, ch. XLI
8. ibid., ch. XII
9. ibid., ch. LXI
10. ibid., ch. LXVII

MIDDLEMARCH
1. *Middlemarch*, ch. I
2. ibid., ch. VI
3. ibid., ch. XX
4. ibid., Prelude
5. ibid., ch. XI
6. op. cit., p. 61
7. *Middlemarch*, ch. LXXIV
8. Joan Bennett: *George Eliot* (1948), p. 167
9. *Middlemarch*, ch. XXI
10. *Partial Portraits*, p. 51 (quoted by F. R. Leavis, op. cit., p. 33)
11. op. cit., p. 75

READING LIST

There are many books about the English novel, including a large number published since this *Introduction* was written. The following suggestions for further reading make no claim to exhaustiveness.

(1) The largest, fullest, 'standard' work is:

BAKER, E. A.: *The History of the English Novel*, 9 vols. (1924–38) Almost any piece of information will be found here, including a long, now somewhat out-of-date, reference list; but as a critical work it is uneven and uninspired. Of shorter 'histories' the best is

ALLEN, WALTER: *The English Novel* (first pub. 1954)

(2) Among less exhaustive general works the following may be found the most useful:

FORSTER, E. M.: *Aspects of the Novel* (1927)

An engaging and extremely readable book which raises more questions than it answers but will set the reader thinking.

LUBBOCK, PERCY: *The Craft of Fiction* (1921)

One of the first (and in many respects still the best) of the attempts to deal with some of the technical and artistic problems of the novel as a serious art-form.

LEAVIS, Q. D.: *Fiction and the Reading Public* (1939)

Despite its aggressive and sometimes infuriating tone this raises brilliantly a host of immensely suggestive critical and historical problems.

LEAVIS, F. R.: *The Great Tradition* (1948)

On George Eliot, James and Conrad this is, most people will agree, out-standing novel-criticism, serious, sustained and rigorous. The general line (especially of the first chapter), the conception of 'tradition' involved and the tone of much of the writing are more questionable.

JAMES, HENRY: *The Art of Fiction* (1948), *The Art of the Novel* (Collected Prefaces), Ed. Blackmur (1934)

The great value of James's criticism is the opportunity it gives to see a highly intelligent and self-conscious novelist in action faced with the actual practical problems of his art.

LODGE, DAVID: *Language of Fiction* (1966)

Perhaps the most thorough and stimulating of recent exercises in novel-criticism.

ALLOTT, MIRIAM: *Novelists on the Novel* (1959)

Though the arrangement is a little odd, this is a most useful book which brings together a great deal of interesting material otherwise widely scattered.

(3) Other general books include (alphabetically):

CECIL, DAVID: *Early Victorian Novelists* (1934)
CHURCH, RICHARD: *Growth of the English Novel* (1951)
FOX, RALPH: *The Novel and the People* (1937)
GILLIE, CHRISTOPHER: *Character in English Literature* (1965)
GREGOR, IAN & NICHOLAS, BRIAN: *The Moral and the Story* (1962)
HARDY, BARBARA: *The Appropriate Form* (1964)
HARVEY, W. J.: *Character and the Novel* (1965)
LIDDELL, ROBERT: *A Treatise on the Novel* (1947)
     Some Principles of Fiction (1953)
LUKÁCS, GEORG: *Studies in European Realism* (trans., Bone) (1950)
     The Historical Novel (trans., Mitchell) (1962)
MUIR, EDWIN: *The Structure of the Novel* (1928)
PRITCHETT, V. S.: *The Living Novel* (1946)
     The Working Novelist (1965)
SCHLAUCH, MARGARET: *Antecedents of the English Novel, 1400–1600* (1963)
STANG, RICHARD: *The Theory of the Novel in England, 1850–1870* (1959)
TILLOTSON, KATHLEEN: *Novels of the Eighteen-Forties* (1954)
VAN GHENT, DOROTHY: *The English Novel: Form and Function* (1953)
WATT, IAN: *The Rise of the Novel* (1957)
ZABEL, M. W.: *Craft and Character in Modern Fiction* (1957)

(4) On particular novels and novelists mentioned in this book: (N.B. In no case is anything approaching a bibliography of the particular author given, merely certain books that may be useful. For a fuller list of books the student is referred to Baker's *History of the English Novel*; F. W. Bateson's *Guide to English Literature* (1965); and *Victorian Fiction*, a Guide to Research (Ed. L. Stevenson) (1964). References to articles in periodicals quoted in the text will be found in the *Notes*)

TALON, HENRI: *John Bunyan* (trans. 1951)
SHARROCK, ROGER: *John Bunyan* (1954)
WEST, ALICK: *Mountain in the Sunlight* (1958) (on Bunyan, Defoe)

WATSON, F.: *Daniel Defoe* (1952)
NOVAK, M.: *Defoe and the Nature of Man* (1963)
WRIGHT, ANDREW: *Fielding* (1964)
SACKS, SHELDON: *Fiction and the Shape of Belief* (1964)
MURRY, J. MIDDLETON: *Unprofessional Essays* (1956) (on Fielding)
LASCELLES, MARY: *Jane Austen and her Art* (1939)
WRIGHT, ANDREW: *Jane Austen's Novels* (1953)
BRADBROOK, F. W.: *Jane Austen and her Predecessors* (1966)
TRILLING, LIONEL: *The Opposing Self* (1955) (on Jane Austen and Dickens)
GRIERSON, H. J. C.: *Sir Walter Scott, Bart.* (1938)
MUIR, EDWIN: *Scott and Scotland* (1936)
DAVIE, DONALD: *The Heyday of Sir Walter Scott* (1961)
CRAIG, DAVID: *Scottish Literature and the Scottish People, 1680–1830* (1961)
JACKSON, T. A.: *Charles Dickens, The Progress of a Radical* (1937)
WILSON, EDMUND: *The Wound and the Bow* (1941) (on Dickens)
HOUSE, HUMPHRY: *The Dickens World* (1941)
JOHNSON, EDGAR: *Charles Dickens, His Tragedy and Triumph* (1953)
FORD, GEORGE: *Dickens and his Readers* (1955)
BUTT, JOHN & TILLOTSON, KATHLEEN: *Dickens at Work* (1957)
FIELDING, K. J.: *Dickens, a Critical Introduction* (1958)
GROSS, J. & PEARSON, G. (Ed.): *Dickens and the Twentieth Century* (1962)
GARIS, ROBERT: *The Dickens Theatre* (1965)
TILLOTSON, GEOFFREY: *Thackeray the Novelist* (1954)
RAY, GORDON N.: *Thackeray: The Uses of Adversity* (1955)
The Age of Wisdom (1958)
STEPHEN, LESLIE: *George Eliot* (1902)
BENNETT, JOAN: *George Eliot* (1948)
HARDY, BARBARA: *The Novels of George Eliot* (1959)
HARVEY, W. J.: *The Art of George Eliot* (1962)

INDEX